# MY FOOT PRINTS IN GHANA'S BLACK GOLD

## DR A. OFORI QUAAH

First published by RMPublishers Ltd, 2020, 2023

Copyright © 2023 by Dr A Ofori Quaah

A CIP catalogue of this book is available from the British Library.

ISBN:

2nd Edition

# CONTENTS

# PREFACE

**February 2019**

Like most children who grew up in the early 1950s in Ghana, particularly in the Central Region, I had all kinds of aspirations as to what I wanted to be when I grew up, but a policeman was definitely not one of them. The reason was although I had two relatives in the then Gold Coast Police Force, one of them very senior, a policeman was the one person that I feared more than anything on earth. If I was doing anything and someone said, "A policeman will catch you," I would stop whatever it was that very moment. It was much later when I heard the oral history of my family that I put one and two together and realised where that phobia had come from.

One of my mother's half-brothers died under very tragic accidental circumstances, which under the law, should have been a coroner's case. He was buried without reference to the police or coroner. The incident managed to attract the attention of the police at Agona Swedru at that time. Several contingents of what was known as "Authority" Police descended on our little town looking for my grandfather. In those days, my grandfather lived in his "Mbanyinfie" (men's house) away from my grandmother, who with her children and grandchildren, lived in her own family house with one of her sisters and their only brother, who was also their last born.

I remember my grandfather coming to our house twice a day, in the morning and in the evening, sometimes several times in between. Having lost my father very early in life, my grandfather was the first really close male figure in my life. As a result, I would often accompany him when he came to visit and would soon wish to return to my mother.

Naturally, when the police did not meet my grandfather in his house because he had apparently gone to his cocoa farm nearby, the first point of call was his wife's house. My grandmother had gone to the market when the police arrived at the family house. This "buga buga" policeman who had obviously been given the names of my mother and grandmother entered the house and called out their names. My mother was nursing her last born, Grace, just three months old. When she answered her name, his first question was "Where is your father?" and before my mother could answer, he just slapped her. The police in Ghana still beat suspects even in 2019!

Her uncle who was just coming out of his room was furious. According to my older sister, our granduncle would have shot that policeman on the spot if his shotgun had been close by. Nana Ofosu, as we called him, had an almighty row with this policeman and the sergeant who followed shortly afterwards. I was a little over five years old and witnessed it all and that was the reason for my fear of and disdain for policemen!

Following the visit of the shepherds to the infant Jesus, the revelations by Simeon and Ann in the Temple in Jerusalem after Jesus's presentation and later when the twelve-year-old Jesus was lost and found in the Temple, St Luke remarked in Chapter 2 verse 19, and again in verse 51, "but His mother kept all these things in her heart."

Apparently, before I was four years old, a string of predictions was made about my future, first by my maternal grandfather, a catechist, a local Imam and a fetish priestess relative of ours, on separate occasions. My mother who incidentally was christened Mary, "kept all those things in her heart."

She had been widowed at 28 (she will be 99 in June and still quite strong, by the grace of God), with no skill except some petty trading and subsistence farming. She had remarried twice, all ending in divorce because she couldn't bear to see any man maltreat her special love child in any shape or form. Not long after that police incident, she sent me off to live with one of her maternal cousins. That is where this journey by God's grace began via a well-appointed bamboo school building. Indeed, as St Paul puts it in Romans 8:28, "We know that in all things God works for the good of those who love him, who have been called according to his purpose." (NIV)

I agonised for several years about writing these memoirs of my life at the Ghana National Petroleum Corporation. A Nigerian Accountant who worked with Lushann, the Ghanaian-Nigerian company based in Houston that formed a partnership with GNPC to resume production of the Saltpond field first suggested in 2001. After my very first meeting of the company's Board, I became Chairman by virtue of being Acting Chief Executive Officer of the Corporation in May 2001. He said, "Why don't you write down your rich experience of exploration in Ghana and Nigeria for future generations?" Several issues got me thinking seriously about these memoirs after I retired in 2013.

First of all, not long after the Corporation began actual business in April 1985, more than a year after the passage of the Law that established it, various myths and half-baked theories began to fly in Ghana about the presence or absence of commercial quantities of oil and gas in the basins of the country. They ranged from those who were convinced that Nigeria was draining Ghana's oil and that all that was required was for Ghana to buy powerful machines and begin to pump and drain her own, to those who believed that Ghana would never find oil until the gods of Nzemaland and the Volta Region had been pacified, to those who thought the GNPC Model Agreement was too stringent on contractors.

Secondly, during sixteen years of involvement in oil and gas exploration in Ghana, I met several people who would influence not only my professional life but my spirituality as well. One of those was my old schoolmate and senior Bible scholar, Giant William Kwami Agbesingyale (WK as his young son called him and Togbe, as we called him in the Exploration Department). Another was a bright young Giant, Anthony Assiamah, with whom I did my last major exploration project in the Corporation in 1999-2000. Sadly, this bright young man died suddenly not long after the commercial discovery was made. "Giant" is the official name of the Old Boys of the Government (now Ghana) Secondary Technical School in Takoradi, several of whom coincidentally played a very important part in the ultimate discovery of oil in Ghana.

An extensive mapping project I did of the Cape Three Points sub-basin of the Western Region in 1992, would turn out to be the major turning point of the whole offshore Ghana exploration effort.

In 2013, I met a former GNPC colleague in London who drew my attention to the fact that two of us, Togbe and I who were so deeply involved in the exploration programme in the early days of GNPC never benefited from the oil largesse. That also reminded me of several young children who missed the presence and love of fathers very early in their lives because their fathers had to travel on official assignments away from home in Ghana or overseas. In many cases, I was part of the reason for those long periods of absence. For the sake of those children and their mothers, those unsung heroes and heroines, something had to be written down for posterity.

Thirdly, there are those generations of mostly young Ghanaians, many of them in my own extended family, who have a sense of entitlement and believe that they can simply acquire wealth, in fact, lots of it, without having to sweat for it. These are the men and women who are being duped big time by false prophets, pastors and so-called men of God as well as "Sakawa" and occultic men and women around the country. I intend to demonstrate that no matter where a person was born and under which circumstances, the grace of God abounds for all and with hard work, any Ghanaian or African, for that matter, can succeed anywhere in the world.

Fourthly I had been on a spiritual journey by the grace of God, with the Lord using me in a small way in the North Accra Circuit and Accra Diocese of the Methodist Church Ghana, culminating in the establishment of a thriving church, the Immanuel Society in the Airport Residential Area in Accra. I read a rather patchy history of the

Immanuel Society a while ago and thought I needed to put the records straight because I was there. As C.S Lewis put it, "My kind of Christianity" had been there with me through it all.

Finally, I had been travelling on a rather shaky truck for sixteen years the revelation of which would only come during ten months of fire-dousing and hoop-jumping at the helm of the Corporation and what revelation that was! However, it was all worth it because, without those twists and turns, Ghana's commercial oil and gas discovery would probably have been delayed for several more decades.

The revelation showed the inadequacies and vulnerabilities inherent in our data and information management systems. Sadly, the benefits to the country of this most crucial national resource could have been greater if the environment had been less political and more welcoming of technical know-how.

Along the way, there were ups and downs, but the Lord used them all to His glory. By the grace of God, I was more productive in my enforced seclusions. Those were the times I had the presence of mind to work so effectively without unwanted interruptions. I was able to practise my seismology alongside petroleum exploration work, travelling around the country as Chairman of the Geological Disasters Sub-Committee of the National Disaster Management Organisation (NADMO).

My only regret is that the constant caution to develop our country with respect for the environment and the laws of nature fell on deaf ears and we are bound to pay a price for it as a nation.

In writing these memoirs I have enjoyed a lot of material and emotional support from my family, my wife, Sabina, and our sons Kofi and Paa Kwesi. Our granddaughters, Maame Ama Sarpomaa and Ewuradwoa Eyiaa kept and are still keeping me on my toes.

In them, I have been able to re-live the periods I missed in our own children's growing years during my regular travels around the world as my footprints were firmly planted in Ghana's Black Gold.

# CHAPTER 1
## IT'S A BOY!

**M**y mother called me her 'special son' and at ninety-nine this year (2019), she believes I have turned out to be exactly that in more ways than one. Apparently, on my father's side of the family, the men always gave birth to a first-born son, followed by a girl. Therefore, it was a major source of 'sadness' for my father that my mother's first-born son died at birth in 1940. My sister was born two years later, and it would be more than six years before I was born on Tuesday, 14th September 1948, but recorded as Tuesday 13th September. According to my mother and grandmother, my birth was a rather difficult one, my mother having laboured, overseen by traditional birth attendants, for about twenty-four hours.

In accordance with Islamic traditions of the day, the local Imam apparently named me Yakubu, just as my sister had been named Hawa at birth. This Imam had apparently recorded my birth as Tuesday 13th September, instead of Tuesday 14th. September. It would be many years after the date had been recorded that I detected the error from Islamic records in the area, by which time September the thirteenth had been used in too many official records to change it.

My paternal grandfather who died in 1960, had not been interested in any religion whatsoever, until well into midlife. He had been married to my grandmother who was a fetish priestess for many years before he converted to Islam with all his children. Subsequently, he tried to convert my grandmother for several years without success. My grandmother who believed that a precipitous abandonment of her "deities" would be detrimental to her family, died a broken woman because all her three sons died within five years of their conversion to Islam.

Apparently, my father was quite ill at the time I was born. As it is the custom in the Gomoa District, my father instructed that I should be named after his favourite grandmother, Nana Abena Eyiaba, five weeks after I was born. He might have sensed that he was not going to survive, and wishing to be remembered long after his death, named me after himself, Ofori, just before he died three months after I was born. That is another reason why I am supposed to be a special son.

My mother remained a Methodist through all this. Apparently, it took a lot of persuasion for her to finally agree to be married to my father, not only because he was a Muslim, but because he was already married with two young children. The other woman left soon after my mother was brought into the marital home. It took more than forty years to be reunited with our surviving sister, who has since become so close to me and my sister. Sister Ekua, as we call her, was another source of my father's 'sorrow' because she was the firstborn from his very first wife and a girl! That is another reason why I was considered so special.

It has taken me a very long time to even contemplate writing these memoirs. But now I feel very strongly that I should put some of my life's experiences into writing so the younger generation of the family who maintains a sense of entitlement, can understand that nothing in the world is simple and straightforward and that "Life is really what you make of it." It is also important to understand that, "When life gives you lemons, you must learn to make lemonade."

Like all mortals, I and several of us in the family have made some wrong choices, resulting in some costly errors that need to be recorded so future generations can learn from and endeavour to avoid them. So, my journey thus far, by the Grace of God!

# CHAPTER 2
## EARLY CHILDHOOD

As I grew up, I realised how really tough life might have been for my mother. My father acquired lands for the purpose of cultivating his own cocoa farms, which was what all industrious young men of his age did in the 1940s. Unfortunately, following his death and that of his two other brothers, their father was so devastated that he literally gave up on life. He seemed to have gone through what we would today call depression. He made no attempt whatsoever to recover the assets that his sons had acquired in various parts of the Central Province at the time, neither did he go looking for the children of his deceased sons, his very first grandchildren, especially those of us whose mothers had not hailed from Gomoa Mankessim where he lived.

The first time I saw my paternal grandfather, I was nine years old and the old man might have been in his early eighties. My mother had remarried twice already by the time I was five years old, and the reason was she could not bear to see any man maltreat her special love child.

In late 1954, she sent me off to live with her cousin Kweku Obrehun on the other side of town. Uncle Obrehun who was fifty-four years old at the time, had just one son, Kwame Yamoah who was in his mid-twenties. Kwame Yamoah had two older sisters, Esi Egyirwa and Yaa. Apparently, their mother died not long after Yaa was born.

Uncle had two other grown-up daughters, Aba Egyirwa and Ama Adadzewa by his second wife, Maame Aba Adawude. Maame Adewude had had eight issues but only the two girls had survived. As was the custom of those days, Uncle had inherited a cousin and married his widow, Maame Aba, with whom he had Yaa Donkor.

Along the line, Uncle Obrehun married two other women, Maame Esi Kyerwaa from Gomoa Broyedur and Esi Sersema from Gomoa Nkran. Therefore, by the time I went to live with him, Uncle had four wives. In those days, a man's worth in society was determined by the number of wives and children he could comfortably cater for. By local standards, Uncle was quite a wealthy man. He and his younger brother Kweku (Budu) Ketseaba had put up a well-appointed compound house, six rooms for Uncle Obrehun and his wives and son, Kwame Yamoah and four for Uncle Kweku Ketseaba and his three wives at the time.

Uncle Kweku Ketseaba had four children in school at the time, Kofi Egyir who was in Middle Form Four, Emmanuel Otoo and Mary Budu who were both in Primary Class Three and Kojo Essel, his stepson from his third wife, Adwoa Guraba, who was also in Class Three.

Although Uncle Obrehun always contributed immensely to every development project in the town and particularly, with respect to the schools in town, he had no child in school. His own son Kwame Yamoah wouldn't go to school because he believed his father was wealthy, and there was more to life for a young man with his kind of privileges than to "go to school to be caned."

Uncle had subsequently enrolled one of his direct nephews in school in the early 1950s, but the boy died tragically in a freak accident on the farm when a fierce storm uprooted a tree that fell on the young boy and killed him instantly. The fact that he had no child in school was a major source of sadness for Uncle. So, when I was sent to live with him, he decided to try his luck with me.

**Primary School**

. . .

In January 1955, Uncle Obrehun enrolled me in Class One, under Master Aikins (who incidentally, was Uncle Nyarko's classmate at Winneba Methodist School). They were both members of the Winneba Methodist Church Choir (together with Uncle Afful, the policeman) when I apparently did my *"ntsii nye yi o eburow"* salesmanship as a two-year-old! Master Aikins had never forgotten that.

I had unofficially followed Sister Efua Antobam to school from about age four, without being enrolled. So, by the time I was formally enrolled in school, I knew much of the English and Mfantse alphabet and could write numbers to about 15. By the end of the second term, I had already read "Fie Na Skuul One", the recommended text for Class One. By the third term, I was reading James Panyin's Class Two books (James Panyin was Uncle Obrehun's first grandchild, who had come to live with him), as well as looking over the shoulders of my cousins, Emmanuel Otoo and Mary Budu in Class Three, to read their books, which sometimes got me into trouble.

At the end of the school year, I and four others; Sampson Enu, Emmanuel Donkoh, Timothy Owu and Peter Aidoo were jumped to Class Three. Uncle Obrehun wouldn't let me because he thought I was too small for Class Three. So, Peter Aidoo, Owu and I went to Class Two, while the other three proceeded to Class Three.

I started school at Nkampor Dan Mu at Gyaman (The magnificent bamboo structure which stood at the northern end of the present-day JSS A football park). When the structure collapsed in a major storm, Lower Primary (Class One to Class Three) was moved to the Gyaman Catholic Church, whilst Upper Primary (Class Four to Class Six), moved to the old Methodist Church building that was demolished after the new building was completed in 1960.

I started Class Two in the small Headteacher's Office in the present day JSS A building because our Class One group of nearly thirty had been decimated to just ten boys and two girls by the end of the academic year. Miss Elsie Sackey, our class teacher, got us to learn up to twelve times, by the second term. Eventually, we did the third term in the present day Primary A building, where because the classrooms had no ceilings, I began to learn whatever those in Class Three were studying. During the final school examinations of 1956, Miss Yamoah, the Class Three teacher, who from time to time had pulled me out of my class to take dictation and arithmetic tests with her class (so I could cane the ones who failed), got me to write the exams with the Class Three group. My friend, Timothy Owu and I were subsequently jumped to Class Four.

My older cousins knew that I had been jumped, but nobody said anything about it at home. In those days, Master Louis Amoah, the Headteacher of the Middle School served as an agent for the Methodist Book Depot, which distributed school textbooks and stationery throughout southern Ghana. When the time came to buy my books for the next academic year, I took my "Class Four" list along with Uncle Obrehun to Master Amoah's depot. While my uncle was talking to his wife, Master Amoah took one look at my list and asked, "Are you in Class Four already?" Master Amoah, a very good musician, came to our class every once in a while, to teach us Mfantse folk songs, so he knew me very well. Uncle did not hear our little conversation and Master Amoah quickly gave me my textbooks and items of stationery and dismissed me because there was a long queue to be served.

While he was adding up my bill, I ran home and began writing my name on the books in ink. It was while my uncle was paying the bill that he realised that I had been given books for Class Four. By the time he arrived back home, I had written my name on the books and it was too late. I was in Class Four after only about twenty-four months in school. The journey to Takoradi had begun in earnest.

## Spiritual Development, The Apostolic Church, Ghana

While his sisters and their youngest brother, Kweku Ketseaba, had all been Methodists (Uncle Kweku Ketseaba had been a chorister in his youth), Uncle Obrehun had never been a religious person. Their mother, Ama Adadzewa, had been a fetish priestess. After the death of their mother, Uncle Obrehun converted to Islam for a while, with the

Muslim name, Kweku Seidu. That did not last very long. He dabbled in occultism for a while, which became a source of friction between him and two of his wives, Maame Adewude and Maame Aba, who were strong Methodists. Maame Aba sang in the choir of the Methodist Church.

Uncle was also something of a playboy and drank very heavily, especially at Christmas. He was one of the few citizens of Gyaman who owned a gramophone player (HMV), which was popularly known as the "Tarkwa Machine." I am not quite sure of the origin of that name, but it would seem that it was first introduced to Ghana by expatriate miners at Tarkwa in the then Western Province of the Gold Coast, from where it spread to different parts of the Central Province and beyond.

At Christmas, someone would usually carry that machine as it played music with Uncle following and dishing out money to people, particularly women, as they danced to the records played on the gramophone.

My mother's side of the family had been Methodists for a very long time. History had it that my maternal grandfather and another person had carried the huge Methodist Church bell from Nyakrom to Gyaman, on foot during the early part of the twentieth century.

However, my grandfather, for reasons I have never been able to discover, left the Church not long after that brave exercise, because even in those days, considering the value of the bell, they could have been ambushed and the bell taken away from them on the way. That notwithstanding, nearly all my mother's siblings had been choristers, and my grandfather's firstborn on my mother's side, Uncle Kofi Amo had been an organist in the church for many years.

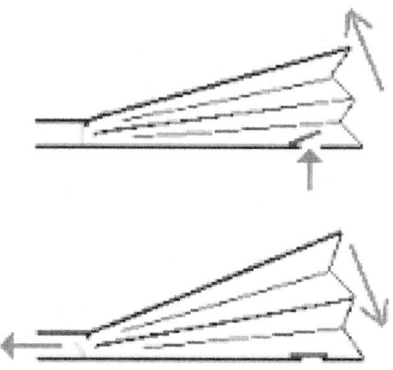

A Bellow Church Organ

The family actually owned one of those "Bellow Organs" until about the late 1960s when it could not be repaired anymore, and of course, following the death of Uncle Kofi Amo in 1959, nobody could play it anymore and might have been thrown away somewhere. In Europe, it could have been sold for a fortune on the antique market.

Apparently, our forebears, Kojo Ata and Kwesi Esiam who went to work in the mines at Tarkwa brought home that organ, together with many other novelty items. They were the two people who from the proceeds of their adventures in the mines, acquired the cocoa farming lands that still belong to the family more than one hundred years after they first began cultivation.

Uncle Kofi Afo, Nana Addow's first son, had learnt to play it and later taught Uncle Kofi Amo and others. Probably, if Uncle Kofi Amo had not died early, he could have taught the next generation and we would still have organists in the family today, just as successive generations have maintained the family choir tradition, especially of alto and tenor singers in church choirs.

Because of Uncle Obrehun's disinterest in church matters earlier, there was not much of an incentive on my part, to attend church services, especially if the head teacher of the Methodist Primary School where I began my schooling was not particularly strict about church attendance. I went in as and when, especially towards the end of the school year when we had to practise for the "Children's Day" celebration when I usually either read a Bible lesson or introduced a hymn. Of course, for the end-of-year school results of the Methodist Primary School, it was compulsory that both students, guardians and parents attended the special church service.

At the end of 1955, the Central Region section of The Apostolic Church, Ghana, organised its annual convention at Gyaman. On the last day of the convention, before the end of the service, a bench was placed in the centre of the large gathering for "everyone who wanted to give his or her life to Christ to move forward and sit on that bench." Uncle Obrehun was seriously drunk but somehow, managed, with some rather unsteady steps, to be one of the first on the bench. My senior cousins and I who were present were all taken by surprise. But that was to be a major turning point in Uncle's life.

The next morning, he prayed what could easily have been the prayer of his life, for more than an hour. In his collection of gramophone records was the hymn, "Abide with Me," which he played most mornings. On this particular morning, after that hymn, he emerged from his room completely soaked with sweat, carrying several wooden and clay figures of a deity that he had acquired at Brekuso in the Eastern Region. I had once eavesdropped on a conversation in which he told an elderly relative that to be able to reach that deity, he had to cross a stream where everyone stripped naked before they could attempt the crossing. He burnt all the figures that morning.

Around the house was a little clearing. He stood there with a bottle of kerosene, and a box of matches and prayed, "Dear God, last night I committed myself to you. I do not wish to have any dealings with these deities anymore. I am going to burn them; if you are really up there, let me see your power this morning." With that, he set fire to the figures and burnt everything to ashes. From that time, Uncle never touched even lemonade again until about 1964 when, following the death of Nana Kweku Otu, his life and that of Gyaman Twidan Ebusua were thrown into turmoil.

The day of Uncle's calling was the day The Apostolic Church, Ghana, was born at Gyaman, because soon after the burning of his deities, he and his cousins Kwame Donkor, and his brother Kweku Baah, another cousin, Kofi Ninsin and their wives began the construction of a bamboo church house, to be joined later by other cousins, Kobena Mensah, Kobena Otsibu, all members of the Gyaman Twidan Clan. Thus, for nearly a decade, the Apostolic Church at Gyaman was known as "Twidanfo Asor" or the Church of the Twidan Clan.

Although I was never officially baptised into the Apostolic Church, because Uncle was one of the pillars of the church at Gyaman, after his conversion, I had one of my earliest spiritual awakenings at a special prayer meeting of the Church in the bushes along the road to Darhom. On that day, I prayed until I was completely soaked with sweat and saw around me a most amazing light I have never seen again since that day. It was in late 1957, I was in Class Four. I was eventually baptised in the Methodist Church on 12th September 1964, the day before my sixteenth birthday.

## A Close Brush with the Law

From late 1948, Nana Kweku Otu had been embroiled in major land litigation with one of the prominent families of Agona Nyakrom, the overlords of the cocoa farming lands where he owned some of the largest cocoa plantations at Nsuansa village. The old man had bought this vast farmland and begun the cultivation of cocoa plantations. Just as the farms were beginning to yield, the landowners sent "land guards" armed with guns and machetes, to drive out the old man, his sons and nephews and their families who worked on the plantations. With more than twelve young men and their children, the old man and his party put up a fight and the case eventually landed at the High Court at Cape Coast.

By 1954 when I went to live with Uncle Obrehun, Nana Kweku Otu was quite old and the prosecution of the case was left with Uncle Obrehun, assisted by Uncle Ansanyi. Uncle Obrehun eventually won the case on behalf of the old man and the rest of the family in 1960, but not until the old man had spent over £12,000 in those days, on legal fees and travelling expenses!

Uncle went to Cape Coast once a month, sometimes more often. He would usually travel to Swedru to join Uncle Ansanyi and the two of them would travel together to Cape Coast, where they spent an evening conferring with their lawyer, one Lawyer Abaidoo, before the court sitting the next day. Sometimes, Uncle Obrehun went alone to Cape Coast.

Uncle had one of those locally made guns in his bedroom. One evening sometime in 1957, following one of Uncle's many travels in connection with the court case, I had just finished sweeping his room when his first grandson, James Panyin, who was in Class Four, came into Uncle's room. Yaw as we called him and I were living with his maternal grandmother, Maame Adewude, as mentioned earlier.

Uncle's gun was in a corner of the room and there was a locally made pellet which was fashioned from small square pieces of thinly rolled copper plate. I took the gun, cocked it and inserted the pellet and said, "Since Uncle had travelled, if a thief came to the house, I would take the gun and fire." Instantly, the gun went off. Yaw was standing by the door, about five meters from where the pellet hit the wall. The mark of that gunfire would remain on the wall for more than a decade.

We were both frightened. I started running and did not stop until I got to my maternal grandfather's (Nana Kofi Enyaah's) house. I collapsed in his arms and would not stop crying the whole night. I spent the night with Nana and he took me back to Uncle's house the next day, by which time Yaw had concocted the story that I said, "Yaw *morotow wo*" or "I will shoot you, Yaw." That became my name in the area, and even later, in school and to this day, a few of my friends who are still alive tease me with that incident, by calling me "*Yaw morotow wo*".

**Near Tragedy in 1959**

Sometime in May 1959, Uncle Obrehun was bitten by a snake just outside the house, an event that nearly spelt disaster for me and a large section of our Gyaman-Afransi Twidan Clan. There had been a funeral in the family and as usually happens in our part of the region, a shed had been raised on the compound for the wake-keeping and large-scale catering for guests.

After the funeral, the palm fronds that had been used to roof the shed had been discarded in the bushes just outside the house. With time, the goats and sheep in the area had fed on the leaves and by so doing dragged the dying palm fronds into the footpath leading to the rubbish dump about one hundred metres outside the house. About 10 o'clock that fateful Saturday morning, Uncle stopped by the palm fronds and tried to move them away from the footpath. That was when he nearly picked up this big green snake. In trying to avoid handling it, Uncle who was wearing open native sandals might have stepped on the tail of the snake, which led to it striking at the big toe of his right foot.

In those days, the first point of call was the local herbalist. Uncle's leg was tied tightly with a piece of clean calico and a fresh palm frond just above the ankle, apparently to prevent the venom of the snake from rising above his waist. He was then given palm oil to drink, to force him to throw up and dispel the venom from the body. Later, I learned in my readings that in humans, most snake bites only affect the immediate area of the bite and the venom rarely ever enters the bloodstream or even affects the nervous system, both of which can be fatal.

Later, an herbalist was brought in from Darhom, all to no avail. By 3 p.m., Uncle was falling in and out of consciousness. Mother who by this time had been at Uncle's side for several hours suggested that he be taken to hospital and actually went to look for Driver Yaw Donkor, who took Uncle to Winneba Hospital where he was given a snake serum that revived him within minutes.

Recounting the journey from Gyaman to Winneba the next day, Mother said she had never seen any driver drive as fast as Driver Yaw Donkor did that afternoon. When I went to see Uncle the next day, he started crying uncontrollably as soon as he saw me. He said all through his ordeal the previous day, there were two people that he worried most about, what would have happened to me and his then two-year-old son, Kwesi Egyir if he had died. He pulled through and was discharged after three days in the hospital.

# CHAPTER 3
# SECONDARY EDUCATION AND BEYOND

Until about the late 1960s, there were only a handful of towns and villages in the Gomoa District with middle schools. Most places had up to Class Six. So, pupils wrote a special entrance examination in Class Six, for admission to Middle Form One. My year group took the entrance examination with Class Six pupils from four other towns, followed by an interview, in November 1959. Sister Efua, together with Brother JK Mensah and Nana Kofi Akwah in Middle Form Four at the time, were part of the group that marked the 1959 entrance examinations. Through Sister Efua and Bro Mensah, I knew I had come first and was sure of a place in the January 1960 Middle Form One Class of 31 pupils, even before the results went out.

I was part of the generation of Ghanaian school children who went through two promotions in 1960 because of the change of the school year from January/December to September/June. So, by September 1962, I was already on my way to secondary school, after only seven years in formal education.

### The Nationwide Common Entrance Examination
I sat and passed the Common Entrance Examination in March 1962.

The examination in those days was made up of three papers, Arithmetic, English Grammar and English Composition. Our Form Three class teacher, Mr J D Otoo, from Senya Beraku, a brilliant teacher, but a very heavy drinker, died suddenly during the Christmas holidays of 1961. Back to school in January 1962, we had no class teacher. Master Amoah and our former Form Two teacher, Mr de Graft Arhin, stopped by once in a while, to assign us work. It was not until about late January, or early February that Mr Quayson, another brilliant product of Peki Training College and a native of nearby Wassa, arrived to take over our class as a substantive class teacher.

Having taken several entrance examinations himself earlier, Teacher Quayson recognised our predicament without a teacher and examinations were only a few weeks away. He went from house to house to beg parents and guardians to allow their wards to stay on after school, for another hour, of extra tuition, free of charge. In March, we travelled to Swedru, to join several hundreds of other children from various towns in the Gomoa, Agona and Awutu Districts, to write the entrance examination.

That year saw the highest ever number (five) of pupils of Gyaman Local Council (at the time) Middle School passing the Common Entrance Examination, and qualifying for admission to various secondary schools.

Just before the end of year examinations of the 1961-62 school year, Master Louis Amoah, (the Headteacher), called me to his office and handed me an open envelope that had come from the Office of the Headmaster, Government Secondary Technical School, Takoradi. I had passed the Common Entrance examination and was invited to attend an interview at the Presbyterian Middle School at Swedru. Later, similar letters would come for two of my Form Three classmates, Emmanuel Donkoh (for the newly established Mpraeso Secondary School in the Eastern Region) and Benjamin Essiam (for Apam Secondary School). Two candidates from Form Two (Kofi Kyem Ampiah, the Catechist's third son, for St Charles Secondary School, Nsawam) and Miss Elizabeth Adjei (my cousin Kwame Donkor's step-daughter), for Nsawam Secondary School.

The gruelling interview involved several sections of written exercises in "Technical Recognition", matching various geometrical figures, followed by one-on-one question and answer sessions with the Headmaster, the late Mr S. M. Adu-Ampoma. Two weeks later, I received a formal offer of admission, subject to passing a medical examination at the Winneba Government Hospital. The medical examination had to be completed by the end of July. The school was to re-open in early September.

**Interview picture for GSTS June 1962**

As a child, I had been plagued by accidents on the playing field, at home and on the farms. Consequently, I nearly always carried one kind of wound or other. Sister Efua Antobam, who had problems with wounds herself, always took me to Swedru Clinic or Winneba Hospital, depending on the seriousness of our wounds, so I knew the route to Winneba Hospital as well as I knew the route from Swedru to Nyakrom, the farthest I had travelled on my own, up to that point. It was later when our son, Kofi was born that I discovered that I am allergic to ordinary plaster, the cause of the festering wounds that plagued my early life.

### Off to Government Secondary Technical School
Later in August 1962, I received another offer from Apam Secondary School, which had been my third choice for the Common Entrance Examinations, but Uncle Obrehun had already begun the

process of buying my "school kit" and I was on my way to GSTS, one of the best schools in Ghana! Also, I always wanted to be as far from home as possible. Apam simply did not feature in my plans for going away from home.

My £3 trunk box was purchased at Swedru, from the proceeds of the sale of my small cassava and corn farm which Maame Adewude (Uncle Obrehun's wife who had been my mother since that first day in late 1954 when Mother sent me off to live with Uncle Obrehun), had assigned to me. I carried the empty trunk to Uncle Ansanyi's tailor friend who had his shop on the banks of the Akora River. He was the one who had been chosen to sew my white suits, shorts, bedding and other items of school clothing, as prescribed in the "School Prospectus."

Later, Uncle bought me two pairs of sandals (Achimota and regular), one pair of black shoes, two cover cloths, towels and toiletries, which we took to the tailor's workshop to be stored in the trunk box. Uncle then bought my wooden "chop box", which we took to Gyaman. At the end of August when my 'regulation' clothes had all been sewn, we brought the trunk with the other items to Gyaman. All was set for me to go to boarding school.

Very early morning on Friday, 7th September 1962, the first day of the school year, Uncle and I travelled to Takoradi, going from Gyaman to Ankamu Junction, then to Cape Coast and Sekondi. From Sekondi, we were advised to take a taxi to the school compound because of my luggage.

Uncle Ansanyi actually paid my Common Entrance Examination fee in January 1962. He was one person who really valued education. Every one of his seven children went to secondary school, although only Kakra and Kojo Ansanyi (post-secondary A) went beyond GCE 'O' Levels. He had been interested in my schooling from the very first week I entered primary school. Our "Gyaman-Afransi Twidan Ebusua", one of the most prosperous in town, was a very close-knit one at the time.

Uncle Ansanyi had come to Gyaman at a time when the deadline for registration for the Common Entrance Examination was approaching fast. Uncle Obrehun had gone to the village, so he gave me the ten shillings to go and register. Uncle reimbursed him later, but it was Uncle Ansanyi who made my choices of schools - GSTS, Mfantsipim and Apam - for the common entrance examination. Later, I would learn that his last son, Samuel Kweku Atta Kakra Ansanyi, whom I had only seen in church on one or two occasions, was in Form Three, going on to Form Four at GSTS.

On school re-opening day, Kakra, as we called him, had been looking out for me and as soon as we got out of the taxi, he came to help carry my things to the Deputy Senior Housemaster (Mr B E Godwyll's) bungalow. I was duly registered but by that time, the cocoa season had only just begun, and Uncle had only managed my "washing fees", house dues of 5 shillings and pocket money of £1, hoping to send me the money for tuition fees and school uniforms later. The school regulations required that we paid for the uniforms, which were supplied by a private contractor, and at least part of the tuition fees. We did not have them and so we had to return to Gyaman. Within a week, Uncle found the money, and this time around asked Mother to take me to school since he had to return to the village for the sale of his cocoa produce.

We went by the same route. Mother knew Sekondi quite well because my cousin, Sister Ekua Akyeamfowa (Kow Morgan's mother), had lived with someone in Sekondi as a young girl and eventually married a soldier from Gyaman who was stationed in Takoradi at the time. Mother had been part of the bridal party at her wedding and had later visited Sister Ekua at least once, with Nana Ekua Addow and also on her own. Once again, Kakra was there to receive us. After I had been registered and assigned to my house (Dodoo House), Kakra took me upstairs, to the junior boys' dormitory, showed me how to make my bed and brought me back downstairs, to bid Mother farewell. At the school gate, Mother thought I looked sad and thought I was actually crying. She asked if I wanted to return with her.

Inwardly, I was elated. The school campus and my dormitory seemed like heaven away from all the chores of Gyaman! Kakra told her, "Maame, don't worry, he will be alright," and with that took my hand and led me to his own Vanderpuye House, from where he took me to the dining hall, to eat with fork and knife for the very first time in my life.


## Making new friends


In the dining hall, I was placed on the "Refugee Table," of boys from different houses who could not find places at their "House" tables, with Senior Bansah a very gentle pianist of the school (who would later teach me Chemistry in Form Four, after Cape Coast University), as my "Table Head"

My very first night in school was "Raws' Night," the Saturday night on which Form One students were made to entertain the whole school with jokes, crowned with a dancing competition. After this night, any kind of "homoing" was illegal and could be severely punished.

During the one week that I waited at home for my school fees and the money for my uniforms, I contracted a kind of infection which eventually took me to Effia Nkwanta Hospital. Because of this illness, one of Kakra's friends in Aryee House, Senior Essiaw, protected me during "Raws' Night." I did not take part in any of the night's activities.

The next day was "white suit and school tie" Sunday for evening service. In those days, we wore Kente Cloth on the last Sunday of the month and white suit and school tie all other Sundays. We had to be dressed up by half past five, for inspection and then, supper before evening service at half past seven.

Many of us from the countryside, in fact, apart from those who attended middle boarding schools, most of us "Raws" did not know how to tie shoelaces or ties, things that are taught in kindergartens in the United Kingdom and our own children later learnt to do in Ghana by age six.

One Form Five student at Dodoo House, Senior Caven, was very good at making the "Raws" in the house feel comfortable and welcome. He taught many of us to tie the 'School Tie' and lace our shoes. He was in the process of helping me 'tie up' when another Form One student, Lawrence Emmanuel Onyeche (LEO) as he would be known for the rest of our time at GSTS, appeared from nowhere and greeted Senior Caven in the Igbo language. Senior Caven introduced me as his new friend and that he was helping me to fix my tie.

I had arrived at school the previous afternoon. Onyeche and I were in the same upstairs, junior dormitory but up till that time, I had only spoken to a few of my mates and so it was good to make a new friend. We formed an instant long-term friendship which got me supporting "Biafra" during the Nigerian Civil War of 1967-70. Onyeche had come to live with his businessman uncle in Takoradi from Port Harcourt in Eastern Nigeria and subsequently gained admission at GSTS. His uncle who owned a huge bakery and a mansion in what was called "Esikafoammbantsem" (nouveau riche) in Takoradi, supplied fresh bread to GSTS and several other schools and colleges in the municipality every morning.

On most free exeat days, I went with him to his uncle's bakery and always returned to school with several loaves of bread that we often had to consume before we got back to school because we could not bring them to the dormitory and "chop box room" was only opened on Saturday mornings before it was cleaned by Form Two students after breakfast.

Having come to live in Takoradi for several months before school reopened, Lawrence knew his way around Takoradi and took me to town and showed me all the interesting places in town. We walked most of the time. We nearly always did UTC from school, then his uncle's bakery, Kingsway, Harbour View, and back to school in time for the 12:30 inspection. Open exeat was half day, 5:30 am to 12:30 pm.

**First hospital attendance**

Kakra was the "school doctor" and had apparently held the position since Form Three. He was in charge of the school's infirmary, popularly known as "Avoid" because it had a sleeping area where anyone who contracted chicken pox or measles was quarantined and isolated from the rest of the school population until they recovered. Those who were quarantined for chicken pox went to the beach in the afternoons to swim because the salty seawater helped the sores to heal quickly.

Because of my infected elbow, Kakra advised me to come and see him at the infirmary on Monday morning so he would give me a chit to go to the hospital. I did. There was a small school van which took those who needed hospital referral to the hospital. The van first went to Takoradi (European) Hospital, then to Effia Nkwanta Hospital.

Sometimes, if there were more than the twelve people the van was allowed to carry, it would go to Takoradi Hospital first and on the way back to Effia Nkwanta, pass by the school gate to pick up those that were scheduled for Effia Nkwanta Hospital.

The mini-bus usually came back at 11:30 or thereabouts, to pick up those who were still in the hospitals, back to school.

I was seen by a European doctor who prescribed an antibiotic for me. I was lucky to have been seen before 9 o'clock. I collected my medication soon after. Kakra had shown me where to get a bus back to school, for three pence. I was eager to start classes so as soon as I got my medication, I went to the bus stop and took the bus with two other students I recognised from the earlier trip and returned to school in time for the last lesson, which was English. Our Form One English mistress was Mrs Robinson, part of a contingent of the Canadian Technical Assistance Scheme at the school. I believed that because of my illness and the fact that I had reported to school late, Mrs Robinson took a liking for me and I became one of her pet students in the class for the year.

Sadly, her husband, Mr Robinson who taught Physics at the senior level, died of cancer at the end of the second term. Consequently, the Canadian High Commissioner to Ghana was invited as the Guest Speaker for the Speech and Prize Giving Day. In recognition of his services and tragic death in the service of the school, Oppon House or House Four was renamed Robinson House in memory of Mr Robinson, a decision that would be reversed about twenty years later following agitation by older students of the House.

. . .

## "Cured" of my Acrophobia

Back home, my cousins with whom I had grown up, did not understand why I could not climb any tree when even the girls among us could climb any kind of tree, including the coconut palm tree. The older boys would often sit among the coconut palm branches and drink the juice of as many nuts as possible, as they tossed the empty shells to the ground for me to pick up. This often happened during the hottest part of the afternoon on the farm when we would be thirsty and dying for something to quench our thirst. No matter how hard I tried, I could never bring myself to climb up to five feet from the ground. I was afraid of heights and would rather head for the nearest brook or stream than try and climb the coconut palm tree.

It was in primary Class Six aged eleven, that I finally managed to climb up an orange tree. I barely managed five minutes on the tree. Instead of enjoying the ripe fruit on the branches like everyone else, I shook the branches to cause a few of the ripened oranges to fall to the ground. Many burst open, but that was all I could manage. At least I had been up there.

At GSTS, juniors (Forms One and Two) slept in the upstairs dormitory with monitors, mainly Form Five and some Lower Sixth Form students. In the old blocks, one had to make a special effort like taking out the mosquito netting, to be able to see the ground, which was fine with me, because I would not make the effort, except when we had to take out and wash the mosquito netting, which thankfully, was done only two or three Friday afternoons in the whole term.

There was a spectacular view of Takoradi Harbour between Dodoo House and the Dining Hall/old Assembly Hall, from where Form One students especially, watched ships enter and leave the harbour. Again, it took me a few weeks to pluck the courage to join my friends, to watch and count the ships waiting to anchor and the ones already inside the harbour. Then there were the water skiers, a real sight to behold.

As long as there were no trains running on the railway line below, I could watch the goings on at the beach and beyond, but the "goods trains" with numerous coaches filled with bauxite and manganese from Awaso threw me into a spin and I would often turn to face the school oval until the last coach passed. With time, I overcame that fear as well.

The Technical Drawing Rooms were on the second floor of the old Administration Block, another obstacle that I had to conquer. Sometimes the last class was a few minutes late and we had to wait on the corridor to go in and I had to look at the playing field with trepidation. Again, with time, I managed to look down without too much trouble. I was being cured of "my fear of heights".

During the long vacation of the 1962-63 academic year, I made a special trip to the village to climb an orange tree, then a mango tree, to demonstrate to my cousins that I was no longer terrified of heights although, till today, I have never been able to make it up a coconut palm tree.

**New Horizons**

Up to this point, the only sports I had participated in were football, volleyball and athletics. Within a few weeks of settling at GSTS, I was playing table tennis, hockey and cricket in addition to football and volleyball. I would continue to play volleyball and hockey through my years at GSTS and at the University of Science and Technology, where I was even invited to the University hockey team, which I declined, preferring to play for my Hall, University (aka Katanga), instead.

Form One went quite well, having finished all subjects in the top ten of my class of 31, considering that I was competing with boys from some of the best middle schools in Accra, Kumasi, Takoradi, Ho, Cape Coast and also from the top boys' boarding schools in Ghana at the time, Salem in Accra, Aburi, Larteh and Akropong. The nearest I had ever got to the French language was listening to "Parlons **Français**" on pre-set radio back at Gyaman. Yet within a few weeks of starting

French classes, I was translating sentences in French and was one of my best subjects, even performing very well at "Scientific French" during my second year at university.

Form Two was challenging in more ways than one. Everyone who went to boarding school in the 1960s and 70s will tell you that most people became haughty during the first few weeks of Form Two, after the trials and tribulations of "Homoing" in Form One. Most Form Two students would not miss the opportunity to "avenge themselves" on the newcomers. I picked on a few myself, often following the crowd. Two of the people I picked on later became my lifelong friends. But my most painful experience was fighting one of those Form One boys who had made fun of me, calling me a villager.

As a boy, people had picked on me at home, on the streets and on the school playground. On most occasions, I would turn and walk away, if I could do so without being called names. This experience in Form Two was one occasion I could but did not turn my back on and it would prove a very costly mistake. Unfortunately, I pushed this boy around and he hit his hand against his metal bedstead and broke his hand. I was suspended from school for five weeks, something that would live with me for the next five years!

# CHAPTER 4
# THE DEATH OF NANA KWEKU OTU AND AFTER

I met the six Wise Men of our clan, Nana Ampiah, Nana Akanambah, Nana Kweku Otu, Nana Kobena Ofosu, Nana Kofi Kwei at Akwamu as well as the two, Nana Kojo Entsie and Nana Kofi Arku who settled at Achiase. They were all very resourceful and formed the solid pillars of the clan, which they held together so skilfully for a very long time. Nana Ofosu was the youngest of both the male and female cousins, but he together with his three older sisters, Nana Esi Ansaaduba, Nana Ekua Addow and Nana Efua Gurabah, jelled very well with Nana Ampiah, Nana Akanambah, Nana Kweku Otu and his sisters, Nana Munkuwah and Nana Mbefowa, to present a formidable and well respected block that brought together the Twidan Clan at Gyaman, Afransi (whose stool incidentally belonged to the unit), Akwamu and Achiase, with links to Asebu and Dabayin.

As far as I can remember, Nana Ampiah was the first to die, followed by Nana Akanambah, Kofi Entsie and Nana Kofi Arku. All these went to join their ancestors in peace, to be joined by Nana Kwei later, but Nana Kweku Otu's death in mid-1963 caused an 'earthquake' whose reverberations continue to vibrate within the clan today. The divisions that single death caused have never been healed, and the once solid Gyaman Twidan Ebusua is now a shadow of its old self.

I am not sure how he managed to do it but Nana Kweku Otu had vast cocoa farms all over the place, Ekuabo, Ahamadonko, Osokor and Akroso. Not only did he settle his older children, Kwansa Panyin (the drummer), Kwansah Ketseaba (Safohen) and Kwaw Edu, who were all very wealthy in their own right, but he also ensured that all his direct nephews - Kwesi Benyi, Kweku Obrehun, Kweku Ketseaba, Kobena Ansanyi (who had some education and later became a master tailor at Swedru), Kobena Mensah and Otsibu - had their own cocoa farms, which they built on. Uncle Kofi Hammond settled at Tarkwa as a prosperous driver and transport owner. Yet Nana Kweku Otu's succession would tear apart these nephews who had been a very close-knit group, and with them, the rest of the Twidan clan.

As our grandmother and grand aunties had always done, Nana Ansaaduba, Nana Mbefowa, Nana Addow and Nana Gurabah got together with their daughters, to look after their "Big Brother" during the latter stages of his life. Nana Kweku Otu was installed Twidanhen in 1957. He was the guardian of a pot of gold nuggets which our great great, great-grandmother (Awo Dena) had reportedly found on the farm about one hundred years earlier. This pot of gold was kept in a safe in Nana's bedroom and was only resorted to in times of major clan crisis. Apparently in his very last moments, his nephews went and drove their aunties out of the old man's room, removed physical cash that was stored under his bed, and managed to find the key to the safe (apparently Uncle Ansanyi who bought that safe, either knew where the key to the safe was kept or according to legend, actually kept a copy of the key for himself). They found some more money in the safe, making a total of £8,000 in cash in those days.

Exactly what happened to the family pot of gold has never been verified first-hand because it was too embarrassing for all involved. Apparently, as the older nephews concerned themselves with the physical cash, Uncle Kweku Ketseaba, one of the youngest of them all, slipped the pot of gold nuggets under his cloth and eventually took it to Odiyifo Kwame Nkansah, Head of the African Faith Tabernacle Church (popularly known as Nkansah Church) at Nkawkaw in the Eastern Region, for "cleansing". Uncle Kweku Ketseaba was a member of that Church.

According to the version that made the rounds at the time, when he got to the Church's headquarters, he was asked to go and put "his parcel" in a special room where such apparently "demonically contaminated" items were kept, and "come back in two weeks." Two weeks later when he returned to claim his "sanctified" possession, it was not there. When he enquired about the whereabouts of his parcel, he was told that if he could not find it where he had placed it, then "the angels had got rid of it to save him from calamity."

A major treasure that had been in the family for about one hundred years and had helped generations before had been lost forever! And that would haunt them, and Uncle Kweku Ketseaba in particular, who died a pauper, for the rest of their lives.

## The Succession Problems

Uncle Obrehum believed that being the son of the most senior of Nana Kweku Otu's sisters, Ama Adadzewa, he was the rightful heir of their uncle. Ironically, Uncle Kwesi Benyi was the firstborn of their mothers but through most of their adult life, he had virtually ceded his seniority to Uncle Obrehun. I have also heard from reliable sources that Nana Kweku Otu singled out Uncle Obrehun as his heir and informed Nana Ofosu to that effect. Had Nana Kweku Otu made a will or even a formal "Nsamansew," as they called it in those days, the upheaval that followed his death could have been avoided.

"Nsamansew" would have involved the old man calling his nephews, sisters and cousins and announcing to them the person he had chosen to be his heir when he died.

As it was, the real battle was between Uncle Ansanyi on behalf of his mother on the one side and Uncle Obrehun with his Brothers Kwesi Benyi and Kweku Ketseaba and their sisters Ekua Gyanwa and Aba on the other side. My direct granduncle, Nana Ofosu, was the Ebusua Panyin at the time. He had the final say in who succeeded his late cousin.

With me being brought up by Uncle Obrehun, it was believed that he would favour Uncle Obrehun, especially since the Old Man had at least mentioned it to him. It was never to be. Within days of Nana's death, money began to change hands like no one's business. Some elders and sub-chiefs at Gyaman made major investments out of that succession battle, and the Ajumako Omanhen, who incidentally was their direct cousin, allegedly bought a saloon car out of the free-for-all largesse.

In the end, Nana Ofosu and the elders decided that since Nana Kweku Otu had a surviving sister in Nana Mbefowa, she had to be the rightful heir ("*Nnamba nnsae a wofoase nndzi adze*"), as was later interpreted. Uncle Obrehun was to take over Nana Kwaw Opan's farms and other properties that had passed to Nana Kweku Otu at his death. With that, Uncle Obrehun was chosen as Twidan Ebusuahen. Nana Opan's storey building was already falling apart by then and his son Kweku Enyan had taken that over anyway. So, Uncle Obrehun's part of the inheritance was just a title and one cocoa farm at Osokor, to go with it. Even Uncle Kweku Ketseaba's coconut plantation which we had all toiled to establish, was taken away from him because that land belonged to Nana Kweku Otu.

By this time, Uncle Obrehun had either sold or mortgaged most of his own cocoa farms and other movable properties. He was a broken man. Nana Mbefowa would later appropriate even the Ebusuahen for her son, Uncle Ansanyi. The break-up of Ebusua Twidan was complete and I became one of the major casualties of that very nasty and bitter family feud. My secondary education was in jeopardy.

Somehow, Uncle managed to find my school fees and other requirements for the first term of Form Two, after Nana's funeral. When I got home for the Christmas holidays, it was obvious that I would not go back to GSTS. In fact, Uncle Obrehun actually took me together with Uncle Kwesi Benyi as a witness, to Nana Ofosu, to inform him that he could not carry on with my education any longer. I had not finished Middle Form Four and by this time my classmates who were in Middle Form Four had already registered for the Middle School Leaving Certificate Examinations. I was stranded.

I could wait and join the next class for the Middle School Leaving Examination the next year or else sit the Teacher Training Examination and go for the two-year (Certificate B) or four-year (Certificate A) teacher training course.

## Ghana Cocoa Marketing Board Scholarship

While I was still considering my options, I went to Swedru one day and decided to visit my old Class Two teacher, Miss Elsie Sackey, who quit teaching in mid-1957, to get married and later went to work for the Department of Social Welfare at Swedru. I had stayed in touch with her after she left Gyaman and had actually written and posted my very first letter in 1957 to Miss Sackey, with a tuppence half penny stamp and got a reply back from her, with a lot of encouragement about how well I had written the letter.

When she saw me, she screamed and might have missed a heartbeat. Why was I not in school at that time of the academic year? I had written to her from school and so she knew that I had gone to GSTS. I told her about my plight, part of which she already knew. She had heard about the troubles that had been brewing in "our family" because she knew some of Uncle Ansanyi's children with whom she had attended school at Swedru.

She asked me to go and bring my Form One school reports. Because much of the cocoa production in the Central Region came from the Agona District, the regional office of the Ghana Cocoa Marketing Board was located at Swedru and that is where the Regional Loans Officer, Mr Kofi Agyarey was based. Mrs Nkrumah, as she had become, asked me to go and bring my Uncle, so we could all go and see Mr Agyarey.

When we met Mr Agyarey in his office a few days later, he was surprised that I had not been awarded a Cocoa Marketing Board (CMB) scholarship after Form One, with the kind of grades I had made in my subjects and the reports that my Form Master, Housemaster and Headmaster had written about me. He asked for £3 from Uncle, to use to write letters to Accra. He told me to come back to check in two weeks. I would visit his office every fortnight for the next two months.

One Wednesday morning in early August, as soon as I entered his office, Mr Kofi Agyarey rose and met me from behind his huge desk with an extended hand and broad smile saying in Twi, "Yeedi nkunim," meaning, "We have won a victory", and with that handed me an envelope from the Director of Scholarships, Ghana Cocoa Marketing Board, saying I had been awarded a full scholarship to continue at GSTS until I finished the General Certificate of Education (GCE) "Ordinary Level," subject to my satisfactory performance at school.

He informed me that a copy of the letter had been sent to the Headmaster of GSTS and that I should prepare to go back to school. A few days later, I received a letter from the Headmaster asking me to report to him on Monday after school re-opened in September 1964.

Although my three school uniforms were still pretty much intact, I had grown out of some of my regulation clothes – white shorts, white shirts and white suits. I could have the coats of my suits opened up a bit and the turn-ups of the trousers lowered to lengthen them. I took them to a local tailor who also assured me he could make those alterations, but I needed at least one new white shirt and a few items of underwear.

I had written to Uncle Nyarko and Uncle Nsedu when my problems began but I did not hear from them. Now the situation was desperate. Besides, by this time, the two sides in the Nana Kweku Otu succession feud had turned to consulting "jujumen" and mediums and Uncle Obrehun was concerned about my welfare and wanted me to stay away from Gyaman as much as I could, now that I was about to return to school.

Mother was not keen about me going to my maternal uncles and her brothers, but my grandmother, Nana Esi Ansaaduba or (Maame, as we called her), thought it was worth giving it a try and actually provided part of the money I used to travel to Koforidua.

# CHAPTER 5
# TO KOFORIDUA AND MY MATERNAL UNCLES

had never travelled beyond Swedru on the Swedru-Nsawam road, but one of my Dodoo housemates, Christian Gyasi Antwi, lived at Nsawam. I had ever heard him say that his father owned a shop not too far away from the train station. Antwi could be of help, so I took the lorry from Swedru to Nsawam. Antwi's father's general merchandise store turned out to be easy to find and he was right there at the store. I told him I wanted to take the train to Koforidua and that I had to be there before my uncle closed from work at 5 p.m. since I did not know where he lived. It was past midday and the afternoon passenger train from Accra to Kumasi via Koforidua had already passed through and there wouldn't be another train till past 4 p.m. I couldn't risk that, so he advised me to take a lorry to Suhum and join another from there to Koforidua.

I was a bit apprehensive, but it turned out to be quite simple. I met Uncle Nyarko at his office at the Ministry of Agriculture. He welcomed me and took me to his wife, Auntie Comfort Addobea (Pastor Nyarko's mother), with whom he had had Yaa (Aba Ansaaduba), who sadly passed away while I was in America. I stayed with Auntie Comfort playing with the two-year-old Yaa until Uncle closed from work and took me to Uncle Nsedu's house at Jackson Park, a short walk from the ministry. I had not seen either of them since they attended Nana Kweku Otu's burial the year before. It was a very happy reunion.

The next day, Uncle Nyarko took me to his Indian merchant friend, Kubchandani from whom he had a line of credit with which he bought most of his personal supplies on credit and paid at the end of the month, to buy me two white shirts, four singlets, a pair of sandals and some provisions. Eventually, Uncle Nsedu settled most of that bill. Uncle Nsedu was working for the Ghana National Construction Corporation (GNCC) that was engaged in a major office complex near the Koforidua Sports Stadium at the time. I met him at the site at lunchtime the next day.

Uncle Nyarko lived near Prince Boateng's house (a former Ambassador and a prominent local businessman). Down the street from where he lived was his caterer, a very pleasant Ada woman who cooked for him in the evenings and weekends and a Togolese 'washer man' who washed his shirts and bedding and was paid at the end of every month. I spent a week at Koforidua and returned to Gyaman, taking the train to Nsawam, and then to Swedru. That was my first experience of travelling on the train, but it would become my mode of travel between Takoradi and Koforidua, for the next six years.

## Back to GSTS

I went back to GSTS on 11th September 1964 with joy and sadness at the same time. Joy because I was returning to school and sadness because I had to repeat Form Two. When I reported to the Headmaster on the Monday after school re-opening which was also my sixteenth birthday, he asked whether I wanted to go on to Form Three. I had struggled with Technical Drawing because I missed the first two classes of "Construction Drawing," in Form One, something I had difficulty catching up with for nearly three academic years. I opted to repeat Form Two since I had only done the first term of Form Two earlier. The Headmaster simply said, then go to Form Two A.

In those days at GSTS, there was a choice between Metalwork and Engineering Drawing on one hand and Woodwork and Building Drawing on the other, from Form Three to Form Five. The A and C classes offered Metalwork and Engineering Drawing while the B classes offered Woodwork and Building Drawing. I had started in Form One B and actually begun Form Two in the B class, although I did not intend to offer Woodwork. Mr A D A Tagoe (ADAT), the Metalwork and Technical Drawing master made life quite miserable for me in Form One, and even though I did better in Woodwork than Metalwork, I still wanted to stick it out with Metalwork.

Soon after school re-opened for the academic year, it was announced that our group would go through a four-year Secondary School Programme, as part of a new policy that was aimed at reducing the number of years Ghanaian children spent in pre-university education. Therefore, instead of choosing our optional subjects in Form Three as was done under the old system, we were to select ours in Form Two.

Geography was an alternative to French. I had done very well in French in Form One and Form Two B and in any case, the Geography Master Mr Kpakpo Allotey had hounded me in Form Two B so for me, the announcement of the four-year programme was heaven-sent on two counts. Firstly, I could choose French and avoid Mr Allotey and secondly, I would complete the Ordinary Levels at the same time as my original classmates!

I had my GCE "O" Levels subjects all set for me: Physics, Elementary Mathematics (compulsory Alternative B at GSTS), Additional Mathematics (which our group began in Form Three, instead of Form Four in the old programme), Chemistry, Technical Drawing, Metalwork, French, English and Oral English (which was also compulsory at GSTS).

For the next three terms or so, everything went quite well for me, both financially and academically. The strict regulations about school uniforms on the school compound and "white-white" on exeat days or special occasions in town meant that everyone, rich and poor, looked the same at school and in town. Uncle Nyarko would usually send me a 'slip' or money order with which I could pay for the transport cost (usually £1), back to Koforidua for the holidays. There was a students' concession ticket for travel on both the trains and State Transport Corporation buses. The train travel between Takoradi and Koforidua was cheaper and simpler than the State Transport bus, as there was no direct bus from Takoradi to Koforidua.

The rich students (vacation time was the only time the difference showed) who went home by bus had to break their journey in Accra and continue on another bus from there. They usually got home earlier. However, most students who lived at Koforidua, Effiduase, Jumapo, Kukurantumi, Tafo and beyond, went on the train. We would usually take the Takoradi-Accra Express Train through Huni Valley, to Kotoku Junction, and join the Accra to Kumasi passenger train from there to Koforidua. The fare from Takoradi to Koforidua and vice versa was ten shillings, plus an additional four shillings for a trunk and "chop box" or just two shillings for a trunk.

Because most secondary schools in Ghana nearly always vacated and reopened the same day in those days, students from several of the schools in Sekondi-Takoradi, the Western Region in general, and even Cape Coast in the Central Region, came down to Takoradi, to join the express train. So, travelling by train was always exciting, although apparently, the overnight train or "Sleeper" from Takoradi to Kumasi was even more exciting because most of the students from the schools in the Central Region who hailed from the Ashanti Region, preferred the "Sleeper" through Obuasi, to Kumasi.

### A bit of mischief

Soon after I joined Form 2A, I made friends with one of the continuing students, Francis Kwami. We were in the same upstairs (juniors) dormitory in Dodoo House, but our friendship actually began in the classroom. Francis was short but quite stocky. He had to stand on one of those wooden platforms in the junior metal workshop to be able to file or saw.

To make up for his height, Francis developed a trick for filling difficult exercises. Instead of filing all the way through, he would mark the metal plate and drill several holes through the portions that should be filed. He would then use the hacksaw to remove the jagged portions, so he would have very little to file away.

This was "illegal" but he did it on the blind side of Mr Tagoe, and he always got away with it because usually there was some drilling to do, although not before the filing was completed. I learnt the trick from Francis Kwami and it helped me a lot.

We played hockey, football and volleyball together and we were always together. In the juniors' hockey team, he played at the old Number 6 position and I played at Number 4. We played in the same positions in the football team. We always covered each other. If you "whacked" at me, you are sure to get a retaliatory whack from Kwami Francis, as we called him. It was the same on the football field.

We studied together for several years and made sure we were always in the same group at Physics and Chemistry practical lessons. When we did "acids" and "salts", we were taught that in all experiments with acids and bases, it was always done alphabetically, acid to base, never the other way around. We decided to test the "wrong" way and see what happened.

On that fateful day after recording all our experimental results and just as we packed away the reagents and test tubes, burettes and pipettes, we did our little experiment and naturally, it exploded and began to burn the bench. We had prepared for that eventuality and quickly put out the fire before the Master could reach our bench. Of course, we pleaded that it was an accident.

Kwami Francis went to Sixth Form at Axim Secondary School and eventually went into teaching. From June 1968 when we parted after "O Levels", we did not meet again till sometime in 1986. GNPC was based at Republic House at the time and I had gone to UTC during my lunch break, to look for something and as I entered the main entrance, there in flesh and blood was my old friend Francis Kwami. We must have spent about an hour reminiscing on the mischief we played on people in the classroom, the workshops and the playing fields.

Years later, I would go through his hometown Logba Tota in the Volta Region on one of my many NADMO field trips in the region. I asked of him then, but he was not in town.

·  ·  ·

**Changed Circumstances**

I began to face difficulties about the third term in Form Three. Sometimes, my slip or money order wouldn't arrive on time or not at all. Occasionally, Uncle Nyarko would write to me or sometimes call me through the school administration office, to go and see his classmate from Gyaman, Mr TK Arko, who also happened to be Uncle Otobaw's brother-in-law.

Mr Arko was a manager at Elder Dempster Lines, a shipping company at Takoradi Harbour. Sometimes, on School exeats or mid-term holidays, which at GSTS in those days was just half a day, from 5:30 am till midday, I went to visit Mr Arko or Mr Odoom, another classmate of my uncle's who was a manager at John Holt Bartholomew, also in Takoradi. Sometimes, I went to Mr Odoom's wife, Auntie Mary, who had sung with Mother in the Methodist Church choir for many years, at Effiakuma. They were all extremely generous to me, and they would usually give me enough money to replenish my supply of toiletries and even 'provisions.'

Since returning to school, I always made it a point not to forget where it had all begun. For the sake of convenience, I would spend the first week of my holidays at Koforidua, go over to Gyaman, then to the village, if Uncle Obrehun was not at Gyaman, on to Akenkausu, to visit Mother and Sister Aba and her family, before returning to Koforidua to prepare to go back to school.

Around 1968, Uncle Obrehun and his younger brother Kweku Ketseaba also acquired cocoa farming lands near Akenkausu, which made life easier for me because I could go to Gyaman, then to Akenkausu and back to Koforidua on the train. On those trips, Sister Aba and Mother always gave me some money, which guaranteed that I would be able to pay my fare back to school and sometimes, even for the return journey home. Right from a very early age, I developed the habit of saving money, so at the earliest opportunity, I opened a Post Office Savings Account at Koforidua. That habit would help me immensely in later life.

On occasions when I did not have anything at all at the end of the term, my friend Christian Gharban from Winneba, who would become my Best Man and life-long friend, would come to me and say, "Ebo, do you have any money on you? I shall go to my uncle and see if I can get something." Chris had an uncle who at the time served as a CID inspector attached to the Sekondi Regional Police Command. He would usually give Chris two cedis in those days. For which Chris would say, "Since you have to travel farther, take one cedi and fifty pesewas and I will keep the fifty pesewas because my mother will pay Mr White anyway."

Mr White was a commercial lorry driver who lived near his house at Winneba and was always dressed in white shorts and white shirts. His wooden Morris trucks (I believe he had two at that time), were painted all white, with the inscription, "Mr White" on all sides and in front. He always took Chris to school and back to Winneba and was paid by his mother.

Not long after Uncle Nyarko joined Uncle Nsedu at Koforidua on transfer from Keta, he met an old friend from his Winneba Methodist School days, Mr Anim, who worked at the State Insurance Corporation (SIC), at Koforidua. Mr Anim introduced uncle to agency work at SIC. Uncle could do it on a part-time basis. Under the scheme, agents canvassed and secured insurance business - life, vehicle, home, etc, and were paid a percentage of the monthly premiums that these clients paid to SIC. With time, uncle got quite a large clientele and was doing very well financially, since it supplemented his salary from his civil service job at the Ministry of Agriculture.

Sometime in early 1965, Uncle began to have some health issues, although, until today, I do not know the exact details. It would seem that those issues necessitated his application for early retirement on health grounds. He applied and got transferred to Kibi, as part of the preparation towards early retirement from the civil service. He was only 41 years old at the time, and I am not sure how it worked out but possibly, it was arranged in such a way that he could retire on health grounds but could not draw his pension until after a certain period, since he began to draw his pension much later, and still receives it today, nearly forty years later! That brief transfer enabled me to spend part of my long vacation of 1965 at Kibi, one of the wettest places in Ghana.

Eventually, Uncle secured early retirement and began to do the SIC agency work on a full-time basis. Soon, his finances began to improve. He even got his friend, Mr Kwadwo Abrokwah who had been made redundant at the Ministry of Agriculture, to join in the agency business at SIC. Mr Abrokwah had moved in with Uncle, as he looked for a new job, but soon after he joined Uncle at SIC, he went and rented his own accommodation at the 'Old Estates' and brought his wife and young daughter to live with him.

Unfortunately, not long after Uncle began the full-time agency business, the more lucrative vehicle insurance part was moved to mainstream insurance, leaving the agency staff with just life and home insurance. Uncle had insured many of the commercial vehicles at Koforidua and the change would deal a major blow to his circumstances.

It would seem that that change necessitated his move from the more central location near Prince Boateng's house to a newly built house at Sorodae. It was a three-tenant, six-room house (a bedroom and a hall each), on the outskirts of Koforidua in those days. There was a large undeveloped plot in front of the house on which I made my own small garden during the Easter holidays of the 1966-67 academic year. Later in the year, we harvested quite a bit of corn and a large amount of tomatoes and pepper. We actually gave so much pepper away to people in the area.

It was during that period that Auntie Grace Glavee returned to Uncle Nyarko's life. Auntie Grace was a very pleasant and industrious woman, who could create different dishes out of corn and cassava doughs, with little effort. Not long after Auntie Grace arrived, Uncle's finances began to improve again. It was from Sorodae that I took my GCE Ordinary Levels. However, by the time I returned to Koforidua for the third term holidays of 1968, Uncle had moved from Sorodae to "Busy Bee", into a house that was owned by one Mr Quist, right next door to Glavee's Art Studios and a short walk from where we used to live near Prince Boateng's house. Mr Glavee was Auntie Grace Glavee's (Ekua Ampiaa's mother's) direct cousin. He had had his Art

Studio in that house for many years. Uncle's finances continued to improve there.

He changed his old, rather heavy sitting room furniture to a more modern set, bought a radio for the first time and an electric pressing iron, thus doing away with his "washerman." He even sent his shirts to Kweku Okyere's Modern Laundry near the Methodist Church, while we washed and ironed our own bedding. Uncle Kojo Benyi had by this time moved to Koforidua and so all three of Mother's brothers were together for the first time in many years. Uncle Nyarko rented one room at Mr Koffie's house, across the street from Mr Quist's house, where Uncle Benyi slept. Kofi Graham, Yaw Mensah and I would join him in that room later. It was at Mr Quist's house that things turned dramatically sour for Uncle, from which I believe he never recovered till he eventually moved back to Gyaman in 2013, and it was not unrelated to his liaisons with women.

## My Uncles' Personal Relationships

I met four of Mother's brothers, Uncle Kofi Amo, Uncle Benyi, Uncle Nsedu and Uncle Nyarko. Mother was the only surviving girl out of three that their parents gave birth to. Nana Ansaaduba (Abawa Hagar or Maame) and Nana Kofi Enyaah had ten issues, five of whom survived into adulthood. Apparently, they were divorced along the line and later got back together again. Nana Kofi Enyaah died in 1957, when I was nine years old, a loss that would live with me for years because Nana had been the first male figure I had really related to as a child after our father died when I was only three months old.

From my very personal attachment to Nana Kofi Enyaah and Maame (Nana Ansaaduba), I learnt that the one thing that caused Maame the most heartache, even more than all the aggravation she received from her younger siblings (she was the most 'saintly' woman I ever met in my life), was the fact that none of her sons settled in a proper marriage in her lifetime. She died in 1967, obviously still nursing that pain. May her amazingly loving soul continue to rest in perfect peace in the Lord.

Uncle Kofi Amo apparently lost his wife (Kweku Ampiah's mother) in childbirth and never married again for the rest of his life, until he died in in 1959. Uncle Benyi never married. As far as I can remember, Uncle Nsedu had a child with Aunt Aba Yaa (she later became a fetish priestess), who lived next door to the family house at Dwokwaafo Mu. It would seem that Aunt Aba Yaa's pregnancy coincided with her "induction" into fetishism. That union never took off and the beautiful girl that was born to it died soon after birth.

Later, Uncle Nsedu had various liaisons with women that were past child-bearing, most with their own grown-up children, during his years in Accra. When he moved to the Eastern Region in the late 1950s with A Lang, which later became the Ghana National Construction Corporation, he first lived at Aburi. Later, his job took him to Koforidua, Mampong, Abetifi and Nkawkaw, as well as short stints at Asesewa, always returning to Koforidua. In his travels, Uncle had a child at nearly every one of these locations. Unfortunately, only two of those children lived past age two, Kwame Ampiah(mother from Abetifi), who was later traced and brought home by Pastor Nyarko when he went to technical school at Abetifi and a Kow Abbam whose mother hailed from Asesewa and whom he never set eyes on again after he left Asesewa.

Uncle Nyarko first met and had a child with Auntie Grace Glavee (Ekua Ampiaa, 1958), while he was stationed at Keta, not too far away from Auntie Grace's hometown of Atiavi. The story I heard from Uncle Nsedu was that Uncle Nyarko married Auntie Grace and actually moved to Koforidua with her and their newborn baby, Ekua. This was about 1959, but within two years, Auntie Grace left and moved back to Atiavi. Auntie Grace had an older daughter with someone else at Atiavi before she married Uncle Nyarko. Her return to Atiavi seemed to have brought some strain between Uncle Nyarko and her cousin, Mr Glavee, from the bits and pieces that I got from Mr Glavee in later years.

After Auntie Grace went back to Atiavi, Uncle met Auntie Comfort Addobea and had a child (Aba Ansaaduba) with her. Apparently, when Auntie Addobea first got pregnant, Uncle bought the customary pieces of cloth, head kerchiefs, a ring, a Bible and hymn book and other items, for the traditional marriage. According to Uncle Nyarko (he told me this story himself and later corroborated by Uncle Nsedu), they carried the items along footpaths through virgin forests and farmlands, for about fifteen kilometres, to Auntie Comfort's father's village somewhere near Mangoase, only to be told by the old man that "He did not want any Fanti man in his family." They went back to the same reception after Kweku Ampiah (Pastor Nyarko) was born in 1965, so their cat-and-mouse relationship continued at Koforidua, away from her parents, for years.

In late 1966, Auntie Grace returned to Koforidua. Initially, Uncle Nyarko did not seem to like the idea because apparently, while she was away from him, she had another child with a fetish priest at Atiavi. The story was that the fetish priest cast a spell on her. Uncle Nsedu was dead against her coming back and it became a source of friction between him and his younger brother. Then Auntie Grace became pregnant with Sammy, who was born at Atiavi in 1968. Later that year, Auntie Grace returned to Koforidua with Ekua and Baby Sammy. Ekua was enrolled in Class 3 at Koforidua Methodist Primary School in 1968. That was the year I finished my General Certificate of Education Examinations (GCE) Ordinary Levels with Grade 1, and qualified to begin the sixth form at GSTS in October. By this time, Uncle had brought Pastor Nyarko and Yaa, as we called his senior sister, to live with him.

Ekua was a brilliant girl, the cleverest of all of Uncle Nyarko's children. When she first arrived at Koforidua, she did not understand a word of Twi. Uncle spoke Ewe like a native and Auntie Grace spoke a bit of Twi, so if the two of them were around, there was good all-round communication. However, whenever I was left alone with Ekua, we had to resort to sign language, but by the end of her very first term at Koforidua, she knew enough Twi to place third overall in class, including beating several of the Twi-speaking children in Twi! My greatest personal disappointment was that owing to the problems that bedevilled Uncle from about 1971, Ekua could not go to secondary school and apparently, it was with some difficulty that she managed to take the Middle School Leaving Certificate Examination at Atiavi, and I could not help my "baby sister" because I was away.

Not long after she arrived back at Koforidua, Auntie Grace began to trade between Koforidua and Atiavi. Sometimes she went for a week or ten days. When I returned from school on holidays, I realised that a young lady who lived in the next house came to our part of the compound house, sometimes when Uncle was away. Often when the lady came around, I would jokingly ask about her business in the house because she was probably my age or just a year or two older. Later, some of the adults in the house would remark about "showing respect to my auntie". At the same time, there was another lady, Miss Comfort Agbenyo, who worked with Uncle Nyarko and, seemed quite close to him. It did not bother me because Uncle Nyarko had never really shown any tendency to womanising, at least not when I was home on holidays.

### Enter Auntie Comfort (Miss Sarah Ampah)

One evening during the Easter holidays of 1969, Uncle and Auntie Grace had a heated argument which could only have been over finances and a woman. By this time, I knew quite a few words in Ewe so I could put one and two together and make intelligent deductions.

Earlier on, I had woken up at 5:30 one morning to see Uncle Nyarko coming towards the house in cloth. I had never seen Uncle in cloth outside his living room, not even at their parents' funerals! He always wore dark or grey trousers and a white shirt. I was not exactly sure where he had come from, but he was definitely not coming from Uncle Nsedu's house because that would have been too far away and too early in the day. Later that day when I asked Ekua about it, she innocently remarked that "he goes to a certain woman around the corner." That woman was Auntie Comfort or Miss Sarah Ampah.

Not long after the argument, while Auntie Grace was on one of her travels, Auntie Comfort came to the house and collected one of Uncle's cover cloths, a bucket, utensils and some other items and took them to her own house. Uncle was really moving in with her.

The details are a bit fuzzy now, but it might have been during the first term of Upper Sixth Form in December 1969. Uncle Nsedu had apparently heard of the goings-on at "Busy Bee" and might have actually spoken to Uncle Nyarko about it in private, but it came to a head that night. The sparks were flying and rightly so because anytime Uncle Nyarko got into trouble, it was Uncle Nsedu who bailed him out, and there had been many over the years. Auntie Grace apparently got fed up and went back to Atiavi with Sammy, leaving Ekua behind. Auntie Comfort moved into the house with her two sons, Kwesi Boateng who must have been three or four years old and Joojo who was lame in one leg and must have been about eighteen months old. There was an older daughter, Maud, who lived with her own father.

There were some furious exchanges between my two uncles, with some of Uncle Nsedu's comments directed at Auntie Comfort, who packed her things and was leaving the house. I went to talk to her in the dark. This episode has been used against me, as having been the one who persuaded her to stay on that fateful night, and there is an even more laughable one about the elders of the Apostolic Church at Koforidua talking her into choosing my uncle over a very rich ex-husband. Auntie Comfort had been divorced from this man for several years before she met Uncle Nyarko, bearing in mind she had two different marriages after that "rich man."


## GCE Ordinary Level


From Form Three when we began to study the physical sciences as core subjects, Mathematics, Physics, English and French remained my best subjects at school. I also did very well in Chemistry, but Technical Drawing was a bit of a headache for me. I always passed it but often around the 60% range, compared with the rest of my subjects. I began to dream of studying Mathematics at the university. However, even though I always did very well in class exercises and mid-term examinations, I nearly always scored higher in Physics than Mathematics in final examinations, which was very frustrating for me. For instance, while I scored Grade 2 in Elementary Mathematics and Grade 4 in Additional Mathematics (long story) at the GCE Ordinary Level, I scored Grade 1 or Excellent in Physics. I had planned to take Physics, Pure and Applied Mathematics in Sixth Form.

Our Class of '68 became an experimental class in many ways than one. We were the first group to study Permutations and Combinations and Statistics as part of our syllabus in Additional Mathematics, as well as Organic Chemistry, at the Ordinary Level. Before then, Permutations and Combinations were part of Advanced Level Pure Mathematics and Organic Chemistry was also studied at the Advanced Level.

Additionally, our group at GSTS was the first to do more filing/bench work than lathe work in the final Metalwork examination - two hours of bench work and one hour of lathe work - because Mfantsipim School offered Metalwork at GCE 'O' Levels for the first time that year. Mfantsipim's only lathes were six or seven very small ones that had been packed in a corner of the Senior Metalworkshop at GSTS for many years. Those small, old lathes were offered to Mfantsipim the year before and to make the playing field fairly level for them, the practical examination was turned upside down, to our obvious disadvantage, since we had done more advanced lathe work for two years, than bench work. We were 'swerved', as we called it in those days!

**After GCE O Levels June 1968**

Secondly, just before the start of the Ordinary Level examinations in 1968, the Ministry of Education announced the cancellation of the Sixth Form physical sciences combination of Physics, Pure and Applied Mathematics. Instead, everyone was to offer Physics, (a combination of Pure and Applied) Mathematics and Chemistry, plus an optional Further Mathematics paper. I had intended to stay away from Chemistry partly because in my Form 5A class, a score of 85% in any examination, mid-term or final, meant fifth position or worse, and partly because I was aiming for mathematics at the university.

Unfortunately, I made a mess of one of my optional questions in the Chemistry paper and ended up with a Grade 4 (the examination was made up of a practical test, one objective or multiple choice) paper and one written paper. In effect, I was stuck with Chemistry in Sixth Form, which nearly cost me a place at the university.

Sometime before the start of the 1969-70 academic year, Uncle Nyarko brought mother's last born, Grace Donkoh, to complete her schooling at Koforidua. I am not sure about the details now but not long after Grace arrived at Koforidua, he also brought my brother Kofi Graham, who comes directly after me, and his half-brother Yaw Graham, to continue their schooling, in Middle Form Four, at Koforidua.

Kofi and Yaw who lived at Obra-twer-Owu, had been attending school at Mankrong Junction, but apparently, an incident that happened in their school for which they were branded ring leaders, led to their expulsion from school. They were both very bright and therefore one of them was almost certainly school prefect, with the other being the assistant or a section leader, as they were called in those days.

I am not sure how much strain the presence of those three put on Uncle's finances, but I know that Uncle Benyi at that time had various painting jobs to support Uncle Nyarko, especially with respect to the one room he had rented across the street for Uncle Benyi and the boys, while Uncle Nsedu had always supported Uncle Nyarko financially. According to my sister Grace, all three of them left Koforidua as soon as they completed their final examinations. Kofi in particular, passed the common entrance that year but when he attended the interview at Pope John's Secondary School, he was deemed "too big" for Form One.

Kofi was not enrolled in school until he was about ten or eleven, by which time he had already been an apprentice shoemaker and could actually make shoes and sandals from scratch.

In the end, having passed the Middle School Leaving Certificate Examination with distinction, he went to teach as a Pupil Teacher and studied privately for the General Certificate of Education, Ordinary Level. He passed six out of the seven subjects he offered, at a sitting, with Grade 1 in Fanti, one of the most difficult subjects at the Ordinary Level in those days. I was in America in 1975 when he achieved those remarkable results and I believe if he had taken my advice to proceed to Post-Secondary A, instead of the private sixth-form college he attended in Accra, his path to the world of work would have been different and possibly more rewarding too.

## Sixth Form

In 1970, the GCE 'A' Level Physics examination was still run by London University, although the West African Examinations Council had taken over most of the other subjects. The practical examinations in the physical and biological sciences took place in late April/early May, followed about a month later, by the two three hour written papers.

To make as much room as possible for each candidate in the laboratories for the practical tests, the examination class was always divided into two groups, the first taking its turn in the early morning, followed in the afternoon by the second group, which was usually "camped" somewhere, to prevent any contact between the two groups as the first group came out of the laboratory. Because of my surname, Quaah, I was always in the second group in any such division.

In May 1970, the Physics practical examination came first. On the afternoon of the examination, as I passed by my old house on my way to the dining hall, I felt a sudden heavy blow on my head. The offending object, a rectangular block of wood had hit me from an upstairs window and fallen with a thud behind me. The blow was followed almost immediately by sharp pain and when I felt the spot, there was blood on my fingers. Then the blood began to drip down my shirt.

One young boy had apparently intended to throw the block at another boy in the upstairs "Juniors' Dormitory" of Dodoo House and missed him with the block flying through the window and into the street below. I was in the right place at the wrong time. The preparation for my new favourite subject was in chaos.

My former Housemaster, Mr E A Teye, took me to the Takoradi (European) Hospital where my wound was stitched in time for me to return for a hurried small lunch and my physics practical examination. Four of us qualified for Sixth Form from Dodoo House in 1968, my best friend, Chris Gharban, (Samuel Entsiwah who unfortunately died at the end of Lower Sixth Form), Cornelius Djameh, who went to Nautical College instead of Sixth Form and I. There were too many of us from the same house. I was sent off to Kennedy (House 7) and Djameh was sent to Vanderpuye (House 2). Fortunately, the rest of the day and the examination itself went very well, in spite of the slight headache that I felt; more would follow later.

The slight headaches continued to plague me through the examination period. My Chemistry practical examination was a major disaster. Somehow, the electronic balance (which we were using for the very first time), that was assigned to me malfunctioned. It would not register any weight. I kept piling the compound to no avail. That was when I should have called the invigilator. I didn't! By the time I finally moved to another balance that had been used by one of my colleagues, it was too late. I believed that I had failed Chemistry and there was no point in continuing with the examinations.

It was once again, my former Housemaster, Mr Teye, who heard about my plight and invited me to his flat and spoke to me for about two hours. He hailed from Asesewa in the Eastern Region with a similar background to mine and because I lived in the Eastern Region at Koforidua in the same region at the time, he took a liking for me soon after he took over as Housemaster of Dodoo House. Mr Teye who was a committed Christian persuaded me to forget about whatever had happened, move on and trust the Lord to see me through. Later, when I was invited for an interview at the Physics Department at UST, he managed to convince me to go and give it a try, for the experience, if for nothing else.

In 1978 while I was working on my PhD at the University of London, I saw him on the escalator in one of the London underground stations. He was going up and I was going down. I went back up, joined him and had a hearty chat with him. His first comment was, "Didn't I tell you that the Lord would see you through it all?" He became a 'Big Brother' to me for many years, after I returned to Ghana in 1984. I stayed in touch with him until he sadly passed away in early 2017. I had spoken to him about two weeks before Christmas and promised to visit him the next time I was in Ghana. He passed away on 6th January 2017. I was shattered!

I ended up with very disappointing A Levels results DB, E, B and S in Physics, Mathematics, General Paper and Chemistry, respectively. Those were the worst examination results of my entire school life! I kept to myself for several days after the results were released. I just couldn't come to terms with myself that I had done so badly in my A Levels.

**After Sixth Form June 1970**

# CHAPTER 6
# UNIVERSITY OF SCIENCE AND TECHNOLOGY, KUMASI

had given up on university, at least for the 1970-71 academic year. During my Sixth Form years, I struck a friendship with Mr Glavee's wife's nephew, James Vinyo, who went to secondary school in Togo and came to Ghana to do his Sixth Form at Ghana Secondary School, Koforidua, and was by this time living with his aunt and her husband. James was one of those politically astute students, very current on national and international politics. He was a year ahead of me, and like me had not done very well in Chemistry and Mathematics in his final A Level examinations. He wanted to go to Medical School and was waiting to re-write those two papers during the 1971-72 academic year.

One morning, James told me that there was a vacancy for a Mathematics and Physics teacher at the Koforidua Technical Institute. He knew the Principal and had already spoken to him about me and the man wanted to see me urgently. I went to see the Principal one Friday morning and he asked me to start the next Monday. James encouraged me to go for it, so I could register for Chemistry and Mathematics, if I wished, at Ghana Secondary School in early 1971.

When I reported to the school on Monday, the Principal asked me to take on First Year Metalwork in addition to Physics and Mathematics for second and third years. I taught several classes during the week. The standards of the students seemed very low to me, compared with students at similar levels at GSTS, but I was prepared to give it a try.

On Saturday morning, as I went to the public standpipe to fetch water to do my usual weekend washing, James came bounding on the street with a big smile and with a loud voice announced that I had been offered a place at the Physics Department of the University of Science and Technology, Kumasi. He showed me the paper, but I had to go and buy a copy of the "Ghanaian Times", which was Uncle Nyarko's regular newspaper, to be certain. My name was there in black and white and I had been assigned to University Hall (Katanga). We were to report to the university in ten days.

The next Tuesday, I received the formal admission letter. In it, was the proviso that I would have to pass A Level Chemistry by the end of the academic year or I would lose my place on the course. I reckoned that it would be simpler to re-sit one paper in the university environment than trying to do it as a private candidate at home, especially since I had no idea about the laboratory facilities at GHANASCO.

I washed and ironed my clothes and packed a few items of toiletry. We went to see Uncle Nsedu that evening, and he was also delighted at the turn of events. Uncle Nyarko gave me an old travel bag and a few items on Monday. In those days, everyone who was admitted to university was awarded an automatic government scholarship that came with a grant of 110 cedis a year, 55 in the first term, 32 in the second term and 23 in the third term. On Friday, 9th October, I took a train with my senior from GSTS Agyekumhene Yamoah (who lived at Effiduase) and who was returning to his third year in the Physics Department, to Kumasi and "Tech", to begin a four-year BSc (Honours) Course in Physics.

I was leaving home as an adult, for the first time and going to live on my own, with no supervision whatsoever, no housemaster, no senior housemaster, not even a "House Prefect". It was an exciting path but one strewn with dangers, for every 'young' person. On the eve of my journey to Kumasi, we assembled at Uncle Nsedu's house at Jackson Park where my two uncles took turns to pray for me, after advising me "to remember my origins, whatever I did at the university." My uncles gave me five cedis and "blessed me on my way." That was the last time anyone gave me money that I did not work for, but I would finance other people for the next forty-five years and I am still paying!

Uncle Nyarko had given me a nice, plastic State Insurance Corporation wallet after I came home from Sixth Form, which I never used till the day I was leaving for university. The wallet was quite long and protruded from the back pocket. At Kumasi Kejetia train station, Senior Yamoah got onto the platform first with one handbag, while I passed our other luggage to him through the window. In the process, someone picked my wallet without me feeling anything. I had come face to face with one of the dangers my uncles had warned me about. Fortunately, I had hidden three out of the five cedis my uncles had given to me in my travelling bag. From that day, I never carried a wallet until I went to postgraduate school in America in 1975.

A week after registration, we were paid the "millions", as we called the students' grant in those days. From my 55 cedis grant, I bought all the prescribed textbooks for the first year, stationery, a slide rule, a large volume of newsprint for rough work (which would last me through the first year and half of the second), and still managed to send some money home to Mother, to pay the tuition fees of my Sister Grace who with Uncle Kweku Otabil's daughter Ekua Otsiwaba, had enrolled at the newly established Gomoaman Secondary School at Afransi. There were opportunities to explore Kumasi and the nightlife it offered, but I was conscious of my uncle's advice and, "remembered where I had come from."

In the Science Faculty in the 1970s, all first-year students of Chemistry, Physics, Mathematics and Chemical Technology, as it was called in those days (now Chemical Engineering), did a common programme - Physics (Mechanics, Wave Theory and Electricity and Magnetism), Mathematics (Analysis, Abstract Algebra and Statistics) and Chemistry (Physical, Inorganic and Organic). When lectures began about the middle of the first week, there was a bulletin from the Office of the Dean of the Faculty of Science saying that those of us who had two A Level passes did not have to re-sit the third anymore. Instead, we would have to pass the subject in which we did not possess A Level pass (Chemistry in my case), at the First University Examinations or we would be kicked out of the university.

**First Year at University**

My First Year University Examinations (FUE) went quite well. I passed all my subjects quite comfortably, with no referrals. I was truly on my way to being one of the first citizens of the Gomoa District to study Science at the University of Science and Technology.

For the then compulsory "Vacation Training" that was part of all programmes at the university at the time, I was posted to the Aboso Glass Factory with a Third Year Chemical Technology student Nyuur, to be joined later by Kojo Wilson, another third-year Chemistry student from the University of Ghana, Legon. My old school senior, housemate and hallmate at Katanga, Derek Faidoo, who was a native of Aboso and a third-year Chemical Technology student, had done his vacation training at the Glass Factory the previous year. He advised me to arrive early because he would speak to the people he knew at the factory about accommodation on the site. Luckily, he was able to secure for me the one-bedroom guest apartment across the road from the factory.

There were no cooking facilities, just a sink, but we ate lunch at the factory. A former classmate of my friend Chris Gharban from his Winneba Methodist School days, Miss Comfort Cole, worked in the Personnel Department of the Glass Factory. Before I left Kumasi, Chris advised me to look her up when I got to Aboso. I did and as soon as I got to the factory, Comfort arranged with one of the ladies in the kitchen, to provide me with dinner from the canteen whenever I wished to eat dinner. The lunch that was provided by the company was quite good but very spicy. That was how I developed a peptic ulcer in my second year at the university. Nyuur and his then-girlfriend Grace, from the University of Cape Coast who was doing private vacation employment in the laboratory, also developed ulcers. Eventually, Grace's cousin who was the Personnel Manager at the time managed to get the kitchen supervisor to provide us with special pepper-free meals.

At the end of July when I received my first "Vacation Training allowance," I went to Takoradi to buy myself a new suitcase, which I would use for the next three years.

My stay at the factory site would have been very lonely but for the fact that El Dorados, the resident band of the Aboso Glass Factory, practised regularly at the Club House next door whenever they were not on tour. The band also played once a month for the staff, their families and the general public. Faidoo who lived in the Aboso Township was doing his Vacation Training at the Bonsa Tyre Factory about twenty miles away. Most evenings, he came to the Club House after work to see me and his townsman and childhood friend, Thomas Mensah, who was the organist for the band. We often sat and talked to Thomas during their breaks or after their band's practice sessions. Faidoo, I and an old German mechanic at the factory, were the regulars at the Club House. This elderly German, Mr Braun, would offer me a bottle of beer. Beer tasted too bitter for me and I often declined it or would nurse a glass of it until he left, which was usually at closing time, then I would give the rest to someone or simply leave it behind and go to bed.

After Vacation Training, I did my regular routine; went through Gyaman, to Akenkauso, where Uncle Obrehun, Mother and Sister Aba and her husband were all cultivating new cocoa farms, then to Koforidua, and back to Kumasi.

The second year went very well. In those days, students offered core subjects in their chosen departments from the beginning of the second year. In the Physics Department, we took courses in Mathematics or Physics, and "Scientific French", which was introduced during the 1972-73 academic year.

The results of the final examinations were always displayed on the notice board of every faculty, department and hall. I did very well with several As and Bs. For Vacation Training, I was posted with another coursemate, Opoku-Adjei and two first-year Mathematics students, Adjei and Ahinakwa, to the Headquarters of the Meteorological Services Department at Legon in Accra, to be joined later by Messrs Charway and Arkhurst from the University of Ghana, Legon.

For my training, I did a very interesting project on the effect of the Akosombo Dam on the local climate with the Deputy Director, Mr S O Tandoh, with whom I later renewed acquaintance at the Leaders' Meeting of Calvary Methodist Church at Adabraka in Accra. It was during this period that my peptic ulcer came to a head. Towards the end of our programme, I reported to the University of Ghana Hospital and was given some medication (magnesium trisilicate). The doctor wanted me to go for a "Barium Meal Test", but we were close to the end of vacation training, about ten days, and would soon leave Accra, so he advised that I should report at the UST Hospital as soon as I got back to the university, which I did. I was put on medication (magnesium trisilicate) and a pepper-free, special diet for the rest of my stay at the university.

## The Move to the University Hall Annexe

The third year again went very well, but during the Easter holidays, I was admitted to the Koforidua Central Hospital, with extreme pain from my ulcer. I spent five days in hospital. Two of the nurses on the ward where I was admitted had boyfriends at the university. When they learnt from my notes that I was a student of UST, they treated me like a king during my stay on the ward. The health system in Ghana worked very well in those days.

For Vacation Training after the third year, I was posted to the Ghana Atomic Energy Commission, again with one course mate, PA Oduro (now Prof Oduro-Afriyie), Chapman from the Biochemistry Department and another gentleman, Aboagye, from the Physics Department of the University of Ghana, Legon. We had a wonderful time at the Commission.

This time around, I did a project on "The effect of the tropical weather on the total body water of Ghanaians, using Tritium as tracer", with the Officer in Charge, Dr BW Garbrah, whom I again encountered later as Rev Professor Garbrah at the Calvary Methodist Church in Accra.

The project was so successful that Dr Garbrah wanted me to return to the Commission after graduation, to continue with the research with the possibility of a scholarship to do a PhD in Atomic/Nuclear Physics. Incidentally, I travelled on the same Ghana Airways flight to London with Dr Garbrah the day I left Accra for London on my way to America. When he saw me on the flight, he asked what I had done with his offer of a scholarship. I could only scratch my head.

Accommodation in the halls was assigned for the whole duration of a student's stay at the university. A change from one hall to another or even from one room to another in the same hall required a special application. I had been assigned to Room 20 in the main hall from the first year with Henry Davies, my classmate from GSTS who was reading Civil Engineering. We renewed our friendship and quickly made friends with several students on our floor of twenty rooms, particularly, Jim Hazel and Kwadwo Ampofo from Mfantsipim and George Ansah from Nsein. We sat at the same table in the dining hall and went to Sunday Church services together. Jim, George and I were Methodists and we also joined the Methodist University Students' Union.

We had become inseparable, but the main halls of the universities were generally very noisy. Henry Davies moved to the annexe after the first year. There was a very "progressive community" on the fourth floor of University Hall Annexe. My lifelong friend and coursemate Lawrence Onyeche was already on the third floor. I applied and got a place on the fourth floor, replacing Senior Yamoah in Room 46 at the beginning of my Third Year.

**Time flies indeed**

.   .   .

The fourth and final year in the university again went very smoothly. After sailing through the first year, I had somehow overcome my "phobia of final examinations." I was doing very well in class exercises, mid-sessional examinations as well as final examinations. I was on course for a good degree!

During the 1969-70 academic year, the government of the Progress Party of Dr Kofi Abrefa Busia introduced changes to Ghana's Higher Education system that did not go down well with a section of the lecturers at UST, particularly those of the Engineering Faculty, most of whom resigned en masse. Many of them went to Makarere University in Uganda. I am not sure about the details now but, I believe it had to do with the periodic allocation of import licences and loans that enabled lecturers to bring in cars from overseas.

Around that time, more than sixty per cent of the senior staff of Ghana's three universities was made up of expatriates. Once a year, the universities, through the government of Ghana, paid for these expatriate staff to return home on holidays and their families outside Ghana visited them in Ghana during the long vacation, (Trinity at UST). It also meant that the government of Ghana had to pick the tab for the retirement benefits of these expatriate lecturers. Those arrangements were getting horrendously expensive at a time when the economy was facing major challenges, particularly with respect to foreign exchange.

One of the proposed changes was the "Ghanaianisation" of the senior staff of the three universities of the country at the time. Under the programme, any student who finished with a First Class or Second-Class Upper Division in any of the universities was to be offered a scholarship for postgraduate studies outside, to return to the university afterwards, to join the senior staff.

The government also proposed a loan scheme to begin during the 1974-75 academic year. The all-grant scheme for higher education in Ghana had become a major burden on the state, which meant that only very few, about four thousand out of over twelve thousand leaving sixth forms around the country every year, could be admitted by the universities. The system needed to be expanded to give the chance to as many students as possible, to gain access to higher education.

Under the loan scheme, qualified students would be given a low-interest loan to cover books and other living expenses for the duration of their courses, to be repaid after they completed their programmes and secured jobs. Although Dr Busia's government was overthrown by Col Acheampong and his friends on 13th January 1972, these policies were maintained in addition to a one-year National Service Scheme during which graduates of the universities and other tertiary education institutions were to work for a fixed allowance in organisations, departments and institutions at locations to be assigned by the National Service Secretariat. Under the scheme, the universities could still select their best students to return to the departments as "Teaching Assistants." The first group of "servicemen and women" took their positions in August 1973.

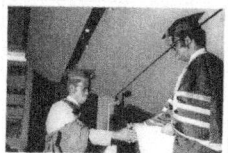

**I received my first degree from Professor Allotey, Dean of the Faculty of Science, the only graduation ceremony I ever attended (February 1975)**

**National Service and Beyond**

Before our final examinations in June 1974, my head of department, Professor Dziwornooh invited me to his office one afternoon and asked me if I would wish to return to the Physics Department as a Teaching Assistant if I obtained a 'good class' in the final examinations. I assured him that I would love to return to the department if I qualified to do so.

I had all my grades for the first three years and by my own predictions, using the low end of each grade of the previous years' examinations, I knew I could gain a Second Class Upper or better in the final examinations. In the end, I scored over 74% overall, which should have qualified me for a first-class, but I got a Second Class Upper and the highest in my graduating class.

In late July 1974, I received an invitation from the head of the Department of Physics to report back to the department on 12th August, to begin my National Service as a Teaching Assistant in the department. On 4th August, Ghana changed from driving on the left side of the road to the right. On the 12th of August, I packed my things and was accompanied by my then-girlfriend Ms Lily Entee, to begin the process that would end with me going to America for postgraduate studies in Geophysics.

I had been teaching Lily towards her re-sit of the GCE O Levels. She was about to take her examinations and her mother decided that she should accompany me to Kumasi, to continue her studies. Fortunately, she passed all five subjects, including Mathematics and General Science, and went on to do the Post-A teachers' certificate, and eventually the specialist diploma at Winneba.

## Flat 3, University (Katanga) Hall

Although I had spent my four years in the university at the University Hall (Katanga), I was directed to one of the rooms in the main hall of Queen's Hall on arrival on Campus because apparently University Hall had hosted a holiday programme and was not ready for occupation yet. It was with some difficulty that we carried my rather heavy wooden box to the first-floor room where we stayed for the night. The next day, we moved to Flat One at University Hall.

That night, I saw some cockroaches and swore never to sleep there again. The Chief Porter moved me to Flat 2 where the sink did not work. At the end of the week, I was moved to the cleaner and better-maintained Flat 3 where I would stay for the rest of my National Service. I had been to this flat before because a member of our Katanga Fourth Floor Annex "Clansmen," Okantey, had stayed there as a post-graduate student and later, Akiwumi who was a year ahead of me in the Physics Department had also lived in that flat for his National Service. It was Ideal and later, we would hold our Katanga "Clansmen" parties in my flat.

When I reported to the department, Prof Dziwornooh asked me to prepare the First Year Degree Physics Practical experiments with Mr Sarhene, the department's research officer and computer programming lecturer. I was also asked to prepare to teach 'Post-Ordinary' Level Physics to First Year Diploma Survey students. I went to work immediately and by the time the university reopened in September, we had set up all the practical experiments for the year - Mechanics, Electricity and Magnetics, Optics and Sound. I had also finished my notes for the first two terms of my 'Post-Ordinary' Level Physics class. In early November, I completed my notes for the academic year and presented the eighteen questions (nine for the main examination and nine for the resit paper), for the end-of-year examinations in June 1975.

About the same time, I began applying to universities in the United Kingdom and America, for post-graduate studies in Geophysics. In the Physics Department at UST in those days, one had to choose two options from Geophysics, Instrumentation, Meteorology and Nuclear Health Physics, in the final year. I had opted for Instrumentation and Geophysics. I wanted to study Geophysics since there was a policy to establish a strong Applied Physics (Geophysics) in the department. Eventually, I gained admission to the University of Leeds in England and The Pennsylvania State University (Penn State) in America. I opted for Penn State and began the preparations – passport, visa and inoculations towards travelling to America, in May 1975.

## Archbishop Porter Secondary School

.  .  .

Three weeks after I had reported to the Physics Department, I received a letter from the headmistress of Archbishop Porter Secondary School in Takoradi asking why I had not reported to the school for my National Service since I had been posted there as a Physics Master. When I showed the letter to Professor Dziwornooh, he told me to throw it away and that the department had produced twenty-two physics graduates that year and it had only chosen one and that if anyone needed one physics graduate from the university, they could go and look for any of the other twenty-one. The letter had gone to Koforidua and Uncle Nyarko had re-directed it to me in Kumasi.

One week later, I received another letter, this time from the Director of the National Service Secretariat, Colonel Kudziku, warning that I was in breach of the Nationals Service Decree and unless I reported to Archbishop Porter immediately, I would be liable for prosecution and sanctions.

Apparently, the then head of state, Colonel I K Acheampong had two daughters at Archbishop Porter at the time, one in Form Four and the other in Form Two. The school did not have a good Physics master and the headmistress had made a specific request to the Head of State to get her one from UST, under the National Service Scheme. I was the "fall guy."

Again, I took the letter to Professor Dziwornooh and this time he decided to go to the Registrar for Academic Affairs. Later that week, he told me never to worry about that letter again and that was the end of the matter.

## Part-time Teaching at TI Ahmadiyya Secondary School, Kumasi

Instead of full-time secondary school teaching at Archbishop Porter Secondary School, I eventually did part-time teaching at the T I Ahmadiyya Secondary School in Kumasi. One of my seniors at the Physics Department, Mr J K Kumah went to teach at the school under the National Service Scheme. Graduate Physics teachers are generally difficult to find the world over, and the reason as my first-year

Classical Physics lecturer, Mr S O Bampo used to say was, "Science is just Physics, everything else is stamp collection!" With a first degree in Physics, a person can go on to do anything, ranging from a Taxi Driver to an astronaut.

In our small graduating Class of 1974, for instance, three of us went on to study Geophysics with two ending up in petroleum exploration and production, the other in mining. Two of our classmates did Wood Technology, one did Nuclear Engineering, one ended up in Metallurgy, another in Water Engineering, two in Meteorology, one as a professor of Atmospheric Physics and a few as teachers of Physics in secondary schools.

Mr Kumah, a soft-spoken and affable man, had apparently been stuck at T I Ahmadiyya Secondary School after National Service. He had taken several classes through the General Certificate of Education, Ordinary and Advanced Levels, with major success, and although he had found other jobs with obviously better career prospects, he could not walk away from the students he had prepared so well from Form three or thereabouts.

With no formal teaching qualification, he was still a "temporary" teacher. In May 1975, he was offered another permanent job by the then Ghana Water and Sewage Corporation as a trainee manager, with a good salary and a much brighter future than an "unqualified" secondary school teacher. He could not afford to let this opportunity slip away from him. He was in charge of several classes from Form Three to Upper Sixth Form. He approached my classmate, Kwame Owusu, who at the time was also doing his National Service with Dr Asihene at the newly established Geotechnical Engineering Section within the Civil Engineering Department.

I had completed my lectures for the Post-Ordinary Level Physics of the Geodetical Engineering Certificate class and was waiting for the final examinations, to grade my examination papers. I only spent time at the department reviewing experiments while I applied to universities overseas, for post-graduate studies. I had time on my hands. Kwame Owusu came to me one day and suggested that I went in with him to "relieve" Mr Kumah, so he could take up his new position with the Water and Sewage Corporation. We could earn some "pocket money" as we waited for the final examinations at the university.

Owusu took on the classes in Forms Four, Five and Upper Sixth, while I took on Mr Kuma's classes in Forms Three, Four and the Lower Sixth, for the rest of the academic year. I did not know where the school was located. In fact, apart from the very central parts of the city, I had not really known Kumasi well enough even after nearly five years at the university. I had to make sure I always went with Owusu, at least for the first three or four lessons, even if I had to kick my heels for an hour or more, before the start of my own lessons. The whole scheme went quite well.

Three years later, one Saturday afternoon while I was staying at the University of Ghana as an Adjunct Student of the Geology Department for my seismology fieldwork in southern Ghana, I went to visit a friend in one of the male halls of the university. As I walked towards one of the main entrances, I heard someone calling, "Sir, sir." I did not think much of it, because I did not consider myself a "sir" at the university. Eventually, I heard running footsteps behind me and turned.

A young student with a broad smile and an extended hand, asked, "You don't recognise me?" "My name is Sore; you taught me Physics at the Lower Sixth Form at TI Ahmadiyya Secondary School. I am in the Medical School here." He became my friend and I met him a few times when he served as Director of Medical Services in the Central Region and eventually, National Director. "Once a teacher, always a teacher", as the saying goes.

## The Death of Mr Kofi Agyarey

Mr Kofi Agyarey had become something of a Godfather to me, after my return to GSTS. He was delighted at my success at the General Certificate of Education Examinations. Over the years, I reported to him during the holidays and would always show him my "End of

Term report." Mr Agyarey always had a word of praise and encouragement for me.

I spent Christmas 1969 with my old teacher Ms Sackey at Swedru. On Christmas Eve, I went to visit Mr Agyarey with a friend who was more streetwise than I was. When we got there, he was so excited at the fact that I had been one of the few people he had helped to secure Cocoa Marketing Board scholarships who managed to qualify for the Sixth Form and university. He set a small table before us with a bottle of whisky, two bottles of Coca-Cola, four glasses and a bucket of ice blocks and said, "Merry Christmas" and excused himself. It was a test I would fail miserably.

My friend poured half a glass of whisky, added some Coca-Cola and ice blocks and took a sip. I followed with my own, and soon, one more glass.

Later, as we asked for permission to leave, Mr Agayrey apparently shook his head and smiled. I did not see much of it. I had a sore throat for two weeks! On 27th December when I went to him alone, to bid him farewell for my return to Koforidua, he asked me if I always drank alcohol and warned of its attendant dangers at such an early age. I could not lift my head for the whole time I was with him. He noticed from my mumbling responses and my croaky voice that I was really a novice. His last comment was, "At least you have found out for yourself and I hope you learn a lesson from it."

I had never drunk whisky in my life before that fateful night, and would not touch it again after that experience, until some five years later when another error of judgement with the American equivalent, "Bourbon," nearly ended in disaster. That was the last time I ever touched hard liquor.

In July 1974, I reported the success of my final examinations to Mr Agyarey and he was full of praise. In September, I wrote to him reporting that I had begun my National Service as a Teaching Assistant at the University. He sent me an uncharacteristically short note praising and wishing me well in all my endeavours for the future. He was apparently quite ill at the time. He died about seven weeks later. It was a major shock to me. A very significant chapter of my early life had come to a close and an important player, encourager and supporter had ceased to be part of my journey.

I attended the funeral in his home town, Abetifi, and as it usually happens, only one of his sons and his long-time male secretary recognised me. As it is said in the famous Akan proverb, "one ought not to attend the funeral of a loved one."

**After National Service, June 1975**

# CHAPTER 7
# POST GRADUATE EDUCATION

## OFF TO AMERICA

I left Accra for London on Sunday, 24<sup>th</sup> August 1975, on my way to State College, Pennsylvania. We had flown to Accra from Kumasi on Friday, hoping to leave Accra on Saturday morning. The second integrated Ghana-Nigeria Games had begun in Accra and all the major hotels in the city were fully booked for officials and athletes taking part in the games.

We were sent to the Meridian Hotel in Tema. I had been to the Atlantic Hotel in Takoradi for a GSTS Old Boys' Association dinner dance, as well as the City Hotel in Kumasi the year before, but Meridian Hotel was beyond anything I had ever experienced.

Interestingly, I spent the following night, Sunday, at the International Hotel at Kennedy International Airport in New York City and it was at par with Meridian at the time, only to return to Ghana nine years later to find Meridian completely run down; so much for our maintenance culture.

**Enroute to Penn State August 1975**

On Saturday morning when we got to the Airport in Accra, we were told that there was a fault on the then Ghana Airways VC10 Aircraft so we could not travel that day. We were to come back the next day. Uncle Nyarko and Uncle Nsedu had travelled from Koforidua to see me off but because of the postponement, they had to go and stay with Uncle (ASP) Afful at his official residence at Kotobabi. I had bought a suit earlier for my graduation in February and bought a few shirts, a Kente cloth, a smock and several three-piece cotton gowns and "dashiki" shirts. I still had 300 cedis left that I wanted to send to Mother. I was not sure if my uncles would return to the airport on Sunday. I went back to the Meridian Hotel to dump my 'travelling' clothes and then headed for Accra.

I went to Aunt Esi Dago at the Fadama Market where she fried and sold doughnuts and handed the money to her, to be given to Mother the next time she went to Gyaman. That would be the first of many instances when I sent money or commercial items home that simply went down the drain! Apparently, Aunt Esi Dago remitted that money in bits and pieces and Mother was not able to do anything meaningful with it.

Eventually, I arrived at State College, the main Penn State campus late afternoon on Monday 25th August, to meet two other Ghanaians, Ernest Yaw Baafi and Emmanuel Kwami Agbolosoo, who had travelled at about the same time as I had done but along different routes from London. Ms Gladys Awotwe-Pratt, the only Ghanaian at Penn State at the time, was so happy to see us. She was serving as the President of the International Students' Association for that year and had been informed by the International Students' Affairs office that three other Ghanaians would be joining her in August/September. We formed a lasting bond, particularly among us men with a Nigerian family, the Alfred-Ockiyas, until Kwami Agbolosoo (Wofa Kwami, as we called him), sadly passed away under very tragic circumstances in 2008.

## Family Responsibilities

My brother, Kofi Graham wrote to me sometime in 1976 that he had sat the GCE "O" Levels privately and passed six out of seven subjects at one sitting. He wanted to attend a private Sixth Form College and needed money. I gave the dollar equivalent to our colleague Ms Gladys Awotwe-Pratt and her relations in Ghana gave the cedi equivalent to Kofi. He had brought his wife and their first-born baby girl, Theresa, to Accra to live with him while he attended this private college. I wrote to advise him that since he had done so well even while studying on his own, he was better off undertaking the three-year Post-Secondary Teachers' course. In those days, the students of the programme were paid a monthly allowance which enabled the more studious ones to study for A Levels while still doing the teachers' course. Successful students had ready jobs as teachers waiting as soon as they completed their courses. Three years after graduation, they qualified for entry into university for degree courses, as mature students on "study leave with pay." I had met a number of them at university.

I reminded Kofi that since his wife had completed her vocational training by then and could sew and bake, according to his own account, part of the money I had given to him could set her up at Obra-twer-Owu, to be supplemented by his own allowance. She would be well-established by the time he completed his teachers' training course. This obviously did not go down well with my brother and, for the next two years, I did not hear from him again until when he needed money to register for his final examinations.

Studying at Penn State was a major cultural and academic

experience. I had gone from UST with a student population of about three thousand five hundred at the time, to a campus of thirty-three thousand students. It would take several weeks after lectures began in early September, to adjust to the new environment. Apart from my African friends and the first American, Steven Tobias, with whom I shared rooms, who was also on the same geophysics programme and who became my lifelong friend till today, my experiences in the courses I took, and on Geophysical/Geological field trips were such that I did not want to do a PhD in America.

## Experiences on Geophysical Field Trips

In the 1975-76 academic year, and in fact, through my 26 months at Penn State, the university operated the "quarter system," according to which the school year was made up of four quarters – Fall, Winter, Spring and Summer school terms, three months in duration. Because of my physics background, my "academic advisor", as they called them in those days, had already selected my course subjects for the first quarter by the time I reported to the department - two courses at the Geophysics Program of the School of Earth and Mineral Sciences, Engineering Mechanics in the Mathematics Department, an "audited" course" in Physical Geology at the Geology Program and another audited course in Computer Science in the Computer Science Department. It was quite a hectic schedule for my very first term in a system that was very different from the British system that I was used to back in Ghana.

"Audited course" meant that I had to pay for the courses, attend all lectures and field trips, and do all coursework and examinations (optional), but any grades I made did not count in the determination of my Grade Point Average (GPA), for the quarter.

I went on a number of field trips on the Physical Geology course. There were stares on these trips because I was the only Black person in this Level 2 class of nearly one hundred students, as would happen in nearly every course I took in the university. I had had racist comments thrown at me on campus, especially when I walked alone to or from lectures or the Library, but what I experienced in the field was something else.

## A Bomb Blast at Erie, Pennsylvania

I had been asked by one of my American coursemates in August 1976, to accompany him on a three-day field trip to western Pennsylvania, to do a gravity and magnetic survey. I was scheduled to begin my own gravity and magnetic survey in September, and with no previous experience in surveying, this was a God-sent opportunity to learn. Three of us made the trip. On the second day, we set up the micro-barograph for monitoring the local barometric pressure of our reference station at a school bus stop.

Because schools had been on summer holidays for about two months, the bus stop was overgrown with weeds and creepers. We covered the equipment with a bright yellow plastic material and some tree branches. My two American colleagues were both from Pennsylvania and therefore knew the state laws. According to them, the school bus stop was public property, so we could use the facility as our reference station.

We returned to that site to record the barometric readings every two hours, as was required for calibrating the gravity readings at the end of the survey. Nobody said anything to us, although we found people in the vicinity every time we returned to take a reading until about 9 p.m. (still quite bright in August). On this last trip to take the final reading for the day, we found police cars flashing their emergency lights as we approached the four-way intersection. The access to our reference station had been blocked.

The leader of our group, and owner of the surveys who was driving the field vehicle parked and approached the nearest police officer. He asked him what was going on. He replied that some people had planted a bomb at the site and they were there to detonate it.

Before he could explain, the micro-barograph was blown up in a controlled blast. My colleague was incensed.

The police officer, said, "Calm down young man, look at the bulges in the clothes of the men around here. They are all carrying guns, and you should count yourselves lucky that we got here first." According to the officer, their station had been contacted with a complaint that three men had set up a bomb in the school bus stop and were waiting for nightfall to move it into somebody's house. The micro-barograph incorporates a clock that ticks as long as it is turned on.

The police had gone near the instrument and heard the ticking of the clock, but they were not sure. They called the local FBI ballistic experts. The FBI officers came and listened and heard the ticking of the clock and also concluded that it was indeed a bomb. All they needed to do was to lift the yellow plastic covering and they would have determined that it was a harmless field device and not a bomb. They used a controlled device to blow it up! Eventually, the Pennsylvania Police Department sent a report to our head of department. The first sentence was "On that fateful day, three Caucasians set up something that ticked like a bomb at a school bus stop, which was reported to the local police, who in turn reported it to the district police and ultimately, the FBI." The head of the department said, right from the first sentence, that he knew the whole report was bogus because there were two Caucasian men and one Black man in the party.

The department decided to pursue the police for the damaged equipment. The police claimed it was the FBI (the experts), who blew it up and therefore the FBI should pay for it. The FBI said it was the villagers who called the police in the first place, so they should pay for it. The university apparently had so much by way of equipment that not every one of them was insured. Our micro-barograph was not covered by insurance and so the university had to absorb its replacement cost.

**Guns Galore**

. . .

Farmers around the world do not like any kind of surveys anywhere near their farms. I have experienced the phenomenon in the United States, the United Kingdom, Ghana and Nigeria. It is all about taxation. The assumption is that any survey is either going to discover undeclared earnings or else will push them into a new tax bracket.

All over southern Pennsylvania, West Virginia and Maryland, there were signs like, "Private Land No Unauthorised Entry." State and Federal Government survey landmarks, elevation points and benchmarks had been deliberately removed to make sure of that. Sometimes a farmer would spot our vehicle and race down to drive us away.

On one occasion, a farmer tried to take a pock shot at me with a rifle. In my effort to carefully manipulate the gravimeter to record the site gravity reading at this roadside benchmark, I heard screeching tires behind me. I had positioned myself between the solid concrete culvert and the road and so I knew I was way out of the road and harm's way. Apparently, this farmer stopped his pick-up truck beside me, went to his farmhouse and brought a rifle. He then peered over his pick-up window, pointed his rifle at me and eventually satisfied himself that I was not up to any mischief and it would seem that my friend Steve's stare through the rolled-down window of our field vehicle convinced the farmer that he had taken a good look at and formed a good picture of him, just in case anything untoward happened to me.

When I returned to the vehicle, my friend was still shaking. We had to stay there for several minutes before he regained his composure to drive again. His voice was shaking; "did you see what nearly happened to you?" "The guy was going to take a pock shot at you, just as well you did not see any of it, you might have reacted, and he would have shot you!" he said.

After this second incident, the head of the department provided bright orange waistcoats and everyone who went to the field was required to wear one of those over their field clothes, but the best or worst was yet to come.

. . .

**One Good Turn Deserves Another**

On this fateful Saturday in October 1976, we had worked on a long line, made up of secondary and tertiary roads and tracks, from Pennsylvania through parts of West Virginia and Maryland. Then we lost our way in the Forest Reserve in Maryland a few stations before the end of the line. It was about half past five in the late afternoon. We drove around till about half-past seven when we finally found our bearings again, by which time darkness was beginning to fall.

The vehicle had been rented for the day and with just four more stations to complete, we decided to work with the vehicle's lights. At about nine o'clock I had just completed the penultimate station and was picking up the gravimeter to return to the vehicle when I heard a voice behind me, "Can I help you?" When I turned around, there was a shotgun pointing at my forehead and a flashlight in my face.

"Oh yes, you can help me," I said. "We are doing geophysical fieldwork in the area; we lost our way and managed to find our bearings just a little while ago. This is the last but one of our stations and so we wanted to continue in the darkness, instead of going all the way back to Pennsylvania to return again for just a few stations."

Hearing my "foreign accent", the gentleman asked, "Where do you come from?" When I said I was from Ghana, the man said, "Sorry about the gun, but this is my land (and it actually had a gas well), I live and work in Washington DC and come here at weekends with my young family. So, when I saw the vehicle and light, I was curious, but between 1962 and 1964, I lived in your country, where the people are extremely friendly and generous."

Apparently, he had worked for the Ghana Geological Survey Department under the American Peace Corps Programme (Steve believed he was CIA and from the proximity of his property, was probably still working for the FBI).

He asked about a number of people he had known at the Geological Survey, all of whom I knew. He then invited us to his house where his wife had baked a very delicious cake. She gave us very large portions of the cake with coffee and invited us to stay overnight and go back the next day. I told him that we had hired the vehicle for the day and had to return it before morning otherwise the department would have to pay for an extra day. Upon which he asked if we had flasks that he could fill with coffee, to keep us awake on the way.

He filled our two flasks with freshly brewed coffee and gave us two basketfuls of peaches that he had harvested from his orchard earlier in the day, bade us farewell and advised Steve to drive carefully back. Our last station was only about a mile away so we took the readings and drove straight back to State College.

It was while we were driving back to Pennsylvania that my friend Steve said, "One good turn always deserves another." He continued as we drove in silence, "If this guy had been badly treated in your country, he could have done you harm, possibly killed you. Two white men and a Black man shot and buried in the backwoods of Maryland, who would ever know what happened if the guy threatened to come after me and my family?"

From that night, I vowed never to knowingly and intentionally cause aggravation to any fellow human being, because "this is a very small world and I never know when I will be on a desert island," to paraphrase old Henry Ford.

# CHAPTER 8
## TO THE UNITED KINGDOM

began applying to universities in the United Kingdom in September 1977 and received a letter from the Head of the Department of Geophysics at Leeds University in England saying that he had passed my details to Professor Blundell, Head of Department of Geology at Chelsea College, University of London and that I should expect to hear from him.

I applied to go to Leeds to work on some geological features in the Atimpoku area in the Eastern Region of Ghana, as the Geophysics Section of Leeds ran a very strong Gravity and Magnetics programme within the Geophysics Department. A few days later, I received a letter from Professor Blundell confirming his interest in the "Seismology of Ghana." He had applied to the Overseas Development Ministry at the time, for a research grant to carry out research into the seismicity of Ghana, which could help resolve the tectonic problem I had identified as being of research interest to me. As soon as I defended my thesis, I went to Washington DC for my visa to the United Kingdom.

On the evening of Friday 28th October 1977, twenty-six months after I first left the shores of Ghana to go to America, I boarded a flight to London Heathrow, to begin what would be a three-year PhD programme at the University of London. One of my hallmates at UST,

Kwadwo Asihene who had joined us at Penn State in 1976, had written to his auntie who lived and worked in London about his friend arriving in London with nowhere to stay and not even having a clue about where his college was located in London. Auntie Comfort, whom I would meet at the University of Ghana a year later when I went to Ghana to do the fieldwork for my PhD thesis, asked her nephew Kwadwo, to give me her telephone number to call her when I got to London. Life was so simple, even in the United Kingdom, in those days.

When I called her from Heathrow on the morning of the 29th, Auntie Comfort asked me to take the British Airways courtesy bus to Victoria Station and then grab a taxi from there to their house at Camberwell in Southwest London, giving me details of the route. On Monday, she advised me to take the underground train to Central London, to look for my Department which was located at Hammersmith at the time. I lived with them for one week after which I found a one-room rental place in Hanger Lane in west London.

In those days, the University of London required PhD students from outside the United Kingdom to register for the MPhil, which was converted to PhD after one year, if the candidate's research was considered to be satisfactory. I did two research projects during the year and my PhD candidacy was approved for me to begin my research. Meanwhile, for nearly one year, my head of department and supervisor, Prof Blundell, waited for approval from the University of Science and Technology, to embark on the project for which the department had received approval for the grant from the Overseas Development Ministry. Dr Michael Bacon who was part of the programme at the Ghana end and was to supervise my fieldwork in Ghana, had already left for Ghana and was teaching Geophysics at the Geology Department of the University of Ghana. Eventually, the approval came in August 1978 and after picking up the microearthquake recording equipment from the Global Seismology Unit at the University of Edinburgh with Prof Blundell, I left for Ghana on 30th October 1978.

It was during my first visit to Gyaman in early November 1978 that I was told that the Methodist Church needed funds for a project and was offering to sell part of its vast lands, to raise the necessary capital. I made a down payment of 500 cedis for the 3000- cedi plot. It would cost me 13,000 cedis in the end. Eventually, I gave the final 1000 cedis to my sister-in-law Janet to "go and pay the money and sit on the Church until she got the receipt and site plan or else take the money back to Accra. That was how I managed to acquire the land on which I built the house which will probably serve the family for generations to come, just as the 'Ebusuafie' that Nana Ofosu built for his mother and sisters served several generations as the family home. In 1978-79, two-bedroom houses were selling for 1,200 cedis in Dansoman. In other words, I could have owned at least two houses before I returned to Ghana in 1984.

From my student allowance, I bought something for nearly everybody when I returned to Ghana in 1978, ranging from half pieces of cloth through towels, to shirts and underwear. I returned to the UK for my data analysis in early May 1979, having spent six months recording microearthquakes in the Greater Accra, Central and Eastern Regions.

While I was in Ghana, I went to visit Uncle Obrehun at Akenkausu and promised that I was going back to complete my course and come back to him. It was not to be. He died in October 1979, aged 79, another heartbreak for me. I sent money to Mother, through Mr Glavee and Uncle Nyarko, for Uncle's funeral, like one of his own biological sons.

On Monday 22nd December 1980, I successfully defended my PhD thesis. The long journey that began at "Nkampor Dan Mu" at Gyaman in 1955, had finally come to an end.


**Phillips Petroleum Company, my first real job**

While I was writing my thesis, I applied to over forty oil and gas exploration and seismic service companies, in addition to various universities around the globe, for a postdoctoral fellowship, to continue with my research. I even applied to a few of the United Nations agencies. With the UN agencies, the response was always, "Ghana has exceeded its quota in this agency."

I managed to save quite a bit of money from my small allowance from Ghana. State College in Pennsylvania was a decent university town in those days. Initially, we took our meals in the cafeteria at a student discount. With time, we realised that we could actually save money by buying groceries from the supermarkets in town, to prepare our own breakfast and lunch while eating dinner in the cafeteria.

I never worked in America because I was not permitted to do so on my student visa, but by the time I was leaving for the United Kingdom in October 1977, I had saved over three thousand dollars from my clothing, living and book allowances.

London was a lot more expensive in comparison, but I did some teaching assistantship for my professor while I was writing my thesis and was able to save some money through that. I had total savings of just about three thousand pounds by the end of September 1980 when I submitted my thesis to the University of London Senate. Soon afterwards, I decided that if I did not find a job or post-doctoral fellowship by March 1981 when I had to leave the country, I would just buy a freezer, a cooker, a fridge and a second-hand car from the continent and go home. I had bought a good sound system from the savings I made while I was in Ghana in 1978-79 and I knew I would be given furnished university accommodation if I returned to UST.

I had met Sabina in early 1978 and we were planning on getting engaged, although returning to Ghana in 1981 was not part of her immediate plans because of the general economic conditions in Ghana at the time. In early December, I attended three interviews, two with oil companies and one with a service company. Three days later, I got a job with the service company, Western Geophysical. They wanted me to start as soon as possible, while they applied for a work permit for me. On 13th December, nine days before I defended my thesis, I got an offer from Phillips Petroleum Company as an Expatriate Geophysicist. I was asked to report on 12th January 1981. When I reported in January, I was asked to bring my passport for the visa and work permit applications.

By 1981, migration, particularly from non-European Union countries, had become such a big issue in the United Kingdom that most companies in the country had literally stopped hiring newly graduated non-European Union students. Phillips Petroleum

Company faced stringent conditions about my experience and qualifications, with respect to their visa and work permit applications on my behalf. I was thirty-three years old, never worked before, except for one year of national service in Ghana and three months in England, both as a teaching assistant. Eventually, the company opted for a "Training Work Permit," which could only be renewed twice and no more. The permit and visa were granted in April and I began work on 13$^{th}$ April 1981, with the assurance from my manager that since Phillips had made a discovery in Ghana, I could always be transferred to Ghana, Nigeria or Cote d'Ivoire if the Home Office would not renew my stay in the United Kingdom. Nearly all the Phillips Petroleum Company exploration offices in West Africa closed within the year, leaving just a skeleton production team in the Cote d'Ivoire.

## Engagement and marriage

I met Sabina in London through an old school friend in early 1978. We went out a few times during the Spring and Summer of that year before I left for my fieldwork in Ghana in October. At the time she had begun her "adaptation programme" to be able to register with the Nursing and Midwifery Council (NMC) of the United Kingdom, as required by law and in preparation for her midwifery training in the country. While I was on my field trip in Ghana, she gained admission for her midwifery training programme at the Bellshill Maternity Hospital in Lanarkshire, Scotland. By the time I returned to the United Kingdom in early May 1979, she was well into her course.

In March 1981, we decided to get engaged. I bought the necessary items and sent them through one of Sabina's friends who was travelling to Ghana. The lady was doing us a favour and could not have travelled all the way to Gyaman, of which she had never heard before. She could not go to my uncles at Koforidua either, because she was in Ghana on a ten-day personal mission. However, Sabina had a classmate and long-term friend, Momo Odai, who lived at Nungua and worked at the Korle Bu Teaching Hospital.

Momo's policeman father had once served as the Police Commander at the Apam District Police Headquarters and had been to Gyaman several times because of a long-running chieftaincy dispute which dragged on in the town from the middle of the 1960s through the 1970s. As a result, Mr Odai knew Gyaman very well and had personal acquaintances in the town. Momo offered to take the items to Mother at Gyaman if the lady called her when she got to Accra. We gave the items and money to the lady to be sent to Momo, who would send them to Mother in her spare time. Mother could subsequently inform my uncles. Apparently, my three uncles felt slighted that I did not pass the items and money through them, so they refused to go along when the time came for the engagement in April 1981.

As was reported to us later, my step-father, Papa Saasi, my brother-in-law, Brother Kweku Benyi, my cousin, Brother Kofi Mensah, my Mother, my two sisters, Aba and Grace, together with some other relatives, went to Accra, to perform the engagement ceremony.

We were married on 29th August 1981. My in-laws, their thirteen-year-old granddaughter, Serwaa (one of the flower girls) and Sabina's junior sister, Janet travelled from Ghana for the wedding, to be joined in London by their senior brother, Eddie and his girlfriend, from Washington DC in America.

My old school friend, Chris Gharban who was getting ready to leave for Saudi Arabia shortly, was my best man, ably supported by his wife, Doris. Auntie Agnes Ampah who lived with Uncle Nsedu at Jackson Park, Koforidua, had moved to London a year earlier, to marry Mr Mike Bondzie, a man she knew as a young lady at Apam. Mr Bondzie, whose father owned a cocoa purchasing company at Mensakrom in the 1940s knew people from Gyaman. He and his wife served as "my parents and close relatives." Several of my school friends from my GSTS and UST days and colleagues at Phillips Petroleum Company came to support us.

My in-laws brought the good news that my sister Grace had gained admission to midwifery school at Winneba and Mother had asked for support for her. Sabina had trained as a nurse in Ghana and continued to Midwifery School in Scotland so she knew what someone who was attending midwifery training required in Ghana of 1981-82. We bought every conceivable item that she thought would help, including textbooks, exercise books, pencils and pressing iron. She added the midwifery books she had brought back from her training in Scotland. Together with things that we had bought for the rest of the family back in Ghana, we filled one suitcase. My father-in-law had paid for excess baggage coming from Ghana so we did not have to pay for the extra suitcase.

Janet took the things to Gyaman as soon as they arrived back in Accra. At that time, Janet was teaching at the Singer Training School at Kaneshie. Sister Aba's first child, Efua Adaboah had finished Middle Form Four and was at home. I asked Janet to try and get her a sewing machine, at a time when there was so much scarcity in Ghana. A young lady in her class got pregnant and was leaving the school. She had brought a fairly new Singer sewing machine, which she believed she would not need any longer. Janet called me about it and I asked her to buy it for Adaboah. She sent it to Gyaman and it was never used because apparently, her father said the sewing machine "did not come with a pair of scissors", which in 1982 cost less than ten cedis!

Earlier on while I was in America, I wrote to Sister Aba and her husband that when Adaboah and Kwesi Arhin (their second born) got to Middle Form Three, they should let them write the Common Entrance Examination and if they passed, I would provide their school kits and fees, to go to secondary school. Having gone through the system, I knew the advantages that secondary education could bring to them. I was determined to create a "backup" for when I finally returned to Ghana because I knew it was not going to be easy carrying that load all alone. It was prophetic. Apparently, my brother-in-law could not find the twenty cedis to pay their examination fees.

**Gratitude to my Uncles**

While I was travelling through the Eastern, Central and Greater Accra Regions during my fieldwork, I encountered several soldiers who had gone on peacekeeping duties in the Middle East and come back with corn milling machines and were doing very well financially. Some had actually quit the army, bought one or two more machines and were even building houses. I also knew of people who had done very well operating that machine at Gyaman and Afransi in the late 1950s and early 1960s. It was a good business.

Within two months of starting work, I ordered a corn milling machine from India, at a cost to Tema Harbour of £1,600, as "thank you" to my uncles, for coming to my rescue when I needed assistance. The shipment was directed to my in-laws in Accra. Janet took delivery of the machine and its parts at Tema Harbour, eight wooden boxes in all. She hired a lorry and took them straight to Koforidua to my uncles. My mother-in-law was surprised when she heard that the things were going to my uncles because, from the introductions at the engagement, she had been under the impression that my mother did not have any brothers.

I had been informed by the manufacturers that the grinders were the parts that were likely to wear out within two years. I paid for an extra eight pairs, just to make sure that my uncles could operate the machine for several years without too much trouble. In 1982, all three uncles at Koforidua were "working for themselves." Uncle Nsedu did steel bending contracts as and when he got them, Uncle Benyi did painting contracts, again as and when he found them and Uncle Nyarko, his agency work with the State Insurance Corporation, which allowed him to choose when and where he sought clients. So, they had enough time on their hands to either work the machine themselves or hire someone and supervise the operations.

Not long after the packages arrived at Koforidua, Uncle Nyarko informed me that they were going to sell one pair of the grinders to "raise the necessary funds to install the machines". I thought it was a good idea. Besides, I felt it was theirs and they could do as they pleased as long as they put it to good use for their benefit. That was not to be. They continued to sell the parts bit by bit.

Later, I heard that Kofi Graham went to our uncles and informed them that he had found a convenient location at Mankrong Junction where he worked. He could set it up and report his sales to them at regular intervals. They could be part of it in the initial stages, to ensure transparency. Our uncles would not hear of it and it became a major quarrel between Kofi and our uncles. He left and eventually gave up on the idea.


**Our first child is born**

Apart from morning sickness nearly throughout the whole period of her first pregnancy, Sabina also had some minor medical problems and was admitted to the Royal Free Hospital in Hampstead, which was the nearest hospital to our flat in West Hampstead. She had had a myomectomy in Scotland in 1980 and her consultant had advised that if she was lucky to have a child, she should opt for a Caesarean operation.

At the Royal Free Hospital, she was lucky to have had the famous Professor Ian Craft, one of the top Gynaecologists in the United Kingdom at the time, as her consultant. Professor Craft had underlined in her prenatal notes that when she got into labour, he should be consulted and in no way was she to have a natural birth.

She had one of those stomach pains and was rushed to the hospital and admitted on 25th March 1982. She was still several weeks away from her due date. But in the evening of first April, after I had visited from work at Victoria and left, the junior doctors in Prof's team decided to play an April Fool prank on us. Apparently, they induced her soon after I left her bedside at 9:30 p.m., hoping she would give birth before midnight on April Fools' Day. Unfortunately, Kofi was rather 'stubborn'; she was in labour all night and much of the following day!

Before I left on Thursday night, she asked me to bring her favourite dish, "boiled rice and chicken stew." When I got home, I prepared the stew, so I would boil the rice the next morning before I left for work. About 6 o'clock the next morning while I was waiting to dish out the rice and set off, I received a telephone call from the Royal Free Hospital that she had been in labour during the night so I should leave whatever I was doing and come to the hospital. When I asked if I should bring the food with me, the lady said no and that she would probably not need it.

I got to the hospital at about 7 am and called my boss, Pete Parker at 8 o'clock to inform him about my situation. He asked me to stay with her and make sure she was as comfortable as possible.

She had been wired and connected to the oscilloscope, so we could observe the baby's heartbeat by the minute. I wiped and towelled her head and upper body the whole time. By 3:30 p.m, she was really frustrated and began to shout at the poor junior doctor who came in and out. She insisted that he went through her notes and read the specific instructions about her delivery.

They called Professor Craft and whatever he said to them, within minutes they were frantically wheeling her to the theatre. Initially, the Sister-in-Charge thought I should join them in the theatre. At the theatre door, she took one look at me and realised that I probably was not up to it. Instead, she gave me a chair at the door and asked me to sit and wait. I could not sit still. For the next forty-five minutes, I might have paced two or three kilometres along the corridor. At 4:45 p.m., one of the nurses, thinking that I could be scared of a new baby, asked me to sit down while another nurse behind her thrust Kofi into my lap.

So, on Friday, 2nd April, the day the British Armada set off for the Falklands War, Kofi was delivered weighing 3.15 kilograms, a few weeks premature, but strong enough to spend just a few hours in the nursery, and then with his mother for the rest of the night and the next few days. He was circumcised by an Egyptian surgeon at the hospital on the 8th and the next day Sabina's Uncle, Mr Quartey-Papafio, one of Kofi's Godfathers, took us home to Edgware, his first home, for the very first time. I had very long nights over that long Easter weekend and for the next thirteen months, I would sing as many of the hymns of the Methodist Hymn Book as I knew, every night, because he never slept before midnight!

Eventually, we bought him a small Frequency Modulation (FM) radio which was tied to his cot and tuned permanently to one of the only two or three FM radio stations in London at the time. He would coo along with the music until news time when he would scream until the music resumed. By the time he was thirteen or fourteen months old, he was singing Boy George's "Karma Chameleon," which would start a love affair with music and singing, culminating in his joining the Calvary Methodist Church, Adabraka, Junior Choir at age six and a bit, when they normally took boys and girls from age eight.

## Our first house

For the first two years of Kofi's life, we were always on the move, looking for somewhere to live or seeking to buy our own house. It began before he was born. The lady in whose flat we made our first marital home, who lived in Côte d'Ivoire at the time, did not want children in her beautiful three-bedroom West Hampstead flat. So, we moved to a four-bedroom house in Edgware in Middlesex, on the outskirts of London a few months before he was born. The couple who owned this house had both retired and decided to go and live with the man's mother in Israel.

After nearly a year in Israel, the lady realised she could not live with her mother-in-law. Nine months into our contract, we received notice that they were returning to the United Kingdom. We had to move. We went house-hunting for several months but could not find a suitable place to buy. At the end of the contract year, we were moved to a block of flats, Embassy Court, adjacent to the Lords in West London, where Phillips Petroleum Company rented some flats for their temporary staff.

Embassy Court was close to St John's Wood underground station. By this time, Phillips had "downsized" to the Little Adelphi on the Strand, making it a very convenient commute for me. However, for Kofi who was eighteen months old, this was not good because we could not go for walks in the park back in Edgwarebury Lane or kick about in the back garden as we did at the Edgware house.

We hit the road once more, with our house hunting, travelling through Kent and Surrey every weekend, viewing houses. Finally, in early March 1984, we found a beautiful four-bedroom detached house in Purley, just south of Croydon.

In May 1984, we moved into our new house. Moving into our own house was good for Kofi who by now aged two, was in his third accommodation since he was born.

Just before we moved to the house in Purley, my boss called me into his office one morning and informed me that the application for an extension of my work permit had not been successful but that the company was going to launch an appeal, although he was not very confident of the outcome. We prayed about it and decided to leave it in the hands of the Lord. It did not work. We had to return to Ghana.

Under my contract, Phillips Petroleum Company would ship all our belongings and pay for our relocation for a month. We could either sell our house and car privately or else sell them to Phillips. The car which was paid for was just a little over two years old. Following independent evaluations, we decided to sell both the car and the house to Phillips Petroleum Company.

We had asked my in-laws to try and look for a place for us to rent for a few months while I looked for a job, hoping that any job I found in Ghana would come with accommodation.

Professor Dziwornooh who had planned to incorporate Geophysics in the Physics Department at UST died in early 1976, and with him, the plan for Geophysics seemed to have died. I could not go back to the University to lecture.

We bought a new fridge and freezer, a gas/electric cooker, a washing machine and other household items, in preparation for the return to Ghana. My friend and classmate, David Kuwornoo, returned to Ghana at the height of the "revolution" in February 1982. One of his two cars was seized at Tema Harbour. He was "being too bourgeois" bringing in two cars at the same time. The poor man and his wife had worked so hard to acquire those cars with the view to using one as a taxi, to supplement their income, but that was never to be. We were apprehensive but knew we would need a car in Ghana. We bought a brand-new Nissan Sunny 1.5 litre car, to be shipped to Tema Harbour.

# CHAPTER 9
# THE RETURN TO GHANA

## WELCOME BACK, THIS IS GHANA!

My wife and I and our thirty-month-old son, Kofi, arrived at the Kotoka International Airport in Accra at about 7:30 pm, aboard a Swissair flight from Heathrow, through Geneva and Lagos, on Tuesday 30th October 1984, some nine years and two months to the day after I first left the shores of Ghana for the United States of America, for post-graduate studies. Coincidentally, I returned to Ghana on 30th October 1978 for a six-month seismological study of southern Ghana towards my PhD thesis at Chelsea College, University of London. Chelsea would later be merged with some departments of Royal Holloway College, to become Royal Holloway University, University of London.

Our first baptism of fire predictably occurred at the Kotoka International Airport in Accra, where the heat and humidity after nearly a day in the air-conditioned aircraft, seemed unbearable. The security lady who searched us thoroughly also wanted 'something', which I did not have. I did not have any local money and was not even going to part with the loose change in dollars and sterling that I had on me. The lady's attempt to search little Kofi met with screaming, "gyae" and for emphasis, "Don't touch me!" To which the lady replied, "Sorry ooo.... little master, but sometimes parents hide money on their children!" There was an acute scarcity of convertible currency in Ghana and all official and unofficial attempts to extract money from travellers were floundering. Earlier, a male customs officer who went through our luggage wanted one of my shirts, which I naturally refused to part with.

What I found really intriguing was the fact that in October 1984 Ghana was supposed to be going through a process of "national self-cleansing" after all the corrupt elements in society were supposed to have been executed, incarcerated or else slapped with heavy fines. Yet there were these "agents of the revolution" openly soliciting, even demanding bribes from travellers. Welcome back to Ghana!

The next memorable spectacle was the near-total darkness that enveloped much of Accra as we were driven by my in-laws to their home in Dansoman where we would stay for the next two years, as we looked for our own accommodation.

When our Kofi was about eighteen months old, something happened that would teach me a lesson about what not to do or say in the presence of a child and that lesson has lived with me till today. Someone crossed us rather badly in traffic in London which made me spit out two not-so-pleasant words, as I tooted the horn. Those two words had apparently been imprinted on his impressionable young mind and been associated with the sound of a vehicle's horn. From that moment, anytime he heard the horn of a vehicle, he let them out! We began to pray about it as we explained to him that what I had said on that day actually meant "stop it."

In the United Kingdom, one can sometimes drive for three months or more without ever hearing the sound of a vehicle's horn. So, after some time, we thought he had forgotten about it all. Not so fast, it seemed. As our Ghanaian diplomat friend would note later, "In Ghana these days, when you are driving, you have to toot your horn, to let everyone know that you also have a car, especially if it is a new one," as there were not that many new cars on the roads of Ghana at the time. As soon as we left the airport there were sounds of car horns all over and each time, Kofi would shout, "Stop it." My in-laws did not understand that. I could only promise to explain later.


**Was I ready for the long haul?**


Although the commercial officer at the Ghana High Commission in London had assured me that I could join the yet-to-be-formed Ghana National Petroleum Corporation on arrival, I wanted to make sure I had something to sustain Mother while I tried to settle back in Ghana after nine years away from home. I bought two STIHL chainsaws, a large one for felling timber, and a smaller one for splitting logs or trimming garden plants. I intended to hire out the larger one and keep the smaller one till I was sure it would all work out.

When I reported it to Mother and Sister Aba, they said I should sell it and give them the money to do something with it. I gave them 5,000 cedis in those days, the price of the chainsaw in cedi terms. Not long after I had given them the money and while I was still debating as to what to do with the bigger chain saw which technically now belonged to me, I was told on a visit to Gyaman that Kojo Ofori, my brother-in-law Kweku Benyi's younger brother, operated a similar machine somewhere in the Central Region and could make money with it for Mother and Sister Aba. I gave it out, to be sent to Kojo Ofori and that was the last I saw of that machine intact. Initially, it seemed to have worked, as Kojo Ofori brought them some money. That arrangement did not last.

Then it was decided that it should be given to another uncle, Kojo Ketseaba, to be used somewhere in the Kadjebi area of the Volta Region. That did not work either. Later, Kofi Graham spent nearly one week roaming that area, looking for Uncle, so he could retrieve the chainsaw. The day he finally brought the machine to Accra, he did not even have enough money to continue his journey to Obra-twer-Owu. I had travelled outside the country and Sabina had to find him some money to continue his journey home.

A few months later, while I was away in Canada on an official trip,

Kofi Graham came to Accra, bullied Sabina with "it is my brother's machine" and took the remaining smaller STIHL chainsaw away. Eventually, he sold both of them. What happened to the proceeds I never knew till he sadly passed away on 30th October 2010, the day before we celebrated Mother's 90th birthday. In effect, everything I brought home from the sweat of my brows had vanished down the drain with nothing to show for it.

**Petroleum Department**

**Off to the Petroleum Department January 1985**

Mr Wilberforce who worked as a student liaison at the Ghana High Commission in London asked me to see Mr TT Fabyan, who was then head of the Petroleum Department, which would later become the Ghana National Petroleum Corporation (GNPC), when I arrived in Accra.

I reported to the Petroleum Department on the fourth floor of Republic House on Wednesday, 3rd January 1985, to begin a process which would lead me to work as a Senior Geophysicist of the department, before the formation of the GNPC.

I served as a Teaching Assistant at the Physics Department of the University of Science and Technology during the 1974-75 academic year under the National Service Scheme, before travelling to America for postgraduate studies. I also did Vacation Training at the Aboso Glass Factory, the Meteorological Services Department at Legon in

Accra and the Ghana Atomic Energy Commission, as an undergraduate student, but this was my first real baptism into the world of work in Ghana, and what an experience it turned to be!

When I presented my Curriculum Vitae to Mr Fabyan, he noticed that I had attended GSTS and advised me to go and see the Secretary of Fuel and Power, as the ministers were called in those days, Mr Emmanuel Appiah-Korang. Mr Appiah-Korang was four years my senior at GSTS. He was the reserve goalkeeper of the famous school hockey team that won the National Schools and Colleges Hockey Championship trophy in 1962, by beating the Presbyterian Boys' Secondary School then stationed at Krobo Odumase in the Eastern Region, at the finals.

He was glad to see me and wanted to ask some questions about petroleum exploration and production. The law establishing GNPC had been passed, but the corporation had not taken off yet. He was about to travel to the Tema Oil Refinery where he used to work and for which he now had ministerial responsibility. Could I wait and go along with him? I had met a few of my old schoolmates but he was the first of the ones in government I was meeting, and I was all too glad to go with him. At the end of our tour, he asked me to go back to Mr Fabyan to give me a job. Without so much as an interview, Mr Fabyan asked me to start the following day as a Senior Geophysicist in the Petroleum Department at the Republic House in Accra.

**I can clean my own office**

In my first few months at the Petroleum Department, I shared an office with two people, a Petroleum Engineer, Mr Adams Alhassan, who I should have recognised from my UST days, and Mr HKN Ashie, who turned out to be a cousin of my Form Two House Prefect at GSTS. Adams, I did not recognise initially because he had put on some weight, as we all do at one time or other in our lives. He was in my first-year science course and also in my Chemistry "Practicals Group".

He had won a scholarship to study in Hungary and returned to Ghana in 1979 or thereabouts, to join the Petroleum Department.

Following the overthrow of the government of President Kwame Nkrumah in February 1966, the Soviets and their Chinese friends were kicked out of Ghana and for nearly two decades, they had no influence in Ghana. Later, after the overthrow of the "rightist" (for want of a better term) government of Professor Busia in 1972, the Soviets and their Chinese and Cuban communist allies began to make inroads into Ghana again. Where better to start than education, with scholarships to impressionable young minds?

There were all kinds of scholarships for studies in the Soviet Block, particularly in science and engineering. I applied for a few and was actually invited for an interview for a programme in the Soviet Union. That was when my senior and now hall mate, Derek Faidoo sat me down and "read the riot act" to me. "If you want to pass your first-year examinations in this university, sit down and focus. On the other hand, if you wish to follow Eastern European scholarships, then pack your books in some corner and concentrate on that full time, but remember if you do not eventually make it, you are stuffed!" That was the end of all my applications and whatever ambitions I had of travelling outside Ghana in those early days and I was ever so grateful for his intervention.

At the time I joined the Petroleum Department, an acute petroleum products scarcity that had hit Ghana for several years still persisted. At that time, the Petroleum Department imported crude oil for the refinery at Tema (GHAIP), to refine for a commission and the products were returned to the department, for distribution. The Petroleum Engineers in the department oversaw this lucrative distribution system through the issue of coupons, while Mr Ashie's Quality Control group ensured that the pumps at the filling stations, which at this point were dominated by semi-legal Burkinabe and Malian operators in the countryside, were properly calibrated. A majority of these foreign sellers employed illegally adjusted pumps at dusty filling stations around the country. Consequently, Mr Ashie was constantly on the move inspecting filling stations and checking their dispensing pumps, while the "Marketing people" went around either collecting debts or ensuring that fuel station operators paid for their supplies.

As a result, I was all by myself most of the week. Because the original occupants of this rather small office were on the move most of the time, the cleaners took advantage of the situation and rarely ever cleaned the office. A few weeks after I moved in, I realised that and decided to confront the man who was responsible for the cleaners and also doubled as head of the security personnel in the office and officers' houses and bungalows, a retired police inspector called Mr Kwamena Sam. He promised to see to the anomaly and actually cleaned the dusty tables himself that morning. It did not last long.

A few days after the encounter with Mr Sam, I found some old seismic sections in a box in the corner of one of the offices at the Geological Survey Department and decided to take a look at them. Back at my office, I asked the people in the adjacent office if there were any coloured pencils and erasers for interpretation of the seismic sections. I was told there weren't any and that if I needed things of that nature, I had to go and see Mr Fabyan, the head of the department. First Mr Fabyan was pleasantly surprised that I wanted to do "technical" work because according to him, "The engineers in this place did not do that kind of thing." He called for the cashier and asked him to provide "petty cash" for the purchase of coloured and lead pencils and erasers for me to work with.

Before I left Mr Fabyan's office, I asked if I could be given a portion of the salary of the cleaner who was responsible for cleaning our small office, since I had been doing it myself for a few weeks. He called Mr Sam and asked why that office was not being cleaned since someone was assigned to do that job. After some discussions, Mr Fabyan cautioned Mr Sam that if I ever reported to him again about our office not being cleaned, he would hold him personally responsible. From then on, our office was cleaned on time every morning, without fail. Mr Fabyan occasionally enquired about its state. As for Mr Sam, he became one of my very good friends in the office until he retired in the late 1990s.

With respect to the supplies, I got several boxes of coloured and lead pencils later, but they were very cheap Chinese varieties that crumbled as they were sharpened. Subsequently, when I had to make an urgent structural map, I had to "borrow" a pack from the pile we had bought for our son Kofi as we prepared to return to Ghana, knowing before we left the United Kingdom that everything imaginable that made life easy was in short supply in the Ghana of the early to mid-1980s!

## Living with my in-laws

I first met my in-laws a few days before our wedding. My mother-in-law (bless her soul), my sister-in-law Janet (and their niece Sylvia), arrived in London five days before the wedding. My father-in-law, my brother-in-law Eddie and his girlfriend, Caroline (from Washington DC) arrived three days before the wedding. My father-in-law and Eddie left soon after the wedding. The women stayed on another three weeks before they left for Ghana. My mother-in-law and Janet came to help out six months after Kofi was born. Their twin brothers came to spend six weeks with us while they were at university. That was the whole time I had known my in-laws. In fact, I had not met Florence the other sister at all before we returned to Ghana.

Yet after just a few months of living with my in-laws, it seemed like I had known them for a lifetime. My father-in-law had become to me what Uncle Obrehun was in my formative years, like my biological father. While waiting to start work, I went to his shop with him during the week. We attended his 'Kwahu Anglican' Church at Adabraka on Sundays together with his grandchildren.

We went "house viewing", together. After a while, Sabina believed that I was conspiring with her father, who adored his grandchildren, to continue to stay in their family house for as long as possible. She believed that I had become more comfortable in the house than she was, thinking that I was not making enough effort to move our family to a place of our own.

Often after lunch on Sunday, Papa, as I called him, would draw me aside and say, "Uncle Ebo, let us leave the women and go somewhere."

That somewhere was usually Ambassador Hotel where we sat and watched Bob Cole and Ajax Bukana sing and dance and tell jokes.

Bob Cole hailed from Aboso in the Western Region, where I did vacation training during my first year at the university. I worked with his junior brother at the Glass Factory and got to know him quite well. I also became good friends with their only niece who was on vacation at Aboso while I was there, but I never met Bob Cole himself.


**First seismic structure mapping**

One Monday morning sometime in 1985, I was approached by Mr Banson who was the Deputy Director of the Geological Survey Department and a member of the first GNPC Board, to make a map of the offshore Accra Basin, for a presentation at a forthcoming investors' conference in London. The conference was to begin the following Monday. In other words, the maps were to be completed before the end of the week.

The final seismic sections of the Geophysical Services Incorporated (GSI's) speculative 2-D seismic survey conducted sometime in 1982/83 were available at the Geological Survey Department. Some of the lines were more than thirty kilometres long. The available hard copies were too long for the tiny tables at the Petroleum Department at the time. We had to go to the Geological Survey Department where they had a long table in the Conference Room, to be able to spread them out.

I was joined by Nii Adzei-Akpor, a Geologist at the Survey Department who was to be seconded to the Petroleum Department and would later formally join the new GNPC. Two days into our seismic interpretation, two other Geophysicists of the corporation came in and wanted us to cut the sections into two so they could work on one-half of the seismic sections. Straight away, I knew they had no clue what was going on. Unfortunately, they had support from Mr Banson, an earthquake seismologist with no experience whatsoever in seismic interpretation.

I offered to do the interpretation so we could do the mapping together if they wished. That was the last I saw of any of them. We worked through the weekend and managed to contour two horizons by late Saturday afternoon.

Later that evening, when I asked why as many as five people were to present those maps in London, I was told that if I thought there were too many people, I should give the maps to others to present and stay at home. Staying at home was not my problem because I did not like the idea of being away from my young family every so often. It was the principle behind it.

Several weeks later, I met the Danish Geophysicist, Niels Neilson, who did the actual presentation and he assured me that the maps and presentation went just fine. That was my first brush with GNPC authority and many were to follow later.

## The birth of Paa Kwesi

Sabina was five months pregnant when we left for Ghana. Before I started work at the Petroleum Department in January 1985 whenever she went to the market on Saturday, I accompanied her to the market, so I could carry the shopping basket to the car park. I received curious glances and taunts and on several occasions, sellers asked: "If I was afraid that she would spend my money recklessly." For those market women, it did not matter if the rather heavy baskets could have negative effects on her health and possibly that of the unborn baby. To them, a man had no business accompanying his wife to the market.

On Sunday, 7th April 1985, I attended "Obo Anglican Church" at Adabraka with my father-in-law, as usual. Sabina was too tired to join us that day. Her mother attended the Emmanuel Presbyterian Church at Dansoman, not too far away from the family home. Soon after we left the house, her birth pains began, and she was rushed to Osu RE Clinic which was run by their family friend and Gynaecologist, Dr K.A. Abrokwa.

By the time we got there, she was being wheeled from the upstairs theatre to the maternity unit downstairs. Kwesi was delivered at 3:58 pm at Osu RE Clinic weighing in at 2.6 kilograms (5 pounds 8 ounces).

Sabina was still drowsy and as I held her hand before she dozed off, she continued to say, "This is the last one, this is the last one." I said "yes" each time and I meant it because two Caesarean operations in exactly three years and five days was not something I could wish on my sister or anyone else for that matter.

I had named Kofi after my father, according to Fanti tradition and named Kwesi after my mother (Kwesi Foh) four weeks after he was born. Two months later, I left for Calgary, Canada, on a three-week trip that turned out to be three months, and by the time I returned, Kwesi was running away from me. It took him nearly two weeks to begin to bond with me again.

Living in the family house with several children around, Kwesi began to walk at eleven months, about six weeks earlier than Kofi had done.

# CHAPTER 10
## THE EARLY GNPC YEARS

## THE MOVE TO THE AIRPORT RESIDENTIAL AREA, ACCRA

We had been looking for a house in a good area. One of our estate agents in London told us that "it is better to buy a rubbish house in a good location than a good house in a rubbish location. No matter how wretched the house is, in a good location, with just a little tender care, it soon appreciates in value." That is what we have always done, including our current house here in Flitwick, Bedfordshire.

Our house in Purley in Surrey, was just beautiful, at a pristine location. Everyone who visited us simply fell in love with it. When we had to leave the United Kingdom, we struggled with what to do with it. Some friends advised that we rented it out so we could use the rent to service the mortgage. The mortgage was big and the premium was quite high. Any slip with the repayment would spell disaster for us. We could lose the house altogether, and we had heard so many such harrowing stories.

Also, a tenant could trash the house and leave us with an empty shell. We fasted and prayed about it as we always did in challenging situations. In the end, we decided to sell it and keep the money in England until we found a house in Ghana. It was a divine intervention because less than a year after we left the United Kingdom, there was a great housing crash which sent house prices tumbling; followed by lots of repossessions. By selling the house, we were able to afford this new one in another pristine location in Ghana.

One Monday afternoon in 1986, one of the numerous estate agents that had been introduced to us took me to inspect a house at the Airport Residential Area. The next day, I took Papa, my father-in-law, to see the house, a rather delightful four-bedroom house with two bathrooms, one of them ensuite, a fair-sized kitchen, two pantries and a garage, plus a very large undeveloped space around it. The compound was overgrown with wild pawpaw trees, bananas and thorn bushes. My father-in-law's first reaction was, "This is a good area, the house is in bad shape, but it can be fixed - just as our agent in London had said several years earlier. We repaired the house in record time and at a reasonable cost, using carpenters, painters and plumbers that my father-in-law had used in the past.

My old horticulturist friend from my Zebra House, London, days, Mr Joe Akoi turned the overgrown space around the house into a beautiful green lawn with a vegetable patch from which we would harvest our own tomatoes, corn, sweet peppers and okra, among other vegetables, for many years. There were palm trees, six coconut trees and two avocado pear trees to which I added two more in the next two years.

We moved into our new house on 26 September 1986, nearly two years to the day after we returned to Ghana. During the period, we looked at numerous houses all over Accra. Simultaneously, the Public Affairs Department of the then Petroleum Department tried very hard to find a rental place for me, to no avail.

A week after we moved into our house, my father-in-law visited us. The first thing he said to me was, "The house is looking really good. Now you have to go and build a house for the old lady." After the family moved to the new house at Gyaman, Mother told everyone who visited that "I was not the one who built the house, it was Sabina who built it", because in her words, *"Gyaman akrakyefo nnsi adan wo*

*Gyaman"*, to wit, "the educated men of Gyaman never build houses at Gyaman."

## Travel woes - stranded at Rio de Janeiro Airport

On Saturday 3rd January 1987, I returned home from a function at Calvary Methodist Church to find a note saying that I was to prepare to travel with the Secretary for Fuel and Power, Mr Appia-Korang to Rio de Janeiro, Brazil, the next day. When I asked about a visa, I was told that Braspetro, the international wing of Petrobras, our hosts, would arrange a visa on arrival. This was the first of several trips I would make to Brazil in the next three years.

Up to this point, I had travelled on GNPC assignments to Canada, the United States of America, the United Kingdom, the Netherlands, Nigeria and Côte d'Ivoire, so I had two sets of travel clothes, complete with underclothes and dressing gowns, one for tropical environments and the other for Europe and North America. Brazil is tropical. I quickly packed two suits, five dress shirts, and two pairs of casual trousers into my "ready-to-go" suitcase and I was ready to travel. When I met the minister and my old schoolmate, Mr Appiah-Korang at the VIP lounge at Kotoka International Airport, he assured me that I would be alright.

We flew by Swiss Air on the overnight flight to Geneva. We were in Business Class and it turned out that Captain Kojo Tsikata, then Provisional National Defence Council (PNDC) member responsible for Foreign Affairs and the Finance Minister, Dr Kwesi Botchwey, were both travelling in First Class on this flight. It was during the night that I saw Captain Tsikata for the first time.

Mr Appiah-Korang went to the corridor to speak to him and I saw Captain Tsikata hand a piece of paper to him. It was the telephone number of Mrs Aggrey-Orleans, Ghana's Ambassador to Switzerland.

We had more than four hours in Geneva before the connecting flight to Rio de Janeiro. Captain Tsikata had sent a message to Mrs Aggrey-Orleans to pick us up from the airport and entertain us so we would not spend that much time at the airport. Mr Appiah-Korang as a minister had a service passport and did not need a visa for international travel, but because I was with him, the ambassador had to make a written undertaking that she would take personal responsibility for us until we left the country. She held on to our passports.

Mrs Aggrey-Orleans took us on a mini-tour of Geneva, showing us the French, German and Italian borders within the city, before taking us home where we took showers, changed clothes and had dinner before she took us back to the airport, to board another overnight flight to Rio.

At immigration the next morning when we asked about our Braspetro contact, we were informed that nobody had arrived for us and it was too early to call because the Brapetro office would not open till 9 o'clock. The minister with his service passport had been whisked through, but I was going to be detained because I had arrived without a visa as required by Brazilian law. The minister decided to stay with me, since it was due to his assurance, on good grounds, that I had travelled without a visa.

Eventually, someone arrived from the Braspetro office to arrange a temporary visa for my stay in Brazil, but not before Swissair had been fined for carrying a passenger without a valid visa into Brazilian territory.

At a dinner hosted by the Brazilian Minister of Petroleum, he apologised profusely and promised that next time if he had ample notice, he would compensate us with a national delicacy, a snake! The minister turned to me and whispered, "*eye se yaamma* notice," (just as well we did not give enough notice).

Back in Ghana a few weeks later, I received a letter from Swissair with a bill for over $4,000, the fine that had been imposed on the airline for our trip to Rio. I sent the bill to the ministry and eventually, GNPC paid it.

**Building at Gyaman**

.  .  .

I spent New Year's Eve of 1985 at Gyaman. With the help of the younger of my wife's twin brothers, I just managed to take delivery of our new car, a Nissan Sunny 1.5 from Tema Harbour on 24th December 1984. It was a close call. We could not leave the harbour early enough to register the car, so I bought a temporary licence plate with insurance and drove it home. We did the formal registration after the Christmas break.

I travelled to Gyaman with Kow Morgan, passing through "Low Cost", Winneba, to be introduced to his in-laws, an introduction that would cause me a lot of aggravation in the following years.

In the course of our stay at Gyaman, I had two pieces of advice that I will never forget. Opanyin Kweku Otu Carpenter (my own Uncle Kweku Otu's half-brother), called me to his bedroom. After the usual greetings and pleasantries, he looked me in the eye and said, "You must build a house at Gyaman because you will never be able to sleep comfortably in your car." The next evening, Nana Kofi Andam, the "Mbrantsehen" of Gyaman said the same thing to me. They both knew that I owned a plot of land in town.

I designed the house at Gyaman myself and showed it to one of my seniors at GSTS, Mr Yartey, a senior architect at the time, with his own architectural company that was doing very well. He also worked for the Petroleum Department and later, Ghana National Petroleum Corporation (GNPC), as Consultant Architect on a retainer basis. Giant Yartey looked at my design and said it was very good but added a veranda all around the perimeter of the compound. I did not like the idea because I believed that:

i) It would make the compound very small, and,

ii) It would make the rooms dark and also reduce natural ventilation, which is common with most Ghanaian architectural designs even today.

I gave my design to one of the draughtsmen in the office to do the formal drawing. Mr Baidoo, the draughtsman, inserted flower pots in the front walls. Again, I removed them because I was afraid that snakes might hide in the pots and cause problems in the house. Somehow, I inadvertently gave out the drawing with the flower pots and so when the masons began the foundation, they inserted the pots. I had to get them removed again.

A few months after we took delivery of our belongings and car from the Tema Harbour, I asked my cousin and best friend, Emmanuel Otoo of blessed memory, whether I could not bring Kwesi Arhin, Sister Aba's second born to Accra, to train as an auto electrician. "Tuutu," as we all called Emmanuel Otoo, had trained as an auto electrician and had done very well working for Kowus Motors in Accra, until the company collapsed in the heat of the "1981 Revolution."

At this time, Tuutu was running his own drinking bar across the road from the workshop of a "body works" garage. The owner of the garage was also his co-tenant and a relative of ours. Wofa Yaw, as he was known around the place, was the nephew of Uncle Obrehun's second wife, Maame Esi Kyerewa, who hailed from Gomoa Brofoyedur. We spoke to Wofa Yaw and he readily agreed to take on Kwesi Arhin as an apprentice. He waived a major part of the traditional fees that he charged his apprentices because according to him, Kwesi "was his nephew too."

For about eighteen months, Kwesi was doing very well and progressing rapidly. He was the favourite at the workshop because he would do anything for anybody. Wofa Yaw depended on him for his records and account keeping because he found him quite bright, not having had much education himself.

Then Kwesi found a girlfriend. Sometimes he would leave the workshop where all the apprentices slept after work on Thursday and only return on Monday morning. When he was questioned, he would give the excuse that he had run errands for me and spent the time with me. I was still living with my in-laws. We had one room with a sealed-off veranda and another room where we stored our suitcases. We could never entertain our own overnight visitors. I only saw Kwesi Arhin occasionally when we went for the meetings of the "Gyaman Youth Association," which had been revived since I had been back from England, with me as Chairman, my cousin John Painstil as Vice Chairman and the late Mr J K Essel as Secretary.

Kwesi's disappearances went on for a while until Tuutu reported them to me after Wofa Yaw had complained to him on several occasions. I went to see Wofa Yaw who subsequently decided to punish Kwesi Arhin by caning. Kwesi ran away to his parents with some flimsy excuse. Eventually, when they learnt the truth about his misbehaviour, they accompanied him to Accra to speak to Wofa Yaw. Wofa Yaw explained to them the disciplinary procedures that everybody who flouted the regulations at his workshop had to go through. Sister Aba and her husband offered to take the punishment on their son's behalf. Wofa Yaw would not have any of it. That was the end of Kwesi Arhin's apprenticeship.

In the end, he served as the "foreman" for the construction of the house at Gyaman. Was that a divine appointment? We shall never know. One thing though, without his supervision and constant "battles" with the workmen, we could not have completed the house in the time we did. So, in this instance, we have to agree with St Paul that, "In all things, God works for the good of those who love Him and are chosen according to His purpose." (Romans 8:28)

During one of my official trips to the United Kingdom in early 1990, I checked and my savings accounts in London had accrued some interest. I cashed the interest plus part of the principal amounts. The next weekend after I arrived back in Accra, I went to Gyaman, picked Kwesi Arhin and went straight to Essikuma. He had told me that he had very good mason and carpenter friends who lived there. I showed the design of the house to the masons and went into negotiations about the cost. I paid them a third of the agreed fee.

Next, we went to the carpenter who would build the profiles and other wooden structures for the foundation and agreed on his fee. I paid him a third and asked him to begin the following Monday. From there we went to my old school senior, Mr Kweku Acquaah who sold cement and cement blocks in the town. I bought and paid for five hundred blocks and one hundred bags of cement.

We then came to Gyaman and arranged for sand, paid for the plot where the sand would be dug as well and paid the labour cost of those who would dig and those who would convey the sand to the building site. We were on our way to building a house at Gyaman.

From there, I went to tell Mother that after church service the following day, she should go to the plot with the Catechist to pray for the start of the house. They had prepared the plot for the planting season and wanted the start of the house construction postponed till after the planting and harvest seasons. I asked her whether she wanted a decent house to live in or a farm.

I had never seen anybody within the family build in my lifetime and it was a major learning experience for all of us. It would take six and a half million old cedis to complete in April 1993, painting, plumbing and all, but the next time we did renovations in 1997, mostly painting, they cost over fifteen million cedis. The latest major repairs in 2010, including roofing, plumbing and electrical wiring, cost over thirty-six million! A new set of repair works in 2016 cost a lot more.

I had intended the house for Mother and my siblings, and that is how the rooms were allocated. As a child growing up, I believed that Sister Efua Antobam was our mother's first daughter or something that close. One of the keys to my early success in reading and writing was down to Sister Efua. I do not remember when she began to take me to school, but I remember that when everybody went to the farm, I would follow her to school. She was in primary school at the time.

After I was formally enrolled in primary school, she always gave me her books for the year, so I never bought any edition of a book that Sister Efua had used before. She was very meticulous, she covered all her books with brown paper as soon as they were purchased, so even though she was in Primary Six when I started in Class One, the books that she handed down to me were always like new. It was her influence and those of Nana Kofi Akwa who lived next door, and my cousins Kofi Mensah, Kobena Onoma and Kofi Egyir that I began to excel almost immediately after I was formally enrolled in primary school.

So even though Sister Efua died a few months before I returned from England, I earmarked one of the rooms for her children in appreciation of what she had done for me as a child. In fact, I was glad that I bought her and Nana Addow a full piece of cloth to share when I was returning for my fieldwork in 1978. I went on to give two more half-pieces to Nana Addow before she died. She became my "sweetheart" before she died. Apparently, she called my name throughout the morning of the day she died and gave strict instructions to Mother to place all the pieces of cloth I had given her in her coffin, so "she would tell her brothers and sisters about me." Nana Addow blessed me before she died.

The original design of the house was made up of eight bedrooms, three bathrooms, two kitchens and two toilets. After the building was roofed, I was told that cooking in the kitchens with firewood would damage the roof. So, I knocked the walls of one of the bathrooms through and built a new two-room kitchen at the back. Those were also turned into bedrooms almost immediately after Mother and the others moved in, making ten bedrooms altogether.

Because Kwesi Arhin worked so hard on the building and missed being crushed by a falling beam in the course of the construction, I assigned one of the first kitchens-turned into bedrooms, much bigger rooms, to him. Since I had planned to give Sister Efua's room to her children, Kofi Ata and Ebo Duncan, I assigned the other to them, so the young ones could be together.

Kofi Ata rented out that room and received rent on it for some time before Kobena Ebo Duncan took it over. Apparently, Kobena Ebo later had a quarrel with Sister Aba and Mother over the constant stream of different women that he brought to the house and decided to move out. He removed his grass-stuffed mattress, placed it under a tree in front of the house over which the electrical wires ran and set it on fire and nearly burnt the whole house to ashes!

Eventually, Maame Esi moved into that room after she gave birth to one of her children at Gyaman and that has become her room.

Adaboah's husband, Kofi Amoh, was a carpenter. He came to see me at GNPC just before the house got to the roofing stage. He told me that he would like to roof the building for me. He would return in a month when the timber that I was putting together for the roofing and other carpentry works was ready. The next time I saw him after nearly two years, he was ill and living in the room that I had originally earmarked for Sister Efua, with his wife and children. He had named one of his sons after me. The boy, Kobena, like me, was born on Tuesday. He had done me a great honour and he was ill, so I couldn't complain. Unfortunately, he died not long afterwards while I was away in England.

. . .

**In search of a helper**

I had always known that without some kind of assistance, taking care of Mother while at the same time helping to advance the fortunes of the family was going to be an uphill task if I was to shoulder it all alone, as my brother Kofi did not seem to be helping in any meaningful way.

Maame Esi was doing very well in school when I returned to Ghana. I invested in her, hoping that she might go on to Vocational School as she had wanted to. It was not to be. She abandoned schooling for motherhood! Later, when I sent her off to our seamstress friend for an apprenticeship, there were all kinds of problems, much of which admittedly, were not her making. We tried another lady who lived near my "adopted daughter", Sophia Bentil-Owusu, and this time, she did very well, but before the formal completion of the apprenticeship, she took off again, this time to be a permanent housewife and mother.

Kwesi Edu did very well at his Basic Education Certificate Examination (BECE) and was admitted without any hassle to Tema Secondary School. There was no accommodation on campus for first-year students. He came to live with us at the Airport Residential Area. He was really struggling to make it to school in the mornings, travelling from the house. One day, Sabina took him with my driver Owusu, to Apam Secondary School where she was promised admission in about a week, but she did not like the water problem in the school. Eventually, that Safari ended with her securing a place for Kwesi at Swedru Secondary School.

He did quite well in his final SSS examinations, but he needed stronger passes in English, Physics and Chemistry. Kwesi re-took those papers and passed English and Physics. He needed to retake Chemistry again. He ran late for the next registration and so decided to go and leave the money for registration under a bed at Gyaman. The next time he went back, that money was gone.

Finally, Kwesi settled on driving, a path of life which would later lead him to some very good skills in Information Technology. Unfortunately, he has not been able to secure a permanent job in IT. However, by taking a bold step to put that first ISUZU mini-bus on the road, without any formal training and just a month after passing his driving test, Kwesi has managed to turn himself into a transport owner and entrepreneur which is all well and good.

I had no intention of buying a commercial vehicle because I knew what happened to Nana Ofosu and also heard about my father-in-law's experience with his own brother. Ato Donkor, Maame Esi's husband, got me involved in it by accident and I got trapped and, but for my senior policeman friend, Inspector Amamoo and his brother at the Driver and Vehicle Licensing Office, I would have lost every penny I invested in that vehicle.

In 2014, when the main door to my part of the house at Gyaman apparently began to fall apart, it was Kwesi who fixed it before I arrived home from England. These days when I get to Accra, without a car of my own, I am sure that I can travel around in safety amidst the chaos of the Accra traffic because Kwesi is always there for me.

Kobena Ebo Duncan was the person who was supposed to drive that ISUZU vehicle. We must have gone to Ato's dealers more than fifty times, to no avail. Just as we were finally about to assume ownership and secure the proper registration of the vehicle, Ebo took off and I never saw him again, literally. I have never really gained anything from that investment, but through sheer hard work, Kwesi now has three vehicles and is able to help with many things in the family, which has always been my intention, a helper!

I met Kofi Ata Duncan during one of my trips to Gyaman in connection with the construction of the house. He needed money to expand his yam farm so we could all benefit. I gave him the money, 13,000 cedis, a lot of money in those days. That was in 1991, and I have never set eyes on him ever since.

From the moment I saw her on my return to Ghana, Grace's daughter, Yaa (Evelyn) became to me the daughter that I never had. I was really praying for another lady in the family, and she was the one

Sometime in 1997, she came to tell me that she wanted to join the

Ghana Prisons Service. She had completed SSS at Krobo Girls' Secondary School in Somanya. I went to see my good friend, Israel Aheto Tsegah who at the time was serving as Commandant of the Prisons Training and Borstal School at Roman Ridge in Accra. He told me that there was going to be a recruitment exercise and that we should look out for the announcement in the newspapers. I told Evelyn to tell her mother when she got back to Somanya where Grace was working, to try and buy one of the daily newspapers regularly. Yaa later came to tell me that her mother said she couldn't afford the newspapers daily.

I bought several newspapers regularly and I could always find one to read in the GNPC library anyway. I am not sure how I missed it but while I was returning from leading the Calvary Methodist Church early morning service one Wednesday, I met Yaa, just as I got to the house. She told me that the entrance examination for the Prison Service recruitment was taking place that day. I drove like a lunatic to get to the examination centre. Mr J K Essel who lived next door to the family house at Gyaman and related to us by marriage (he is Auntie Adwoa Ahema's nephew), was the invigilator for the examination. He was very active in the Gyaman Youth Association at the time. When I told him about Yaa, he said "Oh me nua (my brother), why didn't you come earlier? We have already finished with the first paper and are about to start the second".

He thought for a moment and told me that there was going to be a similar exercise in Kumasi and that if Yaa could get there, she might stand a chance. When she went back to Somanya, the pastor of their church suggested that she could stay with one of their Church's pastors in Kumasi and take the examinations. She did and was selected with 74 others out of over 300 applicants. But then, the successful applicants were warned that even though they had passed the three-day written examinations, there was no guarantee that they would gain places in the training itself because sometimes senior officers whose children could not make the grade substituted their children's names between the recruitment centre and training centre in Accra. When she came to tell me, I went to see Tsegah about her success in the examinations and recruitment. He told me not to worry about it. He wrote her name down and assured me that he would call for the names of the successful candidates from the regions that very day.

Yaa made it. I got her the kit and all the support she needed for the training programme. It was tough, but while many of the male recruits dropped out of the programme, she sailed through it. Unfortunately, I was out of the country at the time of her passing out, but I managed to get her the things she needed for the day and several of our relations made it to her passing out ceremony.

Before the passing out ceremony, she came to tell me about her worries about stationing. I spoke to Tsegah and he informed me that if she chose Accra, it would be very difficult for her to find official accommodation but if she was sent to the regions, she stood a good chance of getting decent official accommodation. Later, Tsegah told me that he could send Yaa to the Central Prisons in Sekondi. That was where she was posted to. I managed to provide the things she needed for her new station. She was going to work for the first time in her life.

The new recruits were not paid for several months. On at least two occasions, she sent SOS messages and I had to send her money, while I went to visit her myself, on two occasions. When things settled down, she seemed to be doing quite well. However, about two years after she went to Sekondi, she was assigned to periphery duties that did not seem too relevant to the level of her training. I spoke to Tsegah about it, but while we were still discussing her plight, I resigned from GNPC and eventually left Ghana. Not long after I left, Yaa resigned from the Prison Service without even telling me.

When Cudjoe (Grace's second child) finished his Senior Secondary education, he came to inform me that he wanted to do the Post-A Teachers' Course. He needed an Education District to sponsor his training. Fortunately, the Tema District of the Presbyterian Education Unit offered to sponsor him. He came to tell me that his mother had told him she could not afford the cost of his Post-Secondary training. About the same time, GNPC paid its staff a percentage of their contributions to the End of Service Benefits Scheme.

At a time, my children were working as cleaners in their school to pay for their lunch in England, I used about 80% of my benefits to ensure that he got a good start for his course at Kibi Teachers' Training

College. He spent his holidays with me and while I was paying his fees and other incidentals, he still went to his mother and sister Yaa, to ask for the same "fees" that I was paying.

When he completed his training, he lived with me for the first three years as he taught in Tema, and later, Accra. When I returned to the UK, I continued to pay the utility bills in the house and even paid for a gardener to tend the garden, when all of them who lived in the house at the time had been to the farm before and could have taken care of the garden. When I decided to rent out the house so I could join my wife and children in England, I gave out money to cover three years advance in rented accommodation for the three of them (Cudjoe, Kojo Baah and Kwame Ampiah), who were living in the house at the time. Cudjoe took his share of the money and went and rented somewhere for himself, leaving Kojo Baah and Kwame Ampiah behind. Having taken a portion of the money, there was not enough left for the others to pay their rent in advance. I had to find extra money for Kojo and Kwamena.

When I started working after university, if someone had paid for my boarding and lodging for three years, I certainly could have saved and done something for myself.

Several years later, Cudjoe sent me an email to say that he wanted to go to university. I was not sure if he had served his bond with the Presbyterian Education Unit. I have done part-time teaching and also supervised several student theses at the University of Ghana, Legon, the University of Science and Technology, Kumasi and the University of Cape Coast. I also knew from my own friends at university that teachers could attend university as mature students after the age of 30 if they passed a special mature students' entrance examination. I knew that if Cudjoe could wait a few years, he could pass the examination and go to the university on study leave with pay.

More specifically, I advised him that while he would gain a promotion after studying at the university as a teacher if he changed career, he could find himself at the bottom of his new profession. In Europe and increasingly, most of West Africa as well, people graduate from university at age 21 or 22 these days. Such a change of career to attend university at 27 or 28 meant that by the time a person completed university education, he or she would be competing with 22-and 23-year-olds for jobs and the prospects were not very bright. An employer would prefer to hire a 22-year-old and train him or her and get 38 years of service than to pick a 30-year-old, and spend money on him or her, for thirty years of service.

Cudjoe obviously did not like my advice. I did not hear from him again till I received another email from him asking if I could help sponsor some kind of attachment in the United States of America. I had just found a new job after I had been made redundant in my previous job. I did not have that kind of money. I did not hear from him for several years until recently when I got a telephone call from him saying he was stranded somewhere in Cambodia. In a rather bizarre twist of fate, our son Paa Kwesi managed to bail him out. Meanwhile, Paa Kwesi did not even remember who Cudjoe was because he obviously had no contact with anybody, but he could find Paa Kwesi when he needed assistance. That has been the trend.

The first time I went to Gyaman after I returned from the United Kingdom, I found out that Uncle Obrehun's last born, Kobena Dadzie was attending Secondary School at Potsin. From that period, I took over his schooling. He would often wait till a few days to school reopening before he would show up in Accra. Sometimes he didn't even bother to come down himself. He would send his senior bother Kwesi Egyir. For all the years he was in Senior Secondary School, I never saw Kobena's school report.

About a year after I took over the sponsorship of his education, my brother-in-law's then-girlfriend, Lydia was posted to Potsin Secondary School as a teacher under the National Service Scheme. When I enquired about my cousin, Lydia told me that the school's standard was so low that if I wanted anything out of him, I should send him somewhere else. Two of my nephews from Uncle Obrehun's side (his daughter Yaa Donkor's sons), Robert and Edward Cudjoe, attended Swedru School of Business. Edward went on to study in Russia soon after I arrived. (He was so appreciative of the pocket money I gave him before he left). Due to some illness, he contracted in Russia, he ended up in America and eventually obtained a PhD in Pharmacy from the University of Georgia in Atlanta. Robert was in

Sixth Form somewhere at the time. So, the school had to be quite good.

About the same time as Lydia told me about Potsin, Robert came to inform me that he did not like the school that Kobena attended and that he could get him a place at his Alma mater. He got him the admission and Kobena transferred to Form Two at Swedru School of Business. I still did not see his school reports. His 'O' Level results were not very good. I wanted him to retake some of the subjects. But anytime I went to Gyaman, I was told he had travelled. Eventually, I found out that he was too ashamed to face me because just around the time, he had impregnated a girl and was about to marry and abandon his education altogether.

The week before Robert reported at Legon for his degree programme in Social Sciences, he came to see us and Sabina gave him bedding, some cooking utensils, cutlery and food – rice, *garri*, cooking oil and "provisions", and I gave him some money to get him going before he received his student loan. Each time he stopped by, he was sure to leave with cooked and raw food. And Robert was ever so grateful.

### Where did I get it so badly wrong?

I have heard accusations of selfishness and ingratitude levelled against me. Selfishness? I have heard reports that I am so selfish that when I travelled outside Ghana, I did not sponsor any member of the family to join me. I went to America on a Ghana Government Scholarship that was administered by the University of Science and Technology, Kumasi, on a student visa that did not permit me to work. So, for two years in America, I depended solely on my student allowance. With that visa, there was no way I could sponsor anyone.

It was the same in England; I came on a student visa and the only form of work I could legally take-up was as a Teaching Assistant offering tutorials to my professor's students. I have already described in detail how Phillips Petroleum could only apply for a "training" visa for me and why I had to leave the company and England after just a little over three years working for Phillips Petroleum Company.

In any case, I had seen so many Africans and Ghanaians in particular, who had come to Europe and North America on an unofficial basis (with little or no qualifications) suffer so much indignity it was not something I would wish for my worst enemy, let alone my own flesh and blood! At least some of my accusers might have heard part of Kofi Graham's "Agege" (Nigeria) stories.

The moment I entered my own room at University Hall (Katanga) in October 1970, I knelt down on the bare floor and prayed to the Lord to guard and guide me so the opportunities He had given me, (the first person to receive secondary and, ultimately, higher education in the family), would be available to the ones after me. I am just human and I might have failed badly, but the Lord God knows that I have tried. I leave it to people's consciences. The Lord Almighty knows I have never intentionally done anything with a bad motive, as far as the family is concerned and as Charles Wesley wrote:


Go, labour on; spend, and be spent;
    Thy joy to do the Father's will;
   It is the way the Master went;
    Should not the servant tread it still?

Go, labour on, 'tis not for nought;
    Thy earthly loss is heav'nly gain;
  Men heed thee, love thee, praise thee not;
    **The Master praises, what are men?** (Charles Wesley, MHB 589)

**Charges of ingratitude**

Apparently, I have been ungrateful to my uncles! I first heard it from Auntie Botwe, Uncle Nsedu's last wife. She had heard that I was building a house at Gyaman, but I had not included my uncles. I told her that I had set out to house my mother and siblings because I cared about my mother, brother and sisters if my uncles did not care about theirs.

The first time I went to Koforidua after I returned to Ghana in late 1984, one of the ladies in Papa Koffie's house asked me to follow her and that she wanted to show me something. After walking for about fifteen minutes, we ended up at the State Insurance Corporation offices. At the back of the building, she pointed at a rusted block of metal. As we drew nearer, she held my hand and stared intently into my face. The block of metal was the stripped engine of the corn milling machine that I had bought for my uncles in 1981. Everything else was gone, the wires, plugs and all. Thinking that I might cry or even collapse, she was holding very tightly to my hand by this time. I didn't utter a word. As far as I was concerned, that was it!

Later, my uncles organised a "welcome party" for me. They made me drive all the way to Gyaman on Friday to pick up Mother to Koforidua for the party on Saturday, drive her back on Sunday and then return to Accra on Monday. This was just before I took up my appointment with the Petroleum Department in Accra. At the party, my uncles and Mother sensed that I was not happy.

A few weeks later, I met a family friend from my early days at Koforidua, in Accra. We had a very long chat. She told me Uncle Nsedu was under a lot of pressure. He had become the sole 'warrior'. Timothy Nyarko was in Technical School at Abetifi, Araba Nyarko was doing catering at Kumasi Polytechnic and Joanna Nyarko was in Senior Secondary School. Uncle Nsedu was shouldering much of the burden. Following that meeting, I relented and went back to Koforidua, for a long talk with Uncle Nsedu. In the end, I paid school fees for each of Uncle Nyarko's children, except Ruth, who might have been in primary school at the time. I went on to pay my two uncles' annual rent for several years.

Sometime in 2012, when Ekua Nyarko's son, Hope needed urgent assistance to secure his admission at Legon, I sent money to make sure that he did not lose his place at the university.

When Nana Addow died in 1986, all our six uncles (from Nana Ansaaduba and Nana Addow), Benyi, Nsedu, Nyarko, Kwame Saah, Kojo Ketseaba and Kweku Otobaw, came to the burial. When we met to discuss the final funeral rites, it was decided that there had to be some renovations of the family house before the funeral. My Uncles promised to send money to Mother to carry out the work. One month to the time when I went back to Gyaman, there were no signs of any renovations. Mother was desperate; all our in-laws would be attending from different parts of the country. We needed to do something.

Kow Morgan was working at the Rural Bank at Afransi at the time. He could supervise the renovations. I bought the cement, and cement blocks and paid for the cost of sand and labour, plus paint. A week before the funeral when I went to Gyaman to deposit the confectionary, coffee, sugar and milk that I had bought for the wake-keeping, I discovered that Kow Morgan had extended the work that we had planned to do, borrowed some bags of cement from Sister Efua Buakoma, in my name and used the paint that had been earmarked for painting the family house, to paint his own rented place at Gyaman, and left the painting in the family house half done. I had to rush to Swedru, to buy new paint. My Uncles later came to find a nicely renovated family home. Mother told them what had happened. None of them gave me a penny or even said anything to me.

Earlier, before Nana Addow's burial service, the Chief, Nana Kweku Donkor imposed heavy fines on my three Uncles Benyi, Nsedu and Nyarko. They had not been to Gyaman for years. Until the fines were paid, the chief was not going to permit the burial. We were in trouble. I stepped in, paid half of the fines and stood surety for them. None of them paid a pesewa afterwards. I had to plead with Nana Kweku Donkor, who assured me that for all the charity work I was doing at Gyaman and for my sake, he would not prevent any of my uncles from settling back at Gyaman in their old age. That was one of the reasons Uncle Nsedu and Uncle Nyarko were reluctant to leave Koforidua for so many years!

Sometime in 1987, Uncle Nsedu came to inform me that Uncle Nyarko had been detained at Koforidua Police Station over some kind of debt, the details of which I was never told. I did not have the money immediately, but I still maintained my account in Bartlesville, USA, from my Phillip Petroleum Company days. I went to speak to a friend who ran a Forex Bureau in Accra. He agreed to take a cheque for $1700. I still have the counterfoil for the cheque drawn on my account at the First National Bank in Bartlesville in my briefcase at Gyaman. When I saw Uncle that weekend, I knew he would die if he spent one more day at the police station. I got him off.

About late 1989 or early 1990, I was returning from taking the early morning service at Calvary Methodist Church one morning when I met Uncle Nyarko at the junction to our house. He had bad news. Uncle Benyi had suffered a stroke and they wanted me to convey him to Gyaman. Essentially, they were afraid that he might die at Koforidua and become a burden for them. When we arrived at Koforidua, I asked if any of my two other uncles would accompany me to Gyaman, and they said no. Poor Mother was to carry that burden. Fortunately for me, Grace who was then working at the Akropong Blind School had come to visit. I asked her to sit at the back of the car with Uncle while I drove. She was reluctant because she had left her two young children all by themselves, hoping to do a quick round trip before nightfall. My plea was that as a nurse she would know what to do if anything happened on the way.

To get to Gyaman, I assumed that it would be quicker to go through Suhum and Bawjiase. It was a big mistake. It took much longer and by the time we went to Gyaman and got back to Accra, it was too late. There was no lorry at the Akropong station. I had driven all day and I could not go to Akropong and come back to Accra, and go to work the following day. Grace spent the night and went back the following morning. Fortunately, her children were alright. In England, a neighbour would have called the police and social services about "abandonment and cruelty to children."

Eventually, Mother and Sister Aba nursed Uncle Benyi back to good health and he was able to go about his normal life until he died in 1992 aged 77. Sister Aba bore the brunt of Uncle's illness and recovery and still carries a back problem from her ordeals in connection with it. None of my two uncles set foot at Gyaman for the whole time that Uncle Benyi was there. I bore the cost of his stay at Gyaman. They didn't even attend their own brother's funeral. Only Timothy and Araba Nyarko turned up for the funeral. I bore the cost of the funeral all alone.

During our visit to Ghana in 2007, I visited my uncles at Koforidua where one of Uncle Nsedu's neighbours at Jackson Park whispered to me that I should try and get him to go and settle at Gyaman. Uncle had the beginnings of Dementia. I broached the subject with him and he was not too keen. Later, Timothy brought him to live in his house in Accra. After a while, uncle's situation deteriorated and he often "vanished" for hours. Eventually, Timothy took him to Gyaman and I had to increase my remittances to Mother, so they could take care of Uncle Nsedu. In late 2008 when he finally went to stay at Gyaman, Mother was 88 with failing eyesight and needed someone to take care of her. Sister Aba again bore the brunt of the care of the two of them.

When Uncle Nsedu died a year later, I bore the cost of his funeral, to which his only son, Kwame Ampiah, did not even attend. Sister Aba again as his carer, suffered further damage to her back. That was why she was adamant about Uncle Nyarko coming to live in the house if he was not accompanied by his wife. Uncle Benyi and Uncle Nsedu had no wives at the time they each went to live at Gyaman. If Uncle Nyarko was coming to Gyaman, he should come along with his wife. I made that clear to him and his wife when I went to discuss the move with them at Koforidua in 2010.

Uncle Nyarko agreed to move to Gyaman. He had always eyed my part of the house, but that was something I had no intention whatsoever of giving up because everything we owned in Ghana was stored there. Besides, after what Sister Aba had gone through with our two older uncles, it would have been most cruel to inflict a third one on the poor woman.

The extension to the house where Uncle Nyarko now lives with his wife was originally meant to be a sheep pen before Grace acquired the adjacent plot. It was going to be difficult to live next door to a sheep pen. The money for the construction came from excess from the earlier repairs on the house. I wanted to use it for something beneficial. I thought about a shop. I had planned for Uncle and his wife to move into the rooms in the back that were originally meant for kitchens but were later turned into bedrooms. During a long discussion on what to do with Uncle Nyarko in 2011, Oforiwaa, Sister Aba's second daughter suggested that I should turn what I was building as a store into a two-bedroom self-contained extension for my uncle. It was a brilliant idea.

Kwame Ampiah had put his own money into the project and had an interest in it. I promised to refund it to him. Sabina eventually paid that refund. When the building got to the roofing stage, I decided that Uncle Nyarko's children should finish it to their taste so that part of the house would revert to them when their parents were no more. They are all patrilineal; Ekua and Timothy, the two older ones, were always the younger brother and sister I never had growing up. Their father had not built anything for them anywhere. They have nowhere else to go except Gyaman, and so are all of Uncle Nyarko's other children. As far as I can remember, the arrangement, facilities and environment of that extension at Gyaman are better than nearly every place that Uncle Nyarko had ever lived, especially at Koforidua.

**So where is the ingratitude?**

I have not written these detailed accounts to win "brownie points" or denigrate anybody. And I am glad that many of the people I have mentioned are still alive. This forms the middle part of my memoirs. I passed it around and asked my nephews, nieces and cousins to fill me in on exact dates and if anybody felt that any section was inaccurate, I would be all too glad to discuss it. Nobody responded.

The Lord knows I am not perfect, but by His grace, I have done my bit. As I was growing up, the whole sub-section of our Twidan clan from Nana Esi Ansaaduba's lineage had one tiny room at the family house. Today, we have twelve. It has been the grace of God. While agreeing with St Paul, I maintain that "I do not consider that I have made it my own. But one thing I do: forgetting what lies behind, I strain forward toward the goal that is set before me." (Philippians 3:13)

There are some brilliant young ones coming up in the family. My goal for the rest of my life is to ensure that as many of those ones as possible get the solid foundation they need for the future, and in that quest, I do not apologise to anyone, even if I should be ungrateful or selfish!

# CHAPTER 11
# SIXTEEN YEARS ON A WOBBLY TRUCK......

As I mentioned in the previous chapter when I joined the then Petroleum Department in Ghana, I was initially assigned to assist the Secretary for Fuel and Power, Mr Emmanuel Appiah-Korang, on Petroleum Exploration and Production matters. Consequently, I spent some time at the ministry, often travelling with the minister around Accra and Tema. Mr Appiah-Korang was a very diligent minister who insisted on understanding every detail of any external communication before he signed or committed to anything.

There were two major live projects going at the Petroleum Department at the time – the Petro-Canada International Assistance Corporation (PCIAC) exploration review programme and the review of a 3,000 kilometre 2-D speculative seismic survey off the coast of the Winneba-Accra-Keta Basin that had been acquired and processed by Geophysical Services Incorporated (GSI).

GSI which had its offices in Bedford, England, at the time, had apparently approached the Government of Ghana, offering to acquire and process 3,000 kilometres of offshore 2D seismic data. The agreement was that GSI would market the data, offering the Government of Ghana 15% of the proceeds of the sales, escalating to 80% with increased sale volumes, until the company had recovered its investment at which time ownership of the data would revert to the government of Ghana.

In the meantime, any company that approached the government about data/block acquisition would sign a confidentiality/sales agreement to review the data and any offer to purchase data would be communicated to GSI. There was a similar arrangement for data review or purchase on the other side.

My first technical task at the then Petroleum Department was to review the report of the data processing and interpretation. GSI had done a reasonably good job processing the data set, but the interpretation left much to be desired. There was no attempt at the depth conversion of the time structure maps. The two-way time maps which had been machine-contoured had lots of "bull's eyes" because there was very little fault mapping.

I reviewed the project report together with the maps and wrote a report on my findings. The company had already presented its report and left and there was not much that could be done about those problems. Some of the local Geoscientists who had been attached to the GSI project were not too pleased with what I had to say about the final seismic maps. The scene had been set for several such run-ins.

## The first Board Meeting

I remember it like yesterday; the composition of the very first GNPC Board was announced in early April 1985 with Alhaji Mahama Idrissu, a member of the Provisional National Defence Council (PNDC), as Chairman and Professor A K Addae, a nuclear engineer attached to the Ministry of Fuel and Power from the Ghana Atomic Energy Commission, as its first Acting Managing Director.

The Board was to meet in a week. Ben Dagadu, a Reservoir Engineer of the Department and I had earlier been tasked with finding an office for the new corporation. We went to inspect a number of places, and in particular, a house at the Airport Residential Area that belonged to one Dr Wadwa, which had been seized and occupied by the area People's Defence Committee (PDC), one of those idealistic groups that had sprung up at the beginning of the 31st December Revolution. Eventually, we settled on three extra floors of Republic House where the Petroleum Department which metamorphosed into GNPC, was based.

We were given one week to get a Board table that would seat twenty people, for the first Board Meeting of the new corporation. We shared the tasks between us. The weekend before this meeting, I commissioned two junior staff members to clean the large room on the sixth floor that was to serve as the boardroom. The following Monday morning, when they showed me how they had perched perilously on the ledge, to clean the windows, I had immediate diarrhoea. If any of them had slipped, it would have meant certain death and it would have been my responsibility!

Through the week and over the weekend, Ben Dagadu trekked between the office and the carpenters' workshop at Farrisco, down the road from Republic House, to ensure that they completed the table and twenty chairs, in time for the meeting. We spent the whole morning on Wednesday, the meeting day, at the workshop. Eventually, the table was completed with the fixing of its last leg about thirty minutes before the meeting began. We both breathed a big sigh of relief.

### Relocation

Soon after the inauguration of the board, Primary Fuels Incorporated (PFI) which had been operating the only producing field in Ghana at the time, the Saltpond Field, decided to pull out of the country. Primary Fuels Incorporated (PFI) was a member of the consortium that inherited the Saltpond discoveries of the early 1970s from Amoco. PFI was contracted by the consortium to operate the field on its behalf, for a fee. By January 1985, the production which began at about 5,000 barrels per day was down to between 400 and 450 barrels per day. It was not economical and with calls from various sections of society to review the agreement, the company decided to pull out and hand the field back to the state.

In the handover arrangement, Primary Fuels Incorporated handed all the equipment and supply vessel, Co-operator II, to GNPC, plus physical cash of $2m to be used to tow the rig to deep sea to be blown up. (That was an acceptable practice in 1985!)

The new duties that came with the take-over of the field, meant that more staff were needed in the office and on the rig, to maintain the facilities, while attempts were made to continue the production or else find a new operator to produce the field. This would not happen for many years.

With the increased numbers, a new home had to be found for the corporation. The Black Star Line building at Osu Kuku Hill fitted the bill. The Exploration and Production Department and a few of the support services moved to share the accommodation with the national shipping line, which by this time, was struggling to stay afloat.

# CHAPTER 12
# PETRO-CANADA IN GHANA

P etro-Canada occupied two impressive towers, one with thirty-three floors and the other thirty floors in the centre of Calgary, Alberta. The mining section alone occupied about a quarter of one of the towers. There was Research and Development that was spread between the University of Calgary, just outside the city and one of the Petro-Canada Towers. There was a huge downstream department and a separate International Exploration and Production Department, which also did projects for Petro-Canada International Assistance Corporation (PCIAC).

PCIAC had apparently been to a number of Commonwealth countries, notably Pakistan and Malaysia, seeking to assist with their petroleum exploration programmes. In the process, it had expended huge resources with little to show for its efforts. As a result, some sections of Canadian society had become frustrated not only with PCIAC but the mother company itself, leading to a groundswell of opposition to further dissipation of taxpayers' money on these forays into "exotic" foreign lands. Various groups, with the support of the small 'independents' and the multinational oil companies in Canada, had begun to advocate for the disbandment of not only the aid wing but the mother company itself. In Alberta and particularly Calgary, there were numerous stickers like, "Fill up at Petro-Canada, I will push my car another three miles."

PCIAC and Petro-Canada needed a success story. One of the international managers of PCIAC, Mr William Soukeroff, who was leading the Ghana project, believed passionately that there was oil to be found in the basins of Ghana. Their very first project in Ghana was to drill two appraisal wells, ST-5 and ST-6 in the South Tano field, a side-step just 500 metres from Phillips Petroleum Company's South Tano discovery wells. And presto, PCIAC had made a discovery in Ghana, giving it a major lifeline.

## The shallow well drilling project

The first real exploration project that GNPC undertook was the shallow oil well drilling programme that was done in conjunction with Petro-Canada International Assistance Corporation (PCIAC).

## The well locations

It was in its quest for further successes in Ghana that Petro-Canada decided to embark on the shallow well drilling programme in the onshore Tano area, believing that the oil seepages in the area could be tar sands, similar to the Athabasca Oil sands in Alberta. Oil seepages had been known in the Half Assini-Tekinta area of the Western Region since the late 1890s. In fact, there were stories locally that some oil production had taken place in the area during the First World War.

Using topographic maps that had been made available by the Ghana Geological Survey Department, Petro-Canada's Geophysicists and Geologists had marked locations to drill in this shallow drilling programme; twenty-two locations in total. These locations had been chosen on the basis of their proximity to known seepages. Unfortunately, without an actual onsite inspection, some of those wells had been located away from the intended seepage sites. The locations needed to be verified.

I embarked on a ten-day field trip with Ben Dagadu, my old school senior, William Agbesinyale, a Senior Geologist of the Ghana Geological Survey Department, who by this time had been seconded to GNPC and a technician of the Geological Survey Department Mr Asiedu, whose wife hailed from the area, and therefore knew the area quite well and also spoke the local Nzema dialect. Giant Agbesinyale, a very experienced field geologist, had participated in the Geophysical Services Incorporated (GSI) speculative 2D seismic processing project in Bedford in the United Kingdom, in the early 1980s.

On this field survey of potential drilling locations, we went from village to village to announce our presence in the area and to inform the people about the impending project. At each village, we called on the chief and his elders, explained our mission and asked for local assistance in tracing the proposed sites. We also enquired about any seepages that were known to them. In the course of the trip, we went through the marshes, forests and farmlands of Half Assini, Tekinta, Edu, Kobenlazuaso, Tikobo No.1 and Egbwazu, among other places, battling the elements. In some areas, we had to crawl in the undergrowth for several tens of metres at a time because there were no footpaths. In other areas, we used small dug-out canoes whose owners had to be coaxed for hours before they would accept the "allowances" that they considered as "peanuts", so they could take us across swollen rivers and streams.

There was a thriving night smuggling business across the Jeunne Lagoon and through forest footpaths across the border to the Ivory Coast. Most of the young men of the villages slept during the day and went to "work" at night. Therefore, getting them to accompany us on our day treks for what they considered to be paltry fees, was a nuisance at best.

Usually, our bait was that when the project took off, it would bring employment for the people of the area and also boost the local economy. To this, the counter argument was that if and when it took off, we would probably bring people from Accra to do the work, which proved prophetic, for political and technical reasons.

We succeeded in verifying all the twenty-two locations, several of which were either bang in the centre of a town or village or else right on the banks of a river. One particular site had been located in the middle of a major stream that flowed through a deep gorge to which access for the rig and other heavy equipment would have been nigh impossible, while another was located in a residential compound in the centre of a village. At this location, the nearest possible alternative was a sacred grove that the people would not even allow us to enter because it was out of bounds to "strangers."

In the end, we managed to replace all the difficult or inaccessible sites with new locations near live oil seepages or close to seepages that had not been part of the original twenty-two sites that had been delineated by PCIAC.

As part of the survey, we took samples from the seepages as well as samples of oil-soaked sands that had been so dried up that they had to be hacked from hillsides and mounds with machetes.

The underlying principle of the project was that the seepages in the area came from tar sand deposits in the mould of the Athabasca oil sands of Alberta and could be extracted in the same way as was done in Alberta. Therefore, the shallow drilling programme was meant to determine the extent of these "oil sands" for commercial exploitation. Laboratory analyses and 'typing' of the field samples, however, showed that apart from the biodegradation as a result of exposure to the atmosphere, the oil that constituted the seepages came from the same source as the oil that had been encountered in the North and South Tano discoveries back in the mid-1970s. Therefore, as a "tar sands mining scheme," the shallow well drilling project was doomed from the start.

## The GNPC Organisation

By the beginning of the Petro-Canada-GNPC/Ghana Government shallow well drilling project in late 1986, the first GNPC board was well-established, with Professor AK Addae, a brilliant but rather tentative Nuclear Engineer and an Old Boy of GSTS, as Acting Managing Director and BK Smith, the Director of Finance and Administration. Mr Cato Browne, a Chemical Engineer who had worked at the Tema Oil Refinery (GHAIP), as the Director of Marketing, making the trio of internal directors of the corporation. The eleven-member Board of Directors had a key member of the Provisional National Defence Council, Alhaji Mahama Idrissu as chairman.

Dr Abbloderpey, a private Mining Geophysicist, served on the Board as one of two "technical persons" (the other was Mr J K A Banson of the Geological Survey Department), with special oversight for Exploration and Production. Dr Abbloderpey was pencilled in as Director of Exploration and Production, but for a 'miscalculation' which forced him to resign from the Board and the corporation.

According to the report which filtered through the grapevine later, the Board began discussions about the acquisition of field vehicles for the Corporation. At its next meeting, Dr Abblodepey presented an invoice from a company that was offering to supply Nissan Patrols from Togo. The prices from this company were slightly higher than those offered by Japan Motors in Accra. While Japan Motors could not supply the vehicles immediately, this company was apparently ready to bring the vehicles to Ghana as soon as the Corporation confirmed its acceptance of the offer, and Dr Abblodepey pushed hard for it, as Director of Exploration and Production.

Unfortunately for Dr Abblodepey, he had brought along to the meeting the company's notepad on which his name appeared as director, which meant a potential conflict of interest situation. Apparently, at some point during the meeting, a member of the Board glanced at the notepad and read the footnote on it. Later, when Dr Abblodepey excused himself to go to the bathroom, the member in question took a sheet from the pad and later confronted Dr Abblodepey about the fact that he was pushing hard for a company in which he had a personal interest. He had no option but to resign from the Board and Corporation, which was a real shame because as a practising Mining Geophysicist, he had a clear understanding of geophysical exploration and what was required and the enthusiasm for the Corporation's exploration programmes.

## Start of the project

I was appointed local Co-ordinator of the drilling project, which meant a lot of running around, applying for permission for the radio transmission and reception equipment from the National Communications Authority, which at that time had another GSTS Old Boy, Giant Kofi Asafua Jackson, as Executive Secretary. I secured the necessary permits for the equipment that was shipped through the Takoradi Harbour and those that had to be flown in by air through Kotoka International Airport. I even made a special trip with engineers from Petro-Canada, to inspect the bridges and culverts between Takoradi and Half Assini, to determine if they could safely carry the weights of the heavy trucks and their loads, especially the land drilling rig and its accessories. In the end, we recommended that special steel plates be placed on some of the bridges and culverts as the trucks crossed them, for the safety of the equipment and the bridges and culverts.

Before the main contingent of the Canadian technical staff arrived in Ghana, PCIAC sent a Geologist, Dr Pepe Pereira, to assist with the geological preparations for the drilling project. Dr Pereira was an excellent geologist and a prolific writer. He and I got along very well. Unfortunately, he arrived in Ghana at a time when the country was still experiencing the economic problems that had bedevilled the country since the early days of the Provisional National Defence Council (PNDC) and the new corporation had very little money. In the process of finding him adequate accommodation, the poor man was holed in a small hotel room for months, which nearly led to extreme depression and had to be sent back to Canada just as the project took off.

Earlier on, Dr Pereira and I held a marathon interview session that began early in the morning till 11 at night, selecting about one hundred technicians, chefs, carpenters, roustabouts, galley boys and other supporting staff that were needed for the project. We later picked security personnel, cooks and labourers from Half Assini and the surrounding villages. The shallow well drilling project eventually began in August 1986.

## A strike on our hands – dousing the fires

The agreement for the Petro-Canada-GNPC/Ghana Government shallow well drilling project stipulated that Petro-Canada would fund the foreign component of the project, including all associated travels to and from Canada, whilst the Government of Ghana, through GNPC, funded the local (cedi) component, including the feeding, insurance, health needs and remuneration of the local staff.

Most of the rig hands we employed for the project were members of a group of Ghanaians, mostly from the Accra-Tema Metropolis who had worked on rigs in Côte d'Ivoire, Gabon and other places in the sub-region at various times and had returned to Ghana, many with no jobs to go to. As soon as the announcement was made for the recruitment of local hands for the project, a few of these "been-tos" quickly gathered themselves together into the "Association of Ghanaian Rig Workers," to lead a crusade for "local skilled labour." A date was scheduled for interested people to present themselves at the new GNPC offices (PFI) at Dzorwulu, near the Motorway.

At the interview, it became apparent that some of those people could be troublemakers. However, our hands were tied. We needed people with some experience for safety and other operational reasons. There was only little time and just enough resources for the most rudimentary training. We had to hire people who had some basic knowledge of rig operations. In the end, we picked all but one or two of the members of the association who had very extreme views about the work at hand and who was best qualified to do it.

Just two months into the project, problems began to surface, beginning with the delayed payment of the wages of the local staff as a pretext. As we had suspected at the recruitment interviews, the leaders of the roustabouts organised a strike action and persuaded the rest of the local staff to join in. Petro-Canada had leased the rig from a private drilling company and every hour during which it stood idle meant incurring standby charges, which in turn meant reduced funds for drilling wells and a shortfall in the project target.

Instead of one of the directors of the Corporation going to Half Assini to speak to the striking workers, management decided I should go and "assess the situation", come back and report. Apparently, there had been a tip-off that any GNPC official who showed up at the camp would be manhandled by the striking workers or at worst held hostage till the wages were paid.

The security for the campsite and the drilling rig had been entrusted to a number of ex-servicemen of the Ghana Army who had been employed from the local area at the beginning of the project. As I would find out later, one of these security men was the landlord of one of my nieces who lived in the Half Assini township. I had not seen this niece for about twenty years, but somehow her landlord mentioned my name in a conversation and she said, "Oh that is my uncle, my mother's cousin."

I left Accra at dawn on Friday with my duty driver, Kabutey. When we arrived in Takoradi, we learnt that word had already got to the project site that we were on our way. A few kilometres before we got to the campsite, we met two of the security men who had apparently been detailed to look out for our vehicle. They assured me that my niece's landlord who was also the head of the security group had made special arrangements for my safety and there was, therefore, no cause for concern.

At the campsite, I arranged for the driver to be fed so he could go and park the vehicle at Half Assini Police Station, just in case there was any kind of trouble. I held a long and testy durbar with the striking workers, with numerous questions about the Corporation's intentions and commitment to the project. I answered the questions as truthfully as I could and made an undertaking not only to see that they were paid as soon as I got back to Accra but to return to meet them again the following week, with answers to the more complex questions and suggestions for the good of the project.

Fortunately, having relayed the seriousness of the situation both for the security of the Canadian personnel and their equipment, the Ministry was able to raise the money to pay the workers within the week. I also returned to the campsite as I had promised. It was a dicey situation and a close call, but it ended peacefully.

### Results of the shallow well drilling project

A total of twelve shallow wells out of the original twenty-two were drilled, with the deepest reaching 700 metres. Two of the wells encountered small amounts of oil. The rest were either dry or else water-wet.

Unfortunately, the results of the analyses of the samples of the seepages that were sent to Canada would not be ready till towards the end of the project. However, major lessons were learnt from the programme:

1. The sample analyses and "typing" of the seepages showed that the oil from the seepages had the same source as oil samples that had been taken from the offshore North and South Tano wells.
2. The oil samples that were taken from the two "successful" shallow wells were similar to the seepage samples.
3. All the oil that had been found in the area up to that point was generated elsewhere and migrated to the basin area.

Later interpretation of a limited 2D seismic dataset that was acquired about the same time as the drilling project showed that:

1. Either the geological structures identified from the seismic data were not in place when the oil migrated through the area; or

2. The oil migrated into reservoirs which were later breached by faulting.

In other words, the various regimes of faulting had caused the oil to escape along the faults, resulting in the seepages that are dotted throughout the Half Assini, Egbwazo, and Tekinta areas.

The second theory seemed more plausible judging from the extent of faulting and the fact that the still active Coastal Boundary Fault that had been partly responsible for the historical earthquakes of southern Ghana, had its origins in the Tano Basin. In that case, as Shell Geologists would remark later, commercial oil accumulation was still somewhere in the area and had to be found.

In early February 1987, with the interest of further exploration in Ghana's basins and the legacy of Petro-Canada's work in Ghana in mind, Petro-Canada transferred all the vehicles and cars that were brought to Ghana to GNPC, together with 15,000 bags of cement and 4,500 bags of drilling mud, for use in later drilling programmes.

Local staff from the district got wind of the donation of cement and spread the news in the area. Some of the chiefs appealed to the Corporation to give their towns some bags of cement for various repair works, especially of school and palace buildings, and standpipes. The corporation did not consent to any of those requests. We had the opportunity to sell the drilling mud to operators who drilled in Ghana after the Petro-Canada project. Again, that was never done. Instead, the cement and drilling mud were moved into storage at Anyako in the Volta Region until they absorbed moisture from the sea and became hydrated. Eventually, senior staff of the Engineering Department of the Corporation were paid to throw away the hardened cement and drilling mud.

Unfortunately for me, I still had to return to the Half Assini area for fieldwork, during which I faced the wrath of the local people as being insensitive to their needs.

•   •   •

## Onshore Tano 2-D seismic surveys

About halfway through the shallow well drilling programme, a 110-kilometre reconnaissance 2-D seismic survey that had been commissioned for the onshore Tano basin began in earnest. The survey was shot by Airborne Geophysical Surveys, out of Calgary and owned by one Fred Foo, an affable Canadian of Chinese extraction. Because of the limestone ridge that is seen in outcrop through most of the onshore Tano area, the energy source of the survey had to be dynamite, to ensure adequate depth penetration.

The acquisition, transportation and storage of the dynamite under the security-conscious Provisional National Defence Council (PNDC) presented a major headache. In the end, we found a house at Half Assini that belonged to one Colonel Hassan of the Ghana Army, for the storage of the dynamite, which also became the operating base of the acquisition contractor, Airborne Geophysical Surveys. The dynamite was transported from Tema Harbour under an armed police guard, and stored in a secured part of the house with a twenty-four-hour armed police guard.

In general, the quality of the data was reasonably good, although deeper reflectors were quite difficult to map, especially in the eastern part of the survey area. As would be a later routine, I did the quality control supervision of the data processing from the office in Tema - from filtering through deconvolution and velocity analyses to final migration. Later, I also did the interpretation of the final seismic data.

Coarse as the grid of the survey was, the results of the mapping pointed to the fact that most of the significant shallow geological structures in the onshore Tano basin had been tested by previous drilling campaigns as well as the Petro-Canada shallow well drilling programme.

Because of the inadequate data penetration in parts of the survey area, it became obvious that the data needed either reprocessing or a completely new acquisition programme was necessary for a better evaluation of the perspectivity of the area. This could be done with the lessons of the reconnaissance survey in mind, by modelling the source and recording parameters.

## The Integrated Data Services survey

The new onshore Tano seismic survey was awarded to Integrated Data Services Limited, the seismic acquisition and processing wing of the Nigerian National Petroleum Corporation (NNPC) in 1988, to shoot a 180-kilometre infill 2-D seismic survey in the area.

With the poor data penetration of the first seismic survey in the Tano Basin and the results rather inconclusive in mind, it was felt that any future such survey ought to be done properly using a top-notch acquisition company.

In preparation for the selection of the best contractor for the job, we wrote to several seismic acquisition companies in Europe and North America and received a number of bids. The results of the analysis of the bids showed that Prakla-Seismos of Germany, possibly the top land acquisition company of the day, was the best in terms of value for money, African experience and technology transfer.

We made the appropriate recommendations, with tables and figures for our ranking and presented them to management. Several weeks after the presentation of the results of the bid analysis, we were informed that in line with a new south-south co-operation policy, the acquisition contract was to be awarded to the seismic acquisition wing of the Nigerian National Petroleum Corporation, Integrated Data Services Limited (IDSL), as mentioned earlier. That was the company's first international acquisition project and it would also process the data, also its first ever international processing project.

I was sent to Nigeria to observe IDSL in the field, spending some time at their seismic processing centre in Benin City in the process. On paper at least, IDSL seemed like any seismic acquisition and processing company that I had come across anywhere in Europe or North America. The problems emerged in the field after the data acquisition began.

IDSL mobilised from Benin City in Nigeria, transporting by road, large volumes of equipment, consumables and people through the Republic of Benin and Togo, then into Ghana, all the way to Half Assini. Getting the necessary permits for the energy source, the dynamite, and communications equipment, was a major project in itself.

As the acquisition got underway, we realised that IDSL operated a kind of quota system whereby the hierarchy of the company, including technical areas where experience should have been paramount, was shared among the major ethnic groups of the country, particularly, the Yorubas and Igbos from the south and the northerners, from the middle belt all the way to the northernmost parts of Nigeria.

As a result, there was intense rivalry among the leaders in the field, which spilt over to the junior staff. Depending on which leaders were on duty at any particular time, recording progress was anywhere between 0.5 to 3 kilometres per day.

For this project, two Quality Control contractors were appointed from Europe on a three-month rotatory basis, to oversee the project. Each time one of them came through the office on his way back to Europe for his home leave, it was a litany of woes. The acquisition project took about one year to complete, but the worst was yet to come at the data processing phase.

### The Ghana geological/geophysical data review project

By the time I joined the Petroleum Department, PCIAC had already commissioned two geophysical/geological consulting companies Teknica and Baxendale and Associates in Calgary and a Petrophysical Company (Van Meurs Economics) in Ottawa, to review all the available geological and geophysical data of Ghana's basins, with a view to delineating prospects and leads for drilling. Baxendale and Associates had, in turn, contracted a Geological Consulting Company, Woods Geological, to review the geological aspect of their work. Van Meurs Economics, the petrophysical company, was charged with providing reserve estimates of all the basins of Ghana, to collate the relevant information for the promotion of further exploration in Ghana to the international petroleum community.

I had the opportunity to work with John Baxendale, a very pleasant and experienced international Geophysicist and former President of the Canadian Society of Exploration Geophysicists (CSEG).

Teknica was owned by Dr Roy Lindseth, another renowned international Geophysicist and teacher whose book, Introduction to Exploration Geophysics, was one of the recommended textbooks for nearly all the geophysics courses I took as a graduate student at Penn State. He was also a prolific publisher and had a string of publications on various aspects of seismic data processing and data analysis. As a student member of the Society of Exploration Geophysicists (SEG), I received monthly copies of the society's journal (Geophysics) and read every article that Dr Roy Lindseth wrote. He was one of my idols in the industry. Then I had to review the work his company had done for Ghana.

In mid-1985, I had the opportunity to go to Calgary to work with John Baxendale and Associates two months after our son Paa Kwesi, was born. I was meant to stay for one month, to bring my experience of the geology of Ghana and knowledge of the geophysical data to bear on the Ghana project. I ended up spending three months, as I mentioned earlier. I returned to Ghana in early July because "Calgary Stampede" (a one-week Summer Festival) time when everything shut down in the city, was approaching and I was not going to be very productive hanging around.

It was towards the end of my three-month stay that I started mapping a huge deep structure in the central part of the Tano Basin. When Mr Baxendale first saw the outline of the structure, he thought it was too deep and would probably be a gas prospect if it came in as a discovery. The Arco consortium eventually drilled the structure as CTS-1 (Central Tano Structure-1) well. It came in with some gas shows, but no further work was ever done on it.

Having worked on various aspects of the review projects, it became my task once again, to write a report on the work of the PCIAC consultants, and again, it was not a very pleasant experience. This was an experience I would later meet over and over again in various parts of the world. Anytime consultants believe that countries especially in the developing world, lack the expertise to scrutinise their work, they tend not to put in their best effort for the heavy expenditures that countries incur to get work done on their behalf.

Baxendale's group worked on the Tano-Cape Three Points area, while Teknica concentrated on the Accra-Keta Basin. Teknica's geologists came to the general conclusion that every fault in the area leaked oil and or gas. They hurriedly assembled a report that was as varied as the number of people that worked on the area, with no common thread whatsoever. Their manager carried the first draft report to Accra with all the typographical and syntax errors.

When I read through it, my first reaction was, "this is not a project report, it is a number of reports that have been hurriedly put together for presentation." Later, the Geology Manager who presented the report admitted that he had, in fact, only read a portion of it on the flight from Calgary to Accra and had not actually read through the whole volume.

My observation was echoed by a United Nations Development Programme (UNDP) Geophysicist who reviewed it on behalf of his organisation. At a presentation in Calgary, I sat next to the Secretary Mr Appiah-Korang. When the gentleman made the remark Mr Appiah-Korang touched the heel of my shoe with his under the table and we smiled at each other. He was at the review meeting in Accra when I first made that comment and there were quite a few unfriendly retorts.

A large contingent, including the then Chief Executive Officer of the Volta River Authority (VRA), Mr Casely-Hayford, had travelled from Ghana to review the results of the studies. At that time, the Ministry and GNPC were trying to interest the Volta River Authority in a gas power plant project that would utilise the gas from the Tano fields, for power generation. The Volta River Authority wanted independent confirmation of the availability of gas supplies to make the project viable over a period of at least twenty-five years, the approximate life span of the proposed gas turbines. The UNDP had an interest because it had financed the review project and were looking forward to the follow-up that was meant to help the government and people of Ghana in the development of the country's energy sector.

At the end of the review, Mr Casely-Hayford was not convinced that there was enough gas available at a reasonable cost to make a gas plant project viable. Following the dissatisfaction with the Ghana review project, Teknica lost a similar project the UNDP was financing in Algeria.

At the cocktail of the final report presentation dinner in Calgary later that year, Dr Roy Lindseth drew me to the side and in a conversation, remarked that he should have taken note of the concerns that I had raised earlier about the work his company did for Ghana. He admitted that he had been very busy travelling around the world trying to secure business for his workforce and had not paid as much attention to the everyday running of his company as he should have done. That was when I told him that he had been my idol for a very long time and I wished the project had not turned out the way it did.

Yes, I worked with John Baxendale's group, but my association with the group apart, they did a much better job than everybody else in the whole review exercise. For instance, the statistics that went into the petrophysics were so poor, that it was difficult to imagine any entry-level petrophysicist accepting the parameters as input for even basic reserve estimates.

## The Petrobras Angle

Certain leads and prospects that had been identified in the Baxendale and Associates structural mapping seemed to be very similar to corresponding structures in the Piaui-Camoccim Basin of north-eastern Brazil about which various technical papers had been published in the international literature. The Piaui-Camoccim Basin is the direct equivalent of the Tano-Cape Three Points sub-basin of the supercontinent Pangea.

It was decided that we got together with Braspetro geologists and geophysicists to compare notes and see what we could learn from each other. There was even a protocol agreement to work with Braspetro officials under a south-south co-operation policy.

Mr Baxendale travelled from Calgary and I travelled from Accra to meet him in Rio de Janeiro. It was February 1987, Rio Carnival time. All hotels in the city had been fully booked for weeks, by the hundreds of thousands that flocked to the city for the annual event. Consequently, our meetings were scheduled for the hills in Friburgo, 100 kilometres away from Rio de Janeiro, and what scenery!

The trip to and from Friburgo was like travelling between Accra and Aburi, except that the mountains are higher. In 1987, about 85% of all vehicles in Brazil ran on alcohol that was produced from cassava and sugarcane. Along the road were cassava, banana, plantain and sugarcane plantations with pawpaw, avocado and citrus trees, just as can be found in a typical farming area in Ghana and Côte d'Ivoire. At a non-technical level, one could conclude that West Africa, indeed, was once attached to Brazil.

**Institutional Structures**

Part of Braspetro's remit in the agreement with GNPC was to develop a detailed organisational structure for the Corporation and the construction or acquisition of an office that would be appropriate for exploration and production, together with adequate storage facilities for the Corporation's gradually increasing geophysical, geological and drilling data that were scattered all over Europe and North America. They were also tasked to review the Tano discoveries, with a view to partnering with the Corporation in the development of the South Tano field in particular.

For the storage facility, I was sent to review similar facilities owned by Petro-Canada in Calgary, Braspetro's in Rio de Janeiro, as well as spending a week at Petroci's (of Côte d'Ivoire) facilities about thirty kilometres outside Abidjan. With seismic data, geological wall cuttings and core sample storage as well as thin section preparation and sample analysis laboratories, Petroci's facilities seemed to be the best option for the Corporation.

Following the presentation of my report from the trip to Côte d'Ivoire, the then Acting Managing Director, Prof Addae, who had also inspected similar facilities in North America, went to Petroci to observe their facility and agreed that their data storage and laboratory systems were the best options for GNPC.

With respect to the Tano fields, Braspetro did their review of all the available data and concluded that development was, in fact, a very viable option but instead of investing in the project as had originally been agreed, they offered to produce the field for GNPC, for a fee, just as Primary Fuels had done for the Saltpond consortium. That also went to confirm my conclusion that the Tano fields were not as good as the Phillips Petroleum Company reports had portrayed them.

**Exploration Manager position**

Sometime in 1988, an advert appeared in the local newspapers and the corporation's notice board, for the position of Exploration Manager. Some of my colleagues encouraged me to apply. At the time, I held the position of Geophysics Coordinator, which with my background and experience, pretty much made me Exploration Manager.

I applied for the position and received a response with an invitation for an interview at a certain date. A few days before the interview, I heard through the grapevine that the position had actually been pencilled in for a former Phillips Petroleum Company colleague, Mr Kwame Apia Kyei, as an inducement to get him to return to Ghana. That was during Phillips Petroleum Company's major restructuring when all the expatriate employees were sent back to Bartlesville in Oklahoma or else let go.

A part of me and also some friends at GNPC urged me to withdraw from the interview, while others suggested that I should go for it, for the experience, if not for anything. Also, some suggested it would give me an idea about how things were done in Ghana. In fact, apart from the Physics Department interview before my admission to university in 1970, I had never attended a proper interview in Ghana. My meeting with Mr Fabyan before I was employed at the Petroleum Department was more or less an induction into the department, I had already been offered the job.

I did not know Mr Apia Kyei before I joined Phillips, but there were very few Africans or in fact, Black people in Phillips in those days. When I started, there were two Nigerians, Dr Imo Izuela, a Geophysicist and Dr Ovuefe Efeotor, a Geologist and Mr Apia Kyei, a Geophysicist.

I had taught Dr Efeotor's wife, Becky as a Teaching Assistant at Royal Holloway (Chelsea) College during my last term as a postgraduate student. Becky was one of several students of Professor Blundell's first-year Physics of the Earth course who struggled with the mathematics of the course. I served as Teaching Assistant and led the four-hour weekly tutorial session. After the second class, Becky asked if I could give her extra lessons, since she was having problems, especially with the mathematics of the course. I told her she was always welcome to see me with any issues that worried her.

Becky's class came to the Geology Department two times a week and would often come to my office after her class. It was during one of the extra sessions that she mentioned that her husband was a Geologist and that he worked for Phillips Petroleum Company. A few days after that conversation, I received an invitation for an interview with Phillips. I mentioned it to Becky the next time we met and she promised to arrange for me to meet her husband before the interview and she did. It was during my meeting with Dr Efeotor that he mentioned that another Ghanaian Geophysicist worked for Phillips Petroleum Company in the London office.

Naturally, Mr Apia Kyei looked me up as a fellow Ghanaian after I had reported for work, took me to lunch and we became friends. I joined Phillips in April 1981 and we were married at the end of August. I invited nearly everybody I had dealt with in Phillips to the wedding, including Dr and Mrs Efeotor and Mr Apia Kyei. My boss at the time Mr Curtis Bratt and his wife really enjoyed themselves as they danced the whole afternoon.

Three of my Ghanaian invitees, Messrs Apia Kyei, Sam Ampadu-Sam and Elliot Asante-Akoi met their future wives at our wedding.

Asante-Akoi and Amapdu-Sam who have both sadly passed away in the past two years were my classmates at GSTS. They had both come to the United Kingdom earlier to study and were working by then. Asante-Akoi and his then-girlfriend Sheila were having problems and had apparently separated for a while, but still spoke to one another once in a while. On that fateful day, 29th August, Elliot called Sheila and told her he was attending a wedding later that day. Sheila told him that she was attending an even better wedding. I had invited Elliot and Sabina had invited Sheila because she is her sister Florence's friend. It was the same wedding and they made up that day.

Sabina invited her friend Paulina Asiedu from her Korle Bu and Bellshill, Scotland, days and she brought her friend, Lydia to join her on Friday night, to help with the cooking and baking. Mr Apia Kyei met Lydia and Ampadu-Sam met Paulina at the wedding. It was all good news that day and has since been a reference point whenever we meet, especially at our children's traditional engagement ceremonies and weddings.

As predicted, Mr Apia Kyei got the Exploration Manager's job and I worked with him like old friends until he left the Corporation after one year, to return to the United Kingdom, to join Arco.

## Another relocation

Petro-Canada's assistance to Ghana and GNPC included the secondment of Petro-Canada-appointed consultants to the Corporation to assist with the consolidation of structures and exploration work. With the shallow well drilling programme over and more serious exploration work to be done, we needed a more functional office than the old Primary Fuels' portacabin offices that housed the exploration and engineering departments. Additionally, all the support services of the corporation were still based at Osu RE in Accra and there were lots of to-and-fro movements between the two sites.

Management had apparently been speaking to the Social Security and National Insurance Trust (SSNIT) about their partly empty district office building near the Tema Fishing Harbour. We joined their staff initially and eventually bought the building which still serves as the Corporation's head office. The building was not totally suitable for exploration purposes, as much of seismic interpretation, well log analyses and geological cross-section construction was still done manually with pencil and paper in those days and needed magnetic walls, which this building did not have. However, it was better than any of the buildings the Corporation had occupied up to this point.

# CHAPTER 13
# IN SEARCH OF GHANA'S OIL

## PROCESSING THE ONSHORE TANO (IDSL) DATA

ollowing the acquisition by IDSL, we pleaded that as a matter of further quality checks, the data processing be awarded to another company. It was common for seismic acquisition companies that processed data they had acquired, to hide misfires and other problems in the field, at the processing centre. If a third party, usually a rival company, did the processing, they almost always brought out the worst in the other through political/commercial point scoring. This was overruled and the processing was awarded to IDSL.

In its bid proposal, IDSL offered to complete the processing in six months. It took five years and that was only after I had provided the processing parameters that a Canadian company had used for the test processing of two lines, one strike and one dip, free of charge. This company had made a bid for the processing at the end of the acquisition. In its proposal, the company offered to process any two lines free of charge and if we liked what they did, we could go into negotiations for the processing of the whole dataset. In the end, we had to pretend that they had not been successful in their bid. Their offer and work saved the day.

During five years of processing this data, I travelled between Accra and Benin City on numerous occasions. On the second occasion, IDSL took me to a hotel on Lagos Island where I spent the night. The next day, I was taken to Benin City in the NNPC Executive Jet, one of the most frightening experiences I have ever had in my life. Thankfully, the aircraft was never available again for any of my later trips to Benin City, but there were other hairy moments!

This was the period when armed robbers (Asika's group and others) were stopping vehicles at gunpoint at fraudulent makeshift police barriers and robbing travellers of money and every piece of jewellery.

My very first trip to Benin City was an eventful one. I travelled with two of the IDSL executive Directors, Engineer Onuozie and Dr Kelwa. About twenty kilometres from Benin City, we stopped behind a long queue of vehicles that had apparently been stopped and robbed about thirty minutes before we got there. Those were the days before mobile phones.

Apparently, one of the vehicles had slipped the net and reported the hold-up to the police in Benin City, but the police never arrived there. About half an hour after we were stopped, one of the lead vehicles took off and everyone followed. We arrived at Benin City without any further incident.

On my last day in the city, I was taken around to see the remnants of the ancient wall of the city with its impressive moat. That was an amazing site, to think that those defences were about one thousand years old.

From the ancient wall, I was taken to the Benin Market, where I had a taste of the real Nigeria of the late 1980s. While we were still haggling over some reproduction Benin bronze artefacts, a man's Pajero was hijacked and as he tried to defend his car keys, the robbers shot him, threw his body out of the car and sped away in his vehicle.

**On the Nigerian roads**

.  .  .

All my later trips were by road after the scare of the NNPC Executive Jet. I would fly from Accra to Lagos on the first Ghana Airways flight to Muritala Mohammad International Airport to be met by personnel of IDSL's Public Affairs Department and continue by road to Benin City.

On the very first of the many road travels to Benin City, we came across a "collared armed robber," a spectacle that I still remember with sadness. This alleged robber sat trapped on the ground with a car tire around his neck like a necklace. His hands had been tied together with a steel wire which passed through the tire and tied his ankles together. The car tire had just been lit as we got to the village. This public-spirited officer blew his horn a few times, hoping to attract the attention of anyone who could help. Apparently, the mob ran to hide in the nearby bushes on the approach of our vehicle. The IDSL gentleman thought it was too dangerous to intervene. He knew the area quite well and so decided to drive very fast to a nearby police station to report the incident.

We found police officers all right, including the inspector in charge, but they had no vehicle or ammunition for such an exercise. The poor man faced a certain and painful death.

On another occasion, there was apparently no official vehicle for the trip to Lagos. The gentleman who met me at the airport came by public transport to Lagos and then to the airport. He hired a taxi to the main Benin City transport station where he paid for three seats on an inter-city taxi, so "his special visitor could travel in comfort." That was the explanation he gave to the taxi driver. I had never experienced anything like that before and I thought it was a very interesting arrangement.

The vehicle on which my travel guide "bought the extra seats" looked so beaten up on the outside that I wondered if it could make the four-hour drive to Benin City. We arrived in Benin City faster than I had ever done in Nissan Patrols and Toyota Land Cruisers! Once we left Lagos Island, the driver hit the floor of this near-dilapidated Peugeot 504 car. Terrified as I was, I still sneaked over his shoulder frequently, to look at the speedometer dial moving between 130 and 140. Anytime we came across one of those gaping potholes that were common on the otherwise superb highway, the driver either rounded the pothole or if there was oncoming traffic, slowed down briefly to go through it.

I had quite a rich experience travelling with different people on different link roads, and onto the main Lagos - Benin City highway, but one experience that will probably live with me for the rest of my life was a fatal accident involving one of the IDSL drivers and a senior accountant just about 50 kilometres from Benin City. I had always prayed fervently on those travels, but for the first time, I became really scared about my travels. The road was always littered with wrecks some of which looked like someone had intentionally pounded an empty milk tin.

I had seen this particular car on the IDSL compound earlier in the morning while my guide for the trip back to Lagos was going through the usual paperwork so we could start our journey. I did not see them start from the car park, but it would not have been more than an hour before we departed.

The car was still lying on its roof on the roadside wedged against the tree trunk that had stopped its further movement. It had rained earlier in the morning and tire marks on the road through the grass indicated that the driver had braked hard for whatever reason, lost control, careered through the bushes, overturned and hit the tree. According to the reports I heard during my next visit, the manager who was sitting in the back seat died instantly while the driver suffered back and neck injuries but recovered later in hospital.

For the first time in my travels on that highway, I became genuinely concerned about travelling by road to and from Benin City. During discussions with the Director of Operations of the company, he assured me that I would always be met by an experienced driver and senior official of the Public Affairs Department who would ensure that the driver abided by road safety regulations and drove at a reasonable speed.

Fortunately for me, the project was finally coming to an end and I made just one more trip after I saw that accident.

· · ·

**Other Experiences**

During the supervision of the processing of the onshore Tano seismic survey, I had some wonderful experiences in Nigeria.

As mentioned earlier, I had a stomach ulcer at UST and ended up being very careful about what I ate or drank at any one time. I have not eaten any hot spices since 1971. By the time of the IDSL project, I could eat quite a number of Ghanaian dishes, if the accompanying source did not have spices, especially pepper. As a result, I was able to sample several Nigerian dishes, including "pepper soup", which I first tasted at the IDSL sports club. Pepper soup especially, was surprisingly more pleasant than its name portrayed it. Having read Chinua Achebe's "Things Fall Apart" in Form One at GSTS, I was keen to try "pounded yam" at the first opportunity and that did not disappoint, with all the 'green-greens' and some really great fish species from the Niger River.

I also participated in some wonderful worship services on the few Sundays when I had to spend the weekend in Benin City and watched many scintillating squash racquet games and competitions at the IDSL Club. Unfortunately, I never had the chance to play any game there, as my schedule was always too hectic during the day and there were always pre-arranged competitive matches on the courts in the evenings.

I had two unintended, but rather eventful extended stays in Benin City in the course of the project.

I travelled to Benin City on 7th June 1993, to participate in the trial velocity analysis for the seismic processing. It was the last week of the presidential election campaign that had pitched the maverick businessman, Chief Moshood Kashimawo Olawale Abiola a Yoruba from Ogun state and the presidential candidate of the Social Democratic Party (SDP) and the young Alhaji Bashir Tofa, a Hausa from Kano state and the presidential candidate of the National Republican Convention (NRC). Election fever was pitch high and the country's borders were scheduled to close at 4 p.m. on Friday the 11th, for the beginning of the election process the next day. However, IDSL officials insisted that they had new ideas that would help finalise the velocity analysis and I needed to be there to approve the final velocities.

We picked and stacked with these trial velocities all week and put in what we believed to be a final batch of velocity trial stacks early Friday morning, hoping the results would be out for analysis by late morning so we could review and approve the final picks. That way, I could leave by noon, to catch my flight back to Accra before the airport was closed. With other departments rushing through various programs, our huge velocity analysis batch blocked the modest mainframe computer. We could not get the results even through the weekend. The airport was shut, and no unofficial vehicles were permitted to move until after the elections. I was trapped in Benin City. I grabbed the opportunity to watch the accreditation and voting process at the Igbinidion Medical Centre, which was next door to the IDSL Guest House where I was staying.

That was the election that was annulled by the military dictator, Sani Abacha, apparently because the prospect of an Abiola presidency was too risky for the military hierarchy to contemplate. The results of the election were being steadily announced throughout Sunday until about 3 p.m. when the news flash declared that the election had been annulled, with very little explanation as to why it was being annulled. It was a most interesting experience.

About two months later, I was again trapped by another computer glitch and had to delay my departure from Benin City. This time around, Engineer Onuozie, the Technical Director of IDSL was travelling back to his hometown, Owerri the Imo State capital. My good friend, Lawrence Onyeche hailed from Port Harcourt (Rivers State) and I had made several friends in Penn State who hailed from Abba (Abia State) and Owerri and this was a great opportunity to see those areas and gain "bragging rights" over my friends.

Having decided to take me along, Engineer Onuozie planned the trip to enable me to see as much of the southern part of Nigeria as possible, especially Igboland. Early Friday afternoon, we took off from Benin City to Asaba, the Igbo enclave in Delta State, through the outskirts of Onitsha, finally arriving in Owerri early evening. First, we went to see Engineer Onuozie's mother and other close relations and retired to his house for the night. Like most Nigerian households, he had dug a borehole for domestic water supply and bought bottled water for drinking.

On Saturday morning, we went to see his friends and more of his relatives who lived in Owerri and surrounding villages. At every home, I was given a taste of Igbo hospitality, very similar to what obtained in the Akan areas of Ghana, and especially, Fanteland.

In the typical traditional Fante homes, all meals are eaten in the open in full view of passers-by or entrants to the family home. The idea is to invite everyone who comes in or passes in full view at mealtime, to join in the meal.

Usually, the invitation is "Ato hɛn ooooo!" To which the visitor will respond, *"Me nsa wo mu"* And the host will say *"Beyi wo nsa"* (You are invited, literally, "my hand is already in the bowl". "Then come and take it out"). At that, the visitor has to take a morsel of food and eat it, to show that he or she has no ill feelings against the host(s).

As described in *Things Fall Apart*, in the early morning the head of every compound we entered brought white cola nut and sweet pepper. He would bite a piece of each and give them to me in turn, to do the same, which I did promptly on each occasion. Afterwards, everyone was given his own full piece(s) of cola nut and pepper.

Later in the morning, there was often a pot of palm wine, to go with the cola nut and sweet peppers. Here again, the visitor is expected to drink from the same pot as the host. The idea behind the symbolism of eating from the same pieces of cola and sweet peppers and drinking from the same pot is that the host does not have any ill feelings/intentions about the visitor and the visitor does not come with any evil intentions. Refusal to eat from the same piece or drink from the same pot means the visitor has bad intentions and vice versa.

On Sunday morning, we went to bid farewell to Engineer Onuozie's sister and mother and several other close relations and prepared for the trip back to Benin City, leaving late morning rather than later in the afternoon, which turned out to be a smart move. We came back the other way, through Port Harcourt, Warri and Sapale Junction.

My former Phillips Petroleum Company colleague, Dr Ovuefe

Efeotor, hailed from Sapele and I would have loved the detour to see his hometown, but by the time we got to the junction, it was beginning to rain and the forecast on the radio was that it was going to be a tropical downpour, very typical of that part of the country. We skipped Sapele.

Along the highway between Port Harcourt and Warri, we had to take a diversion through a newly constructed tertiary road no more than one hundred metres long. Even at that early part of the day, the diversion was getting quite muddy. As we learned on Monday, dozens of vehicles were trapped behind other vehicles that were stuck in the mud. Many of those drivers had to spend the night in their vehicles until they were towed by tractors on Monday. In effect, we left Owerri just at the right time.

**Personal security**

I returned to Accra on Tuesday evening with rather bad news. As usual, I was met by a driver from the Public Affairs Department of the Corporation. As soon as he packed my suitcase into the vehicle and I sat down, this driver thoughtlessly blurted out, "Oh Doc, thieves broke into your house while the family was sleeping and stole some things." I was dumbfounded. All I could ask was, "When, was anyone hurt?" The short five-minute ride from the airport to our house could well have been five hours.

Apparently, the thieves cut the mosquito netting, removed two louvre blades, slipped through the gap, entered the living room and used the key, which at that time was left in the keyhole, to open the front door. It would seem like there were quite a number of them because they quickly passed the television which they had disconnected from the power source, along our long driveway into the street and were attempting to enter the library when my wife began to scream, "Thief, thief," at which the neighbours also started shouting and they ran away.

The next day, my friend Dr Kwasi Addae, fixed burglar-proof nets around the whole house, including the garage.

The Corporation provided watchmen for senior officers' homes, but only if the house belonged to or was rented by the Corporation. I lived in my own house, so I did not qualify for a corporation-assigned watchman. I got a dog.

On another occasion, thieves jumped over the wall behind our house and made away with one of our gas cylinders. I heard footsteps and shouted "thief, thief." The dog would normally bark furiously at anyone who passed within a mile of the house. Why had it not barked this time around? The thieves had thrown poisoned meat over the wall. It died the next day. After the second theft, I went to the Director of Finance and Administration and told him that unless I was assigned a watchman, I was not going to leave my family to go on any overnight assignment, not even in Ghana, let alone travelling outside the country.

Somehow, the rule, which apparently was not written anywhere, was changed for me. At that time, all senior officers of the Corporation either lived in Corporation houses or bungalows that had been inherited from the old Petroleum Department. I was the first senior officer to own my own house, which came with its own troubles. For the next three years, I was assigned a stream of unreliable watchmen until I got a puppy from Gyaman that my gardener, Issifu, turned into a fierce dog, by syringing *"akpateshie"* (a local alcoholic brew), into its nostrils before it was three months old.

My first watchman was an elderly gentleman who won a substantial amount on the National Weekly Lottery, popularly known as "Lotto", by staking my car's registration number, 5070, in various permutations and combinations. The story as he told my wife later was that he dreamt that the National Lottery had "dropped" my registration number and he staked it the next morning. In other words, he had been sleeping on the job.

We called him "Baba." When my wife asked Baba how he could be dreaming at night when he was supposed to be watching the house, he said he did not sleep, he only closed his eyes for a few seconds and saw the number.

With his winnings, Baba first painted his house at Tesano, bought a new bicycle and then married a second wife, in that order. His new wife who lived at Madina, would often meet Baba in our house in the evening and spend the night with him in the garage from where he watched the compound, occasionally walking around the perimeter of the long security wall. On more counts than one, the dog was actually more useful as security than Baba.

Unfortunately, for him, the head of security at the time, Kwamena Sam, paid a surprise visit to the house one night, found Baba's new bride in the garage and got him changed. I never found out which unfortunate senior officer got my Baba.

Next was Nuhu, a younger man who seemed to be related to everybody in his part of Achimota because nearly every week, he lost one close relative or another. He would sometimes come to the office during the day, to inform me about a funeral because of which he would either not come to work at all or else come in late. It was when an electrical gadget broke down one evening that I found out that Nuhu also doubled as a radio repairer/electrical technician. Apparently, he often went home in the morning to work on his customers' gadgets and so wouldn't have enough sleep before reporting for work or sometimes he went off completely and so missed work altogether.

Life had to continue and so I carried on with everyday work while ensuring that my family was as safe as possible.

# CHAPTER 14
# MORE TECHNICAL WORK

*Many people, especially ignorant people, want to punish you for speaking the truth, for being correct, for being you. Never apologise for being correct, or for being light years ahead of your time. If you're right and you know it, speak your mind. Speak your mind. Even if you are a minority, the truth is still the truth. (Mahatma Gandhi 1869-1948)*

As part of the new phase of increased exploration activities, a sniffer survey was conducted of the whole offshore area of Ghana's territorial waters in early 1988. Rather surprisingly, pockets of very high gas readings were recorded in the area between Accra and Keta, which were referred to in general terms as the Accra-Tema and Keta Basins.

Generally, in exploration in "virgin" areas, the tendency is to look for signs of oil and gas in previous geological mapping or even road construction activities. The Saltpond Field had been produced for some time, which in petroleum terms established it as an oil and gas province. As mentioned earlier with respect to the Petro-Canada - GNPC shallow well drilling project, there had been a detailed mapping of seepages in the onshore Tano area. Additionally, there was the Phillips Petroleum Company gas discovery in the Cape Three Points area as well as the oil and gas discoveries in the Tano Fields.

In exploration terms, those occurrences showed that oil and gas had indeed been generated in the offshore area between Saltpond and Tano and the onshore Tano area. They had to be found.

With the passage of the Petroleum Exploration and Production Law (1984) and promulgation of the Petroleum Income Tax Law (1987), several Petroleum Agreements with international oil companies such as Atlantic Richfield Corporation (ARCO), Amoco, and Diamond Shamrock (Onshore Keta) were executed. The Canadian government, acting through Petro-Canada International Assistance Corporation, made substantial investments in support of GNPC in acquiring extensive 2D seismic data in the offshore Tano/Cape Three Points Basin in 1984, 1997, 1998 & 1999.

The Government of Japan in a bilateral cooperation agreement also assisted the Government of Ghana by acquiring offshore 2D seismic data for GNPC in 1987. This data covered the area from the Eastern border of Ghana to Cape Three Points, the same area that had been covered by the Geophysical Services Incorporated (GSI) speculative seismic survey. The GSI survey had been a reconnaissance one, and therefore, of a coarser grid. This new survey was planned to fill the gaps and provide a denser coverage of the area.

**Saved by the Bell**

In August 1988, GECO, a seismic acquisition and processing company based in Orpington, England was contracted from a long list of bidders to acquire 2D seismic data in the Saltpond and Cape Three Points sub-basins. For the quality control of the acquisitions, a Quality Control consultant, also from England, was appointed to supervise the acquisition, with one of the young GNPC Geophysicists, Gabriel Osatey, as his understudy, as we always did on all corporation projects, as part of a scheme to develop a local skilled workforce.

By mid-afternoon of 8<sup>th</sup> August 1988, the day the vessel was scheduled to sail to the Saltpond field for the start of the surveys, the quality control supervisor had not arrived, having apparently experienced some hick-ups at the Ghana High Commission in London with respect to the issue of appropriate visas and permits. At about 4:30 pm, just before the close of business, the Exploration Manager, Mr Apia Kyei, walked into my office and asked me to go home and get ready to board the acquisition vessel at Tema at 6 p.m., to undertake the quality control supervision for the survey.

That turned out to be divine intervention because going away in a hurry that day saved me from investing £9,000 of my savings in England in a venture that collapsed within days of my leaving for the survey.

About a week earlier, my old schoolmate, Kwaku Osafo Antwi had informed me that the Ghana Textile Printing Company (GTP) which had been facing foreign exchange problems with respect to production inputs, had made a proposal whereby people who had savings overseas could invest in its production operations. According to the scheme, approved investors could be given pieces of cloth of their choice, according to the quantum of their investment, to sell as they pleased. Kwaku had actually invested in the venture before and made a good profit and could therefore testify to its viability. He also knew people who had returned to Ghana from England and invested in the programme.

On that fateful Monday, I took my Natwest chequebook to the office, hoping to sign a cheque for £9,000, which I would send to Kwaku's house on my way home in the evening. In the haste to sort my office, go home and return to Tema before the vessel sailed at 6 pm, I forgot to sign the cheque. On the drive home, I thought of signing and leaving it with my wife to forward it to Kwaku Osafo Antwi. However, leaving for the field for nearly one month at such short notice required that I wrote down detailed instructions and cheques towards the running of the house. In the end, I forgot even to bring out the NatWest chequebook. It was still in the pocket of my briefcase when I returned four weeks later.

A few days after we sailed from Tema, I heard on the radio that

GTP had folded and been placed into receivership. According to the news, it had little or no assets, except ageing machines. I had been saved by the bell!

### In the eye of the storm, Oil found in the Volta Region?

Sometime in the middle of 1989, one of our colleagues announced at a meeting of the Exploration Department that someone had reported an oil seepage in the Hohoe area of the Volta Region. My first reaction was "That could not be possible." The Keta Basin, sometimes wrongly called the Volta Basin and confused with the much larger Voltaian Basin, consists of a narrow strip of land no more than five kilometres by about fifteen kilometres between Ada and Anyako. Hohoe is further north of this rather shallow sedimentary basin.

Unfortunately, as always happens with all petroleum issues around the world, there were political undertones, as the Corporation was engaged in exploration activities in the southern part of the Volta Region with well-publicised seismic surveys and well drilling programmes. Since I hailed from the Central Region where the then abandoned Saltpond field had been produced for a while, dismissing a potential oil discovery in that part of the country out of hand meant "depriving the people of the area of a potential association with and benefit from oil production".

The matter was apparently taken seriously and reported to the Castle, the seat of government at the time. A high-level representation was made to the Corporation about the displeasure of people in high places with the manner in which the report of "oil find" had been dealt with.

Fortunately, one of the new geologists in the Department was born in the area. I scheduled a trip for him, a driver and another geologist to go to the area and verify the report. Their assignment was to go to the village where the report had come from, announce their presence and mission to the chief and his elders and ask for people who knew the "oil find" and the person who had made the report, to visit the site, study the vicinity of this "oil find" and take samples for testing as we had done in connection with the Tano seepages.

Apparently, a large contingent of young and old men joined the party. When they arrived at the site, our field geologists noticed what seemed like a trail of dirty oil and followed it for several hundred metres until they came upon an abandoned automobile workshop. That was the source of "the oil find" in the area.

### The Cape Three Points seismic interpretation

Sporadic exploration work had been going on in the Cape Three Points sub-basin since Mobil drilled the GH5-A1 well in 1970. Various vintages of seismic data existed over the area. However, data coverage had been sparse and unrelated, since nearly every survey had targeted a different objective.

It was not until 1983/84 that Petro-Canada International Assistance Corporation (PCIAC) in conjunction with the then Ministry of Fuel and Power, undertook a fairly comprehensive 853-kilometre 2D seismic survey in the area. In 1987, the Japan National Oil Company (JNOC) acquired another 75 kilometres of 2D seismic as part of a 4200-kilometre survey in the Central Basin in a Japanese Government bilateral aid programme. For all but regional mapping purposes, the seismic data coverage for the sub-basin was still sparse.

In September 1988, therefore, GNPC acquired 3200 kilometres of 2D seismic to bring the coverage in the area to a respectable 2 kilometres by 2 kilometres in the western and southern parts of the area where the 1984-97-series were acquired and 3 kilometres by 5 kilometres in the other areas where only the 1988-GNPC data existed. Having been part of its acquisition and processing, I knew this dataset so well it was natural that I did the interpretation, which I began during the early part of 1992.

The purpose of the study was to integrate all the most recent, mostly migrated data, in a structural interpretation with a view to determining:

1. If the poor results of the old wells in the sub-basin were due to poor well positioning
2. Whether there were still drillable structures in the study area
3. Whether there were good stratigraphic leads in the area that could be developed into drillable prospects, and
4. The future of geophysical exploration in the sub-basin.

Four time horizons, Intra-Lower Albian, Lower Albian, Middle Albian and Albian, were mapped and later converted to depth using a polynomial equation that was derived from the handful of time-depth data pairs in the existing wells.

## Results of the mapping exercise

This exercise would later prove to be such a major turning point in the whole offshore Ghana exploration programme that its main findings have been reproduced as a scanned Appendix A, ring binding, yellowing pages and all, at the end of the book.

## Stratigraphic Prospects

As stated earlier, this was essentially a structural interpretation exercise. However, at the very early part of the seismic interpretation, five out of the many stratigraphic "features" that were identified were noted and later studied in more detail. In particular, a very prominent reflector that enveloped all five features was mapped and included in the prospect catalogue.

In describing this "enveloping" reflector, it was stated that "

If it is assumed that oil has been generated in the south and southwest and been moved northward (as per oil shows in GH5-A1, GH5-B1, Dixcove 4-2X), then locations like Axim 4-3X and Takoradi 6-1 should be filled to capacity. Unfortunately, this does not seem to have happened in the area. This would seem to support the earlier assertion that oil in the sub-basin tends to accumulate in the highest regions of the sub-basin. In this case, the structural locations of these stratigraphic prospects would not be favourable. However, since these turbidite-like features are, in most cases completely encased in shales, they must be of major exploration interest."

This is what turned out to be the game changer, the turning point, in Ghana's oil exploration effort as the conclusions and recommendations that have been reproduced below show.

## Conclusions and recommendations for further work

1. A detailed interpretation exercise has been undertaken in the study area. The quality of the available data, especially the 1988 vintage, has been found to be reasonably good, although it will benefit from specialised processing for stratigraphic interpretation.
2. Structurally, the study area is very complex, having gone through several phases of faulting and vertical and lateral movements. The study area is consequently bounded by faults on its northern and eastern boundaries, all of which seem to be related to Atlantic megashear zones.
3. The study area seems to be divided into two structural provinces along a line west of the Cape Three Points-1 well location. To the west, the structural features trend east-west, while the ones in the east trend northwest-southeast.
4. Available data seem to indicate that the Upper Cretaceous source rocks have the best potential for hydrocarbon generation in the sub-basin. However, there is the potential

for other deep-seated sources, particularly in the Lower Albian, to generate hydrocarbons.

5. Several of the structural highs have been tested with limited success. A series of tilted fault blocks seem to be the remaining structural features with the potential for the accumulation of commercial volumes of hydrocarbons.

6. Generally, Upper Cretaceous sands appear to be the best-developed reservoirs in the area. Thus, the tilted fault blocks and stratigraphic features that were discussed in sections 5.2 and 5.3 respectively, need to be studied in more detail. The Upper Albian structural nose described in section 5.1.4 has a very good potential for finding oil in the Cape Three Points area. Because the feature is big, any oil find in it is likely to be commercial. With respect to the structural features that were mapped, the two closures designated D and E at the Middle Albian level, are the only ones worth further attention.

7. The stratigraphic features that were presented earlier in the "Prospect Inventory Book" need to be examined in more detail. Colour attribute processing, particularly amplitude, phase and instantaneous frequency, will be most appropriate.

8. A detailed interpretation of the "tilted fault blocks" has been done. The results of the mapping are presented as Appendix B of this report.

This project was completed in 1992 and fifteen years later in 2007, Kosmos made the biggest oil discovery in West Africa for decades in what was described as:

"The discovery of the Jubilee field in the Tano Basin of Ghana opened a new play in the deep water of the Atlantic transform margins. The field is a **late Cretaceous (same as Upper Cretaceous)** combination structural-stratigraphic trap associated with topography created by the transform tectonics during the opening of the Atlantic. Prior to the drilling of the discovery well, the African transform margin had seen very little deep-water exploration with only nine wells drilled over a margin more than 2000 km (1243 mi) long. The field was discovered in **June 2007 with the Mahogany 1 well,** which encountered 98 m (322 ft) of high-quality oil pay in a Turonian-aged **(Upper Cretaceous, as predicted in 1992) fan sequence trapped in a combination structural-stratigraphic trap.** Subsequent to the discovery, accelerated appraisal and phased development resulted in the first production in November 2010. **The field is currently producing more than 100,000 BOPD and has a planned peak production of 120,000 BOPD. The discovery has resulted in an industry-wide exploration campaign of over 50 wells in the last 8 years. These have resulted in a number of additional discoveries and to date at least one additional development."**

**The first 3-D Seismic Survey**

In 1989, GNPC funded the acquisition of 2430 square kilometres 3D seismic survey, first ever in Ghana, over the South Tano Field. The data was acquired and also processed by GECO at their office in Orpington in England. Once again, it became my lot to supervise, in fact, I did a lot of the processing of the data between Orpington and Tema.

By this time, I was supervising the Saltpond, Cape Three Points and onshore Tano processing projects in Swanley by Simon Geolithic, and Isleworth by Western Geophysical Company all in England, and Benin City Nigeria, by IDSL, respectively. These projects would go on for several years.

Shooting the first 3D seismic in Ghana was exciting. It became top priority. This data acquisition was part of the effort to develop the Tano fields. I went to Orpington to participate in the selection of the initial processing parameters, deconvolution, filtering, multiple attenuations, stacking velocities, etc, and to learn what I could about the quality of the data and any geological features that could be of significance, in preparation for a series of meetings that were scheduled for Arco's office in Plano, Texas. From the initial processing, I took along with me hard copies of the brute stacks of a number of inlines and crosslines.

Phillips Petroleum Company's 1980 handing over notes had stated among other things, that the South Tano Field alone had in-place reserves of some 350 million barrels of oil, plus associated gas and condensate. I never worked on Ghana data while I worked for Phillips Petroleum Company, but I knew people who did and from interactions with them, I always knew that if there had been that much in reserves, Phillips would have at least sought farm-in partners for their Ghana blocks. They would never have simply walked away from their discoveries in the country.

## Into the wilderness

Soon after we moved to the former Primary Fuels site where I had a proper desk and some storage space, I assembled the available geological data and 2D seismic sections of the North and South Tano discoveries and did my own quick interpretations and reserve estimates. That early work confirmed my suspicion about the figure of 350 million barrels in place in the South Tano discovery area. I suspected that there had either been a typographical error which nobody spotted or else it was a political gimmick that Phillips Petroleum Company had sprung on the government of Ghana at the time, as they tried to highlight how much the company had invested in the country and what results they had achieved. Firstly, test results showed rather poor reservoir parameters – size, porosities and permeabilities. Secondly, the areal extent of the whole North and South Tano structure was very limited. Like the Saltpond Field, the Tano structure consisted of the remnant of an ancient dome that had been eroded and left standing by itself like a sore thumb. It was not related to anything in the vicinity. Therefore, even the two fields together could not possibly contain that much in oil reserves. The brute stacks of the 3-D processing reinforced my earlier deductions about the Tano Fields.

From Orpington, I joined a meeting in Plano, Texas, where the merits of the Tano Field development project were presented to the Arco partnership and other potential investors. After the presentation, the Chief Executive Officer, Mr Tsatsu Tsikata, called the GNPC group of my old comrade Ben Dagadu, Dr Rauwerda, the Petro-Canada Consultant Geologist attached to GNPC and me, to a private meeting, to review the results of the earlier meeting. The Chief Executive asked each of us in turn, to give our honest opinion of what we thought. I was, in particular, asked to additionally report on what I had brought from the stage of the 3-D seismic data processing.

I presented my quick interpretation of the brute stacks and noted that what I had learnt up to that point from the 3-D processing indicated that the Tano fields were not that big and that the reserves were probably not as high as had been presented in the Phillips Petroleum Company handing-over report. Unknown to me, this view had not gone down very well. Plans for the development of the Tano fields seemed well advanced and my opinion seemed to present a clog in the wheels of the project. That was the beginning of my problems at GNPC, the beginning of my years in the wilderness.

## Act of disobedience?

From the meeting, I returned to Orpington to continue with the data processing there and elsewhere in England. After a total of six weeks away from home and family, the initial parameter testing phase of the 3D processing was complete and the other projects were progressing steadily. I was ready to return home. My return flight to Accra had been confirmed and I had written to my wife that I would be home that weekend. There were no mobile phones in those days, and not many functioning landlines either. I wrote to my wife two or three times a week.

Our boys were excited that I was returning home after such a long time away from them. They had already made plans about the things we were going to do over the weekend since I was scheduled to arrive on Friday night.

Late Thursday afternoon, I received a message that I should go to Benin City to supervise an aspect of the onshore Tano 2D seismic data processing before returning to Ghana. I called the office and tried to explain my fears about travelling to Lagos with my luggage, and then to Benin City at such short notice, without being able to communicate directly with IDSL in Nigeria. Instead, I suggested that I would go to Accra, rest over the weekend and without extra baggage and potential dangers that entailed and continue to Nigeria on Monday.

This apparently did not go down well in Accra and Mr Bill Stinson the Exploration Manager at the time, left a terse message on the phone for me.

Bill is African American, and one of the most practical geophysicists I ever met in the industry. He came to Ghana with Arco as Chief Geophysicist and worked very closely with me during the Arco consortium's operation in Ghana.

Bill was a very good friend of my last Chief Geophysicist at Phillips Petroleum Company, Mr Peter Parker. Pete as we called him, lost his first wife under tragic circumstances and met his African American wife a few years later through Bill Stinson.

Before he came to Ghana, Pete Parker told Bill Stinson that one of his former colleagues at Phillips Petroleum lived in Ghana and probably worked for the national oil company and would be a good contact. Bill looked for me the day after he arrived in Accra and not long after that first meeting, I got him out of a sticky situation.

Arco had brought in a two-way radio communication unit which ordinarily required a permit from the National Communications Authority to clear out of customs. The equipment had been carried in the luggage of one of the Arco officers, which was then set up in their temporary office near the Tetteh Quarshie Roundabout. Someone went to the office, heard the unit being used and reported to National Security that some Americans had set up a listening post at a secret location and were sending and receiving information from Accra. The Executive Secretary of the Authority, Mr. Kofi Asafua Jackson, went to the office with armed security men and seized the equipment and asked Arco to report to his office within hours.

Mr Jackson was a Giant (Old GSTS), and had become "My Uncle" since meeting him at Calvary Methodist Church in Adabraka. Arco's local office facilitator, who also worshipped at Calvary knew about my relationship with Mr Jackson and asked Bill to come and see me so we could go and talk to him. Mr Jackson was a well-built six-foot-four man. Bill is a six-foot-six basketball player. When we arrived at Mr Jackson's office, he rose from behind his desk to shake hands and his first reaction was, "I don't like people who are taller than me." He went on to explain that Bill and his people were not supposed to import the equipment into the country, let alone setting it up, without permission from the National Communications Authority. However, the unit was not even as powerful as it had been made out to be. Mr Jackson asked Bill to complete the necessary application forms, I witnessed them and the equipment was released to us the next day. Bill was ever so grateful for my intervention.

Back from Orpington on Friday, I went to report to Bill as soon as I arrived in the office on Monday morning. In his characteristic Washington State twang, he told me that "the Chief wants to see you, he is cheesed off!" So, I went. It was a rather cold reception. He simply told me to give the details of the seismic processing programme to my old Giant senior, Mr Agbesinyale, to go to Benin City. I was happy to do that, at least I could spend my first week back home, with my family.

Seismic data processing is a very specialised discipline of exploration geophysics. As I mentioned earlier, the onshore Tano processing project had not been an easy one and the Nigerians appreciated the effort I had put into it. Not surprisingly, a week after Mr Agbesinyale returned from Benin City, IDSL sent an urgent message that they needed me to join them for some crucial tests. I went and eventually, adapted the parameters that had been used for the Canadian test processing, to complete the IDSL project, nearly five years after it began! Seeming so special to the project also deepened my life in the wilderness at GNPC.

Reflecting on my reception back form Orpington later, my mind went back to my Phillips Petroleum Company days when I had to go to Bartlesville, Oklahoma, on a six-week training programme in January 1983. Our first son, Kofi, was not quite one year old and my boss, Mr. Curtis Bratt, was so concerned about sending me away from my young son he arranged for me to make one extra telephone call every week to my wife, in addition to what the company had earmarked for all participants, at company expense. Here I was in Ghana, with no telephone contact, yet unable to return home to my family at a scheduled date, after so long away from them.

**The final dataset**

The velocity analyses turned out to be the most troublesome and time-consuming phase of the whole processing exercise. The GECO processing team on the project sent me several different stacks they had produced by automatic velocity picking. Those stacks bore no resemblance to the known North and South Tano geology. They were picking multiples and spurious reflectors. In the end, I had to go and pick all the velocities manually. I picked twelve horizons which were then extrapolated to twenty-two. These were then edited and refined, to generate the final stack and then, migration velocities.

The final dataset was made up of time slices, stacks and migrated sections. Later, GECO sent tapes with the old SEG-Y format, for use on interactive platforms.

**3-D seismic interpretation**

The interpretation of the Tano 3D seismic data went through a number of false starts. First, it was going to be done interactively with Braspetro in Brazil, we actually made a trip to Rio for discussions on that. That fell through for reasons that seemed at the time to be related to the fact that the Brazilians painted a glossy picture of the Tano developments but then declined to invest their money in the venture. Instead, they wanted to be contracted to produce the fields on behalf of GNPC, for a fee, the kind of arrangement that Primary Fuels made with Agripetco, the Texas Group that owned the Saltpond field until it was relinquished in 1985.

In that arrangement, the owner of the field bears all the costs and risks involved in the development and production, the contractor can walk away unscathed if the project does not go according to plan, which is what happened in the case of the Agripectco Consortium.

Another plan to undertake the interpretation in Europe also fizzled out. Then in September 1990, the corporation acquired a small mainframe computer and the newly emerging Zycor workstation interactive interpretation system. In late November, the vendor sent a representative to Tema to install the workstation and software and provide ten days of training. Naturally, using a sample dataset that this trainer had used on numerous occasions, it was easy for him to run through the training manual. Unfortunately, loading and doing hands-on interpretation of real data for the first time is not that simple. Additionally, the computer was to be shared with other departments, which caused it to freeze the very first time we tried to look at the seismic data on our own. With the time zone difference between Ghana and the United States of America, getting assistance from the vendor proved even more difficult.

We tried it at different times during the next several months with little success. Eventually, we had to abandon the whole exercise. One bright Monday morning in 1992, the exploration Manager, Bill Stinson, walked into my office and said, "Do the 3D interpretation because it is needed for the forthcoming Tano field development." That was it.

I had done a course in 3D seismic interpretation at Phillips Petroleum in 1984, using time slices but I had not practised it ever since. I assembled three sets of data, stacked, time migrated and time slices. From my earlier quick interpretation of the available 2D seismic data, I knew what the Tano structure looked like. After one week of practising with the time slices, I settled on the time-migrated sections, picking every twentieth crossline and inline and began the interpretation.

At the same time, I was also doing various projects, including the Quality Control of the IDSL onshore Tano 2D seismic processing in Nigeria, the nearshore-shallow marine seismic survey of the whole coastline and the Cape Three Points 2D processing which was mercifully nearing completion at the time.

The nearshore shallow marine survey was a particularly difficult survey to process because the flat-bottomed boat that was required to do it had been lying fallow in Nigeria for more than twelve months before the corporation contracted it. There had been just basic maintenance on it before the survey began. It emerged during processing, that there were numerous missed shots which the contractor had not recorded, literally hiding the problems. Every shot had to be edited before processing could begin, costing a lot of man-hours and money!

For the 3D interpretation, I picked eight horizons through the whole survey. In all, the interpretation took about ten months. Then I had to cross-check every tie. I wrote notes as I went along and used a colour-coded scheme to mark troublesome areas, misties and interesting geological structures.

Fortunately, by the time I was ready to digitise the horizons, the Exploration Department had been boosted by eight new graduate entrants that had been posted there by the National Service Secretariat. Most of these "servicemen and women" had graduated in physics, geology, mathematics or geotechnical engineering from the universities in Ghana and Eastern Europe with no experience whatsoever in seismic processing or interpretation. In fact, none of them had ever seen a seismic section before. It was a perfect opportunity to introduce them to the concept of seismic in petroleum exploration.

After taking them through the theory of seismic acquisition and processing, I used them for the digitisation of my interpretation. As I called out the two-way travel times for the picked horizons, they posted the figures at the shot points on the seismic sections in sequential order, beginning with the youngest or shallowest horizon to the oldest or deepest. Later, when I transposed the travel times on the fault maps and began contouring, I realised that the exercise had gone very well because there were very few "bulls' eyes." Those few often resulted from a figure having been missed or written down incorrectly. Those were very easily corrected by re-timing the horizon at the affected shot point(s).

## Depth conversion

To convert the time structure maps to depth, I used all the available time-depth data and the final average and interval velocities in the 3D processing to generate average and interval velocity maps for the whole survey, a sort of velocity tomography. After several iterations of the velocity maps, editing out extreme data points, I tested the accuracy of the velocity maps by picking times at random shot points and depths, determining the depth (velocity multiplied by half of the two-way time) and comparing with the measured depths in the wells. Having ascertained that the technique gave reasonably accurate depths, I used a simple Time-Depth linear equation to convert each of the eight mapped horizons to depth.

In fact, I wrote the equation together with Bill Stinson on a hand calculator with a printer. Bill came to my office one day and informed me that we needed to design a geological profile for a new well in the South Tano field development programme. Over lunch break that day, we argued until we got the algorithm right. It was a simple linear time-depth equation. It worked so well it would later be the source of a major problem that nearly destroyed the Exploration Department and with it, the whole Corporation. By this time, I was something of a pariah in the Corporation. I was not to be quoted anywhere but I was doing all the relevant exploration work. My 3D interpretation was carried to America, pencil interpretation, hand contoured maps, side notes and all, for a "consultant" to machine digitise my interpretation and simply remap them on the computer, at a huge cost to the Corporation.

As part of my "incarceration," National security operatives were made to follow me everywhere, even to funerals at Gyaman and other places. It did not take long for me to find out though. First of all, a very good friend in another department who had ears within the inner circles at GNPC took me out of the office for a walk one day and in the centre of a park in Tema, warned me to be careful around the office and even in my house. Fortunately, I did not have a telephone in my house at the time so I could not be bugged.

The next Sunday after my friend alerted me, a security man at Calvary Methodist Church also warned me to be careful at work. This man was a former officer of the Ghana Police Service. I did not know his rank or what he had done in the service. But he said some people had come asking questions about me at the church premises. Calvary Methodist Church was made up predominantly of Fantis and Asante. Anyone who went there speaking Mfantse or Asante with a funny accent was bound to raise suspicions.

A few weeks after these incidents, a driver of one of the Corporation's vehicles who carried the surveillance team that had been following me around hit and killed a cyclist in a fatal accident because he lost me in traffic. As related to me by one of the drivers later, in the pursuer's frantic effort to trace and reconnect with me, he hit the unfortunate young man at speed.

I came home early that day and decided we should go and visit my mother-in-law who was not well, at Dansoman. On our way back to the Airport Residential Area, I took a turn at Mataheko to visit my niece who lived in that area. It was a spur-of-the-moment decision and so this driver who was apparently several vehicles behind did not realise that I had turned. It was after he entered the main Kaneshie-Kwame Nkrumah Circle Road that he discovered I was not in the traffic. In those days, the road was not as sophisticated as it is today. He tried to turn and head back to Dansoman. That was when he hit the poor young man.

A few days later, one of my neighbours, a retired officer of the Ghana Army, told me about a taxi driver who had been staking out on my side of the road. The next day, as I drove home from work towards our gate, I saw the taxi with the same registration as had been described to me just off the turn into my driveway. I stopped beside the driver. There were two other men, one beside the driver and the other in the back seat. I asked the driver what he was doing outside my house. Before he could answer, the gentleman in the backseat blurted out that the driver was on a public street, serious error. He was less than ten metres away from my driveway causing an obstruction. The driver rather apologised and moved away.

The next day, they parked two houses away across the street from us. My wife went to see the lady who lived there and together, they drove the 'intruders' away, threatening to call the landlord, a retired Brigadier of the Ghana Army if they did not move. That was the end of the rather amateurish surveillance of our house, although it continued in other guises. Of course, I knew they were there!

In the mid-1970s when I first went to America, there was still a lot of racism, especially when I did geophysical fieldwork in southern Pennsylvania, all the way into Maryland, Virginia and West Virginia, beyond the Mason-Dixon Line.

On campus, apart from one course in Engineering Mechanics that I took with one Nigerian colleague from the Geophysics Program and a half-Brazilian, half-American student (her mother was a White American lady and her father a Black Brazilian Professor) from the School of Engineering, I was always the only Black person on every course I took at Penn State. Soon after I arrived on campus, whenever and wherever I met racism, I adopted the attitude that I was better travelled and better educated than most of the people I came across on my courses and on field trips. I would therefore not take to heart any unpleasant situations I came across. That served me very well then and later when I went back to America to work at Phillips Petroleum and others. It sounds arrogant, but that was my coping mechanism.

Soon after I joined GNPC, I became a born-again Christian and with that came the belief that whatever I did in any aspect of my life, I did for the Lord and not human beings. "Whatever your task, work heartily as serving the Lord and not men," (Colossians 3:23) "The master praises what are men?" That kept me going during my years in the wilderness at GNPC. In fact, I got so much done because apart from departmental meetings, it saved me from participating in long and mostly unproductive meetings.

. . .

**The first directional well in Ghana**

Possibly the most important result of the South Tano 3D interpretation was the discovery of a new sand body that had not been tested in any of the previous wells in the Tano block. To be able to test the full extent of this sand body, a horizontal or at least a directional well had to be drilled. We did well design with a pencil and ruler and a hand calculator

Using our linear equation, the top of the new and exciting sand body, the primary target, was predicted at a depth of 2438.40 metres (8000 feet), while the top of the regular Tano sand, the secondary target, which had been encountered in all the earlier wells, was predicted at 2712.7 metres (8900 feet). The well, ST8-ST (South Tano 8 - Sidetrack), was designed to test the secondary target and secure it in readiness for development. It would then move back to drill from the point of contact of the new sand body at an angle of 30 degrees to the horizontal, to test the whole 200 metres of the primary target. This was the first directional well to be drilled in Ghana, possibly the whole of West Africa. It was most exciting!

The first part of the well design was achieved without a hitch. The top of the "new" sand was reached at 2437.8 metres, 0.61m (just 2 feet) short of the true depth, a feat that was hard to achieve even in the North Sea of the 1990s with a very high well density.

It was during the testing that a tool was lost in the well and had to be "fished" out, the industry term for recovering missing tools. Unfortunately, a drilling mud consignment that had been imported into the country could not be cleared out of the port for reasons that had no bearing on the technical capabilities of the Corporation. In desperation, a water-based substitute had to be used in drilling through the shale seal, causing it to swell, and leading to the fishing tool being stuck in the well. At a standby charge of about $100,000 per day, the fishing process was getting very expensive and after three days, the tool had to be cut off and the exercise abandoned. With it, the exciting directional drilling was abandoned and along with it, the prospect of testing this new exciting sand.

. . .

## Bill Stinson deported from Ghana

This ambitious drilling exercise had been touted as a major breakthrough by the Corporation and had therefore been given screeching headlines in the national print and electronic media as well as some of the private print media at the time. Earlier, as the preparation for the drilling programme got underway, there were unfavourable headlines in the private press about the number of rigs and other marine assets the Corporation had acquired when it was not producing oil or even drilling by itself. So being able to drill its own well, and a complex one for that matter, was seen as a major achievement. Then things began to go wrong and the news began to find its way into the private press.

A committee was set up to find where the leaks of the unfavourable news to the media had been coming from. Soon after the committee began to sit, some staff of the Exploration Department including the Exploration Manager, Bill Stinson, were suspended with pay. There was unease in the Department. Nana Asafu-Adjaye was promoted to Principal Geophysicist and made Acting Exploration Manager. Overnight, one of my subordinates had become my boss. I continued to do my work as usual.

Bill Stinson came to Ghana with his African-American wife. Somewhere along the line, he met a local woman Sheila. Bill loved his life in Ghana and like many African Americans before him, decided to make his permanent home in Ghana. So, when Arco sent him back to America, he resigned and came back to Ghana joined GNPC as Exploration Manager and soon got married to Sheila. Sheila has both Fanti and Ga ancestry, so Bill became my "brother-in-law."

Their first child, a girl, was born on Tuesday, the day of my mother's and my birth. I gave her the name Abena and elected to be her Godfather and both stuck. I visited them regularly and Bill visited my house once in a while. He loved okra, a long species of which I grew on a part of my very large compound. I learnt from Bill how to fry the raw okra for use as filling in sandwiches. It is so good I still do it anytime I can get my hands on fresh okra even in the United Kingdom.

Bill still lived in the Corporation rented accommodation down in the valley in East Airport, so I usually took his letters, which his secretary, Mabel, regularly brought to me, to his house after work and if it was a Friday, after church service on Sunday, so I could have some time with little Abena. Although like most African Americans Bill might have been born and bred a Christian, by this time he had become a Buddhist, possibly adopting the faith in California or during his working life in southeast Asia. We did not discuss it, but we respected each other's faith. He admired my Sunday Kente and local men's clothing outfits.

Across the street from Bill's house was an uncompleted building where some young men loitered most of the day, and sometimes well into the night. Not long after Bill's suspension, I was alerted by one of the Corporation's drivers and confirmed by one of my childhood friends who worked in some kind of security outfit that those young men who "loitered" in the uncompleted house across the road were, in fact, part of surveillance teams and were recording the registration numbers and details of everyone who visited Bill's house. Bill was my friend and I could not stop visiting him, especially when he still had important mail being sent through me. Instead, I decided to go alone each time I had to deliver his letters or visit him, so I could not put my family in harm's way in any shape or form.

Along the line, the Chief Executive Officer of the Corporation had sued Bill Stinson for something like One Billion cedis and Bill had filed a countersuit seeking damages of Two Billion cedis through his lawyers, Akuffo-Addo and Prempeh and Company.

One Saturday morning in July 1996, I went to play squash at the Polo Club down the road from our house, as I did every Saturday morning, and even some Sundays, before going to church. Just as I was finishing my last match for the morning, one of my colleagues signalled from the gallery to say that my wife was looking for me. Sabina never came to the squash court, so I knew there was something wrong. When I came out of the court she said, "Bill Stinson had been arrested the previous night and detained at the Airport Police Station."

We drove to the Airport Police Station and asked to see him. When he came out of the cell, we were both shocked to see him. He wore just a white cotton vest on a pair of trousers and barefooted. Overnight, the mosquitoes had feasted on him badly. Bill is very fair and the sites of the mosquito bites showed on his face, arms and down to his feet. My wife advised that he needed anti-malaria medication immediately. I spoke to Bill for some ten minutes during which he asked me to go and see his lawyers who had been informed earlier in the morning.

I went to a nearby chemist's shop, bought the medication that my wife had recommended, brought them to Bill and made him take the recommended dosage immediately with instructions to take more at appropriate intervals during the day. From there, I drove home and took a shower, changed clothes and headed straight to Akufo-Addo & Prempeh and Company at Adabraka.

A secretary took me to Nana Akufo-Addo (now the fifth President of the Fourth Republic of Ghana), in his plush office with antique furniture. After listening to me for a few minutes, he asked me to see Mr Philip Addison one of the lawyers at the practice, who apparently was handling Bill's case. I had never met Mr Addison, but I knew his father Dr Addison, a Giant and entrepreneur, through another of my Giant "uncles", Nii Ayi Ayitey, the Managing Director of Kabelmetal in Tema, although I did not know about the relationship at the time. Dr Addison owned a factory that manufactured cement bags in Takoradi but was also interested in cement manufacture. Uncle Nii, as I called him, arranged for me to meet and talk to him about the limestone outcrop in the onshore Tano area.

I spoke to Lawyer Addison for some time and we eventually drove together to the Airport Police Station. According to Mr Addison, Bill lived and worked in Ghana on a visa and work permit that was secured by GNPC. His appointment with the Corporation had been terminated and his immigration status revoked. There was not much that could be done under the circumstances, especially on a Saturday. Bill had to plead for voluntary repatriation from the country. Mr

Addison advised me to contact the American Embassy and ask for their assistance in Bill's safe and orderly removal from the country.

As my socialist friends used to say, this was part of "communist inferior tactics," which was incidentally used very effectively under the First Republic of Ghana. The Law does not allow a person to be arrested after 6 p.m. in civil cases or be imprisoned without appearing before a court of justice. But he can be arrested and placed in police custody before 6 pm, ostensibly to bring him to court on Monday. However, in the case of the Preventive Detention Act, the victim would be in detention and in the case of deportation, he would have been removed before the courts opened on Monday morning.

I called the American Embassy and spoke to the Counsellor who put me through to the Ambassador. The Ambassador's view was that under the circumstances, the only assistance the embassy could provide was to see to Bill's safe removal from the country as soon as possible and that they were working on his being repatriated the following night. He assured me that he would provide an escort to accompany Bill to the aircraft and ensure that he was safely seated on board. I relayed the message to Bill and then to Mr Addison. The embassy did and a few days later, Bill informed me through Sheila, that he had arrived safely in his native Seattle.

Sheila and the children lived in a house that was rented by the Corporation and they had to vacate it. She moved to their family house at Adabraka, where I continued to visit, even though I knew that the house was being watched. Eventually, she managed to buy a new house at the Regimaunel Estate at Sakumono and moved there before they finally left Ghana to join Bill in the United States of America.

In spite of all that he went through in Ghana, Bill still found it in himself to assist several Ghanaians, including former employees of the Corporation, to settle in America.


**The Corporation drills its own wells**

· · ·

Using the results of the South Tano 3D seismic data interpretation, GNPC drilled three further wells in the South Tano Field in 1994, using its acquired drillship (Discoverer 511), in furtherance of the proposed Tano Fields Development Project that was aimed at using the gas from the fields for power generation. That really confirmed my conclusion that the Tano discoveries were, in fact, gas discoveries and not the 350 million barrels of oil in place that had been reported by Phillips Petroleum Company.

The South Tano 3D data is still among the best seismic data ever acquired offshore Ghana.

As part of the integrated Tano Fields development project, the corporation ordered a power barge to serve as the offshore plant for the power generation project, with the corresponding onshore infrastructure located at Effasu-Mangyea and power transmission lines at Essiama and Elubo in the Jomoro District, to tie into the national grid.

## The 1999-2000 Deepwater Tano 2D Seismic interpretation, my last major geophysical interpretation project

In late October 1999, I began a 2-D seismic interpretation of the Deepwater Tano area using every available seismic vintage that had ever been shot in the area, 1200 kilometres in all. Earlier in the year, I had done some preliminary seismic studies with Anthony Assiamah, a bright young Giant who had done his National Service at the Exploration Department about a year earlier and had subsequently been employed as a Geophysicist after his service. He showed a lot of promise and was eager to learn.

After selecting the seismic sections with coverage of roughly two kilometres by two kilometres (slightly denser in some areas), I highlighted the relevant lines on a base map and asked him to put together the sepia copies of the seismic sections and have the mapping section print two copies of each section. He assembled the seismic sections, together with fresh base maps within two weeks.

After checking all the seismic sections, I told him that our task was to interpret the Upper Cretaceous and basement horizons and pick every stratigraphic anomaly in between. I picked the two horizons on a loop of about six kilometres by six kilometres, tied them together, and interpreted stratigraphic anomalies that I had identified in the course of tying the loop. I then took him through the process of tying those horizons to ensure that he was comfortable with picking the two main horizons and identifying stratigraphic anomalies.

We resolved to meet mid-morning every Monday after our regular weekly sectional meeting that involved everybody, to review our progress. However, if he had any problem anytime during the week or day, he could always call on me.

Working very closely together, we picked ten very large anomalies each and seven minor ones. We interpreted, hand digitized and contoured our picks over six months and by the end of the year, all the maps had been drafted by the Mapping Section.

The largest of the stratigraphic leads which I nicknamed "Whale" straddled the Ghana-Côte d'Ivoire border. That lead is so large and clear even on the older vintage 2-D seismic data that I have always suspected that the Ivorian border agitation of a few years ago could have been triggered by one of the companies operating in that country identifying that lead. Since we completed that project, I have kept my ears to the ground waiting for an operator to drill that prospect.

Unfortunately, it seems the blocks in the area have been awarded to political big "wigs" that have neither the technical nor financial capability to do any serious exploration in those blocks.

Sadly, my young friend Anthony Assiamah with whom I did the interpretation passed away suddenly about four years ago.

As a spin-off of the exercise, I took advantage of the quality of the deep reflectors in the Tano and Cape Three Points areas to map the Coastal Boundary Fault all the way to the Keta Basin. I have just submitted that paper for publication.

# CHAPTER 15
## MY SPIRITUAL DEVELOPMENT

From my primary school days, I attended church services fairly regularly and was involved in various church activities either with my mother and siblings in the Methodist Church or with Uncle Obrehun in the Apostolic Church. At GSTS, I began to read the Bible every morning along with my Scripture Union friends, although I never formally joined the Union. I read through the Bible twice before I finished secondary school. This routine would continue through my university days in Ghana, America and the United Kingdom.

Unfortunately, my church attendance faltered when I arrived in the United Kingdom until we moved to West Hampstead after I started work with Phillips Petroleum Company. The reason was that none of the places I lived during my first three years in London, including Kings Road Chelsea, had a church within easy reach. It was in West Hampstead that we found an Anglican Church (where we were eventually married and Kofi was christened), within walking distance of our flat. The Immanuel Parish Church was so welcoming that we kept our membership there after we moved to Edgware and Saint John's Wood and continued our membership of that Church even after we settled in Purley until we left for Ghana. I participated actively in the Church's activities, taking offertory during Sunday services and manning harvest stalls at Harvest time.

However, my closer walk with the Lord began when we went to live with my in-laws in Dansoman, which would culminate in my true spiritual growth and new birth in Christ at Calvary Methodist Church, Adabraka.

When we first went to live with my in-laws in Dansoman, we attended church services with my father-in-law, sometimes at the Obo Anglican Church at Adabraka and sometimes at the local Anglican church near my in-laws' residence where Paa Kwesi was baptised. The Obo Anglican Church at Adabraka did not have a resident vicar and so just before Paa Kwesi was born, my father-in-law advised that we should go to the nearby Anglican church, to pave the way for the "baby to be baptised without too much hassle."

### Calvary Methodist Church

While we lived with my in-laws, I met my cousin, Rev EK Dadson, who by this time was the Superintendent Minister at Calvary Methodist Church by chance, in Accra. I had only met him briefly since my return to the country at a funeral at Gyaman in late 1985. He mentioned that he was stationed at Calvary Methodist Church in Accra and that if I needed a place to worship, I could always come to his church. I had not been able to visit him until this chance meeting when he came to Dansoman to visit one of his parishioners.

When we moved to our own house at the Airport Residential Area in late September 1986, we realised that the nearest church in the area was the Accra Police Church which was Methodist-Presbyterian. Sabina had been baptised Anglican and we had been married in the Anglican Church, but there was no Anglican Church anywhere near the Airport Residential Area.

It had to be Calvary Methodist Church. So, the first Sunday after we moved into our new home, we decided to try it out and so began our long association with Calvary Methodist Church at Adabraka. In line with Methodist tradition, we appeared before the Leaders' Meeting later that week, for formal enrolment into the church and were assigned to the "Airport Bible Class", under the leadership of Brother Kwesi Abbey Sam, as the Methodist Church required every member to belong to a Bible class.

During my later years at GSTS and at University, I worshipped at the Koforidua Methodist Church during the holidays, where the service was always in *Twi* and English. There was, therefore, no incentive to read *Mfantse*. I had not read *Mfantse* since leaving Middle School Form Three, to go to GSTS, apart from the occasional personal letters that I wrote to my mother after I left the shores of Ghana.

Not long after we joined our new Bible class, I was asked to lead one of the weekly class meetings. That involved reading the *Mfantse* Bible. I soon became a regular feature on the class meeting leaders' rota, which meant that I had to brush up on my *Mfantse* reading, which did not take that long.

The Airport Class, as it was known at Calvary, was very vibrant. Several members of the class held various positions in the Church. Every Bible class was required to nominate one male member in the course of the year, to join the "collectors", those who took and counted the offertory during church services. About two months after we joined the class, I was nominated to join the next batch of collectors, a job that I would do for the next two years.

Our Airport Class made great strides spiritually and materially in the late 1980s, especially after Brother Abbey Sam returned from the Christian Leadership Training Programme at the Haggai Institute in Singapore around the middle of 1987. The programmes of the class were expanded to include teachings by Spirit-filled Christians from Calvary and even outside the Methodist Church. It was such a joy to belong to the class and members looked forward with anticipation to Thursday evening, especially the last Thursday of the month when we met for prayers and testimonies.

It was during this period that I found a deep and very personal relationship in my walk with Christ the Lord, culminating in my being co-opted into various leadership positions in the church. Some people can point to dramatic Pauline conversion experiences, mine was gradual.

## Spiritual Growth

Before Rev E K Dadson ended his tenure at Calvary Methodist Church, he embarked on a radical, perhaps revolutionary idea of attracting and retaining young people into the church through a special 'Youth Service', a concept which has now become a Connexion-wide youth evangelisation success phenomenon within Ghana Methodism.

With the approval of the Leaders' Meeting, a workshop was organised for the young people of the church ranging in age from 12 to 25, to discuss the worrying trend of the younger generation of Calvary Methodist Church members and the Methodist Church nationwide, flocking to the new "charismatic" and "evangelical" churches. Eight of us who were deemed to be "young adults" - Brothers Abbey Sam, Kingsford Amoah, Ato Ockan, Kwamena Hazel and I and Sisters Dinah Hayford, Dorcas Ocran, Karen Essiful-Ansah, Paulina Esar, Joanna Sam and Rose Adjei - led the one-day workshop.

## The Calvary Methodist Church Youth Service

At the beginning of the workshop, which was very well attended, the young people were divided into eight groups. Each group was assigned one or two leaders. The task of the leaders was to listen to the young people's concerns and their reasons for hanging around the church premises on Sunday mornings conversing instead of participating in the services and why some, including young people whose parents held prominent positions in the church, either did not attend Sunday services or else had left the church altogether.

The leaders of the groups collated the views and reported to the whole workshop at the end of the day. The views were many and varied. They ranged from the fact that sometimes the *Mfantse* that was spoken by preachers went over the heads of the young people in the Church, through services being too conservative, to lack of opportunity to express themselves as young people or be used in some shape or form, as the future leaders of the church. Even more importantly, they did not fit in at the adult Bible Classes of the church, even where their own parents led those classes in their homes.

In other words, the young people lacked spiritual nourishment, which they could find in the newer churches or for those in the secondary schools and universities, only when they returned to their various campuses. So, for those in boarding institutions, the holidays were times of "spiritual wilderness" and for those in day institutions or the younger ones still in junior schools, a worse phase of spiritual inactivity in their lives.

Most of the young people who attended the workshop were secondary school or university students who belonged to various Christian groups like the Scripture Union, Youth Fellowship and Methodist Students' Union. At these organisations, they were able to sing, clap, drum and dance, as and when the appropriate musical equipment were available. These opportunities were not available to them in the mainstream church on Sundays.

The findings of the workshop were summarised into a memorandum that was presented to the Leaders' Meeting of the church, with the recommendation to set up a "Youth Service", with a slightly modified format.

The Youth Service was to be led mostly by the young people with guidance from the elders who were to be called "teachers" and who were also given "notes to preach," so they could serve as preachers for the service.

Under the format, the first forty minutes of the Sunday morning service involved Bible studies, as was done at the adult Bible Class. There were eight groups, each with no more than twelve or fifteen young people under one teacher and one of the young people as his or her assistant. The teachers and their assistants met two Wednesdays in a month and "taught themselves" with one of them leading the discussions. That way, at any time on Sunday morning, every group (class) dealt with the same topic. The materials for the Bible studies were printed and distributed to the young people ahead of the class, so they could study and make meaningful contributions during the Sunday class meeting. The very first Youth Service began at 9:30 am on Sunday, 22nd March 1987 with twenty-one young people and seven teachers.

As fate would have it, an Electrical Contractor member of the Church, Mr J E K Taylor, won a major contract of ten million cedis in those days and decided to donate his (10%) tithe on the project towards "youth work." Therefore, the Church decided that part of that money should be given to the Youth Service towards the purchase of a set of musical instruments. We purchased a set of drums, keyboard, percussion and a trumpet.

Low and behold, within a few months, of starting the service the young people were flocking back to the Church and participating meaningfully in the Church's programmes. On a good day during school holidays, attendance could be as high as 100. The classes had spilled to the corridors and more chairs had to be brought in from elsewhere, to accommodate the numbers.

Of the final twelve teachers of the Youth Service, only Brother Abbey Sam was an accredited Local preacher. The rest of us took the route of being teachers of the Youth Service into the Church's Lay ministry. Having been given "notes to preach", we had to attend lessons in preparation for the "Local Preachers' Examination." The weekend before the first opportunity came to take the examination in June 1989, I was sent away to Ethiopia for six weeks, to participate in a geophysical data processing programme and there would not be another examination till 1994 when I finally took the examination and was commissioned a full local preacher later that year.

Within two years of starting the Youth Service, two of our teachers, Brother Kwamena Hazel and Sister Paulina Esar were called to the ordained ministry. Some of the young members became Assistant Class Leaders, while a few left the service for ministry in the new churches around Accra and beyond. The Calvary Youth Service was soon to become part of the whole Church's Youth Evangelical Ministry.

.  .  .

**Some exciting times of my spiritual journey**

One Sunday evening not long after I began preaching, I took an unplanned service at Calvary Methodist Church which will probably live with me for the rest of my life. I had gone to the service early that evening, as another member of the congregation. While we were waiting for the service to start in about fifteen minutes, the Superintendent Minister, Rt Rev Ebe Arthur came and whispered to me that the preacher for the evening was not coming and could I take the service. Apparently, this preacher who had sent his hymns and Bible readings earlier was suddenly taken ill.

We had read a very touching Bible passage and commentary from "Light for our path", one of the daily devotional resources of the Methodist Church Ghana at the time, for our family devotion that morning. I asked for and was given a copy of the magazine from the Manse. I scribbled down a few notes and as I mounted the pulpit to start the service, I came face to face with Most Rev Kwesi A Dickson, the President of Conference himself! He was in cloth and a jumper. I prayed under my breath to the Holy Spirit to lead me.

By the grace of God, the service went so well that several people came to congratulate me at the end of it. The President of the Conference and the Superintendent Minister called me and together, congratulated me for leading the service at such short notice. The President remarked in his characteristically beautiful intonation, "If you preach like this after ten minutes of preparation, I wonder what it would be like when you have fully prepared for your own service. Well done." I thanked him and went home. I had met the Most Rev Dickson when he served as Superintendent Minister of North Accra Circuit during his preparatory year before he took office, but this was the first time I met him as President of the Conference.

**In unfriendly environments**

. . .

While attending the series of seismic acquisition and processing workshops in Ethiopia back in 1989, I came across true persecution of the Church of Christ for the first time in my life. When I travel, I always leave my Bible and devotional reading materials on my bedside table. Mengistu Haile Mariam who led a communist military dictatorship in Ethiopia at the time had embarked on a major persecution of the Church and Christians were only meeting in secret in homes. Somehow, not long after I arrived in Dire Dawa, which is now in Eritrea, word got around that a new Christian had arrived in town. One of the many local secret cells decided to seek me out. An emissary was sent to meet me on a deserted street one late afternoon after lectures.

I was invited to one of those secret meetings. I instinctively agreed to go, without asking any questions. I was taken through back alleys with decoys, and camouflage until we arrived in the back room of a large house. After prayers, I was introduced as the new "Brother" (Wadanya in Amharic) from Ghana. We had a lively Bible discussion that night. I went a few times, but it was later after I had returned to Ghana that I learnt from people who lived through the persecution that although I could technically not be touched as a guest of the government, sometimes there were mistaken identities, to put it mildly. The Lord's hand had been with me.

## Leadership in the Church

As a result of being made a Leader in our Airport Bible Class, I was inducted into the Leaders' Meeting of Calvary Methodist Church, which also entitled me to membership in the North Accra Circuit Meeting. I went to the Calvary Leaders' Meeting as one of the youngest people there. Because of my work in seismology and environmental protection, I began to participate actively in the deliberations of the Leaders' Meeting not long after I joined the bi-weekly meeting. Some people thought I was bold, even audacious to make contributions that early after my induction.

One way or the other, it won me many friends among the older members of the Leaders' Meeting. That was even before I became a Local Preacher of the circuit. One of my elderly friends was Mr B A Yankson, a well-mannered lawyer of the old school who had a practice in his hometown of Agona Swedru as well as Accra.

Mr Yankson was a member of the editorial board of Calvary Methodist Church's magazine, *The Christian Sentinel.* It was a small local quarterly publication which apparently began in the 1980s and was edited first by Mr Ribeiro and later, by Mr U K Hackman.

When Mr U K Hackman passed away in London under rather tragic circumstances, the editorship passed to Mr Yankson.

Even before he became the editor, Mr Yankson had encouraged me to write articles for the magazine. I wrote one article for the magazine as a contributor, but Mr Yankson had bold plans for the magazine. He believed that the future of the Church and its organs, especially in the wider readership of its newspaper, the bi-weekly *Methodist Times* and soon-to-be Connexional *Sentinel,* belonged to the youth of the Church. He reconstituted the editorial board with new members, including some members from the other societies in the circuit, St John's Methodist in Achimota and Gethsemane at Mamprobi, making it a North Accra Circuit magazine.

I was included as the youngest member of the board. Mr Yankson encouraged me to write a column on environmental issues. This was 1994. I soon became a regular contributor and a familiar face not only in the circuit but the whole Accra Diocese.

By this time, I had also been drafted into the Technical Sub-Committee of the Accra Metropolitan Authority, from where I was detailed to make presentations on earthquake preparedness to the various Sub-Metro Assemblies of the authority. I even appeared on radio talk shows and television discussion panels. The presentations and radio and television appearances for good or ill, again exposed me to the public, sometimes not in very pleasant circumstances, as some of the things we had to say about building and other environmental practices in the Metropolis were not palatable to everyone. Eventually, I was drafted into two sub-committees (Infrastructure and Geological disasters) of the newly inaugurated National Disaster Management

Organisation (NADMO) and appointed Chairman of the sub-committee on Geological Disasters.

Then late in the afternoon of 6th March 1997, while the nation was still celebrating its 40th independence anniversary, a medium-sized Magnitude 4.9 earthquake struck Accra and its environs and threw the country into a panic. There had been minor tremors in 1996, but this was the largest since 1969. I had been giving talks to secondary schools and church groups since joining NADMO. This earthquake raised the profile of our NADMO sub-committee in the public domain.

**To my first Synod and Conference**

I attended the Accra Diocese Synod of 2000 by accident. Brother Abbey Sam who was one of the Circuit Stewards of the North Accra Circuit was scheduled to attend as one of the automatic members of Synod, but an emergency occurred in his office a few days before Synod began and he suggested to the Superintendent Minister that I replaced him.

In 2000, there were still issues in the local media about the earthquake of 6th March 1997 and because it affected many areas in and around Accra, the issue naturally came up to the floor of Synod to which I contributed. That again gave me some exposure, this time at Synod itself. When the time came to elect members to Conference 2000, my name was seventh in the number of votes cast. I had been elected to Conference, the highest decision-making body of the Methodist Church Ghana!

At the end of the election, I was reminded by one of the veterans and fellow members of the Sentinel editorial board, Mr Abadoo that I was the first person ever, to be elected to Conference at his first appearance at Synod. That record apparently still stands today.

On Synod Sunday, I was chosen with a minister, Very Rev Sackey, to attend the Sunday service at a Methodist Church deep within Madina. One of the receiver-transmitter stations in the microearthquake recording for my doctorate thesis was located at the University of Ghana's Nungua Farms and so I passed through Madina regularly during the six-month period of my research in Ghana in 1978-79. Since returning home, I had also been to Madina several times but I had never been to this part of the township. It was a new experience. I was so blessed by that service that day, the singing, the worship and ultimately, the preaching were all very uplifting.

I landed at my first Conference (Accra 2000), with a bang. There were moves in the North Accra Circuit, apparently backed by the President of Conference, Most Rev Dr Samuel Asante-Antwi, who had very ambitious plans for the expansion, growth and development of the Church, to create a new Diocese in Accra. The process had split the Leaders' Meeting of Calvary and later, North Accra Circuit. Other Circuits in Accra looked at it as "another move by the Akans, mostly Fantis, to cause trouble in the Church once more." They had forgotten the fact that Most Rev Aboagye-Mensah had been denied Chairmanship of Tema District at one point because he was not a Ga.

The lot fell on me, an innocent first-timer, to move the Memorandum for the creation of the Accra East and West Dioceses, with the support of the Chairman of the District, Rt Rev C R A Pappoe. I moved the first notice for the Memorandum and it was seconded by Rt Rev Pappoe, but at the afternoon session, it emerged that some of the mainly Ga circuits were not too pleased about the plan to divide the Accra diocese. They tried to prevail on Rt Rev Pappoe to withdraw his support for the Memorandum. That got several members of the Winneba Diocese delegation led by my old senior from Essikuma, Brother Kweku Acquaah, to pledge support for the Memorandum. The first stage motion eventually passed.

To his credit, Most Rev Asante-Antwi in his time, moved the Church to another level with the establishment of the Methodist (Donewell) Insurance Company and the Methodist University College, among other theological innovations. The new dioceses are apparently in the process of being established now.


**Conference Saturday**

.   .   .

The practice at the Conference is that on Conference Saturday, a delegation of two members, one clergyman and one layperson, is chosen to visit superannuated ministers who are no longer able to attend the Conference, to extend Conference's felicitations, give each a token envelope and report back to Conference about their well-being.

On this occasion, I was sent with Very Rev. Ofori Donkor to visit Most Rev T Wallace Koomson. He had lost his eyesight by this time so he had to be guided to the meeting in his living room by a lady caretaker. After the conversation which lasted about fifteen minutes, he prayed for us and asked each of us to pray for him in turn. He seemed to have been touched by my prayer and asked my name again. He wished me well and we left. That will not be the last meeting with the famous minister and former President of the Conference because about a year later, he attended an early morning (7:30) service that I led at the Calvary Methodist Church.

Just after midnight that Sunday morning in 2001, I received a telephone call from Rev Kwaku Dua, then a junior minister at Calvary Methodist Church. He could barely speak on the telephone. His voice was gone. He had been planned to take the early morning service but by Saturday morning, his voice was gone. He had been calling all day trying to find someone to take his service to no avail. I was his last hope.

Rev Dua was married to Rev Ofori-Rockson's daughter. Rev Ofori-Rockson, the immediate past Superintendent Minister of the North Accra Circuit, was the Protestant Chaplain at UST while I was in the university and had actually witnessed my very first passport as a minister of the Church of Christ. So, when we met again in Calvary in late 1986, it was like a great reunion. He had been transferred by 2001, but the familial ties were still there. I could not refuse Rev Dua. He had already picked his hymns and lectionary Bible readings for the service. I sat down till 2:00 a.m. and wrote a sermon.

The Calvary Methodist Church's 7:30 am service was all English, another of the Calvary firsts that was adopted throughout the Connexion and even, later, among other denominations.

The service went very well and unknown to me, Most Rev T Wallace Koomson who had been brought to the service by a guide that morning, had sat in the corner away from the pulpit. While I was recessing and praying with the choir, he sent for me. Had I done something wrong? When I met him at the vestry, he shook my hand and congratulated me on "a good service and a very good sermon." The Old Man prayed for me and wished me well for the future. I was thrilled. Another former President of the Conference had heard and appreciated my sermon!

**Conference 2002**

I was elected to the 2002 Conference in Kumasi by an even larger vote coming in fifth overall. At the Kumasi Conference, I was appointed to the drafting committee where the memoranda and resolutions were drafted.

Unfortunately, Kumasi would be my last Conference as I joined my family in the United Kingdom later that year. Mr Abadoo would never forgive me for "abandoning" him because he had apparently begun a grand plan meant to put me up for the position of Lay President of the Conference.

**The birth of a vision, a new Methodist Church in the Airport Residential Area**

At one particularly heavily attended Bible class meeting sometime in early 1993, thirty-five out of the total roll of about fifty-five members made it to the meeting, with more than half arriving about the same time. There had never been that many people attending one meeting. The class spilt over as far as the dining room of Brother and Sister Abbey Sam. Everything that could be used as a seat was brought out for use. It was at the end of the meeting while we were dispersing that a "Sister" suggested to Brother Abbey Sam that the class could actually be turned into a church. A seed had been sown!

Following that extraordinary class meeting, it was decided that the class had overgrown the Abbey Sams' bungalow and that it was time to effect some changes, to encourage its further growth. A suggestion to divide the class into permanent and independent smaller classes met with stiff opposition. A compromise had to be found, which was that the class should be split into sub-divisions to be known as "Groups," that would meet separately but would follow the same teaching programmes and study topics. All groups would, however, come together on the last Thursday of the month, for the usual prayers and testimonies.

Subsequently, the class was divided into four groups. Brother Abbey Sam led the first group that continued to meet in his bungalow, assisted by Sisters Christina Arhin and Mercy Abbey Sam. The second group which was made up of people who lived in the Roman Ridge area was led by Sister Alice Acquaye, assisted by Sister Naana Ampratwum and met at Sister Naana Ampratwum's bungalow at Roman Ridge, the third group made up of people living at Legon and Kwabenya, was led by Prof de Graft Johnson and met in his house at Kwabenya Junction, while I led the fourth group, made up of people who lived at the Airport Police Station and our part of the Airport Residential Area, assisted by Sisters Gloria Ghartey and Lily Adjei and met in Mrs Boateng's house. The arrangement worked incredibly well as everyone travelled shorter distances to their new class meeting places, and together the Airport Bible Class shone brightly throughout the North Accra Circuit.

## Beginnings of the preaching post

The vision of establishing a church as the class's contribution to evangelism in the Airport Residential Area, which at that time only boasted of a small Action Chapel in a private house adjacent to the diplomatic shop, would not die in spite of initial opposition at the mother church, Calvary Methodist.

With the enthusiastic support of some senior members of the

Calvary Leaders' Meeting like Brothers Atta-Peters, Kingsford Amoah and Yaw Ofori, the Calvary Methodist leadership agreed that the Airport Bible Class could start a "Sunday evening service" and a Sunday School within the Airport Residential Area. Similar "evening services" had been running at Palladium, Teshie-Nungua and Kanda Estate for years, with no vision of ever becoming full-fledged churches.

With that approval, the Airport Class now needed a meeting place. As fate would have it, one of our members, Sister Effie Ayayee, was the headmistress of the nearby Association International School. When she was approached, Sister Effie consulted with the management of the school which readily offered two large classrooms with a connecting movable wooden curtain in the primary section. So, on 19th April 1994, Brother Kingsford Amoah led the first evening service in a double classroom of Association International School, preaching on **"Blessed are those who have not seen and yet believed,"** based on John 20, verses 29-31. He 'prophesied' about great things to come.

A new thriving Sunday School and an evening service thus began at the Airport Residential Area. Brother S. A. Mills-Robertson, while maintaining his membership at Calvary, became a very enthusiastic teacher with Brother Abbey Sam and me, for the whole period that the Sunday school was held at the Association International School. Our two sons, Kofi and Paa Kwesi, still read and write *Mfantse* today because of the excellent tuition they received at the Sunday School.

Even Muslim children of Dagomba parentage who lived on our Fifth Street attended the Sunday School. During my last visit to Immanuel Church about three years ago, I discovered that a number of the very young children who attended the Sunday school at its inception are now adult members of the Church, with several holding responsible positions in the Church and society at large.

**Temporary cessation of the service**

Although the Airport Bible Class and some individuals had financed most of the initial requirements like a lectern, public address system, organ, tables and chairs, a lot of items were still required to make worship as comfortable as possible for members and visitors. Therefore, the elders (we were still a preaching post and could therefore not constitute a traditional Methodist Leaders' Meeting system for the administration of our preaching post) decided to hold a fund-raising anniversary service, to raise funds for the new "preaching post." It was held on 29th October 1995 and officiated by the Reverend Professor Emmanuel Asante who at the time was the Rector of the Trinity Theological College at Legon. Rev Professor Asante based his "prophetic message" on Mark 4:30-32, **"The mustard seed."**

Unfortunately, a heavy downpour late that fateful Sunday afternoon disrupted the function, but that did not prevent us from raising a very substantial amount of money. When it was reported at the next Leaders' Meeting at Calvary, the amount of money raised immediately became the subject of a major debate. According to the Superintendent Minister, Rev Joseph Ebe Arthur, under Methodist Standing Orders, that money had been raised in the name of Calvary Methodist Church and therefore ought to be paid into that church's chest. There were some rather "unchristian" exchanges at that meeting. Some members, in whispers, even let out the notion that "Brother Abbey Sam and I were using the Airport Preaching Post to collapse the Calvary Youth Service" and we had to be stopped.

The Youth Service at the time had ten teachers, of which only two of us were involved at the Airport Service. How could two out of the leadership of ten teachers possibly collapse a service which by this time had been going for about eight years and had already produced two ministers for the Methodist Church, another for one of the "Charismatic" Churches in Accra and several youth leaders for Calvary Methodist Church? Unrealistic as this perception was, the "Airport Evening Service" was brought to an impromptu, if temporary halt.

By the time the issue was resolved, and approval given for the resumption of the evening service, the Church of Pentecost had begun a new branch in the spacious twin classroom that we had been using earlier. We had to move to two smaller classrooms at the Junior Secondary section of the school, which did not have the "movable wall" facility. The two classrooms catered very well for the Sunday school, but for morning services, they were grossly inadequate.

### Approval for the Preaching post

It would seem that some members of the Calvary Leaders' Meeting had supported the idea of an "Evening Service" at the Airport Residential Area with the hope that it would remain one of those 'toddler' sites that never moved on from being an "Evening Service." For, not long after we resumed the evening service, we were reminded that it was only an evening service and could therefore not hold "Leaders' Meetings." Information had reached Calvary that we "were planning big things," but the Lord's purpose could not be thwarted by mortals. We called our planning meeting the "Elders' Meeting"

Eventually, in late 1996, approval was given by the Calvary Methodist Leaders' Meeting for the Airport Evening Service to become a full-fledged "Preaching Post" under Calvary Methodist Church and the North Accra Circuit. Brother Kingsford Amoah again conducted its very first-morning service on 21st January 1997. There were seventy-five adults and children at that service. Brother Amoah 'prophesied' that "the Lord was going to do mighty things with the "little outpost." It did not take very long for that "prophecy" to begin to materialise. At the next Sunday morning service, there were seventy-six adults and twenty young people. A separate children's service had to be started that day, led by Sister Ayikailey Sam, and the Church has not looked back ever since.

In early June 1998, the Airport Preaching Post became a full-fledged Society in the North Accra Circuit and adopted the name, Immanuel Methodist Church, Airport, out of four names that had been chosen by the membership. On 3rd June, it held its first Leaders' Meeting chaired by its first minister-in-charge, the Rev J K Bassaw and attended by its first set of leaders: Brothers K Abbey Sam, Dr Ofori Quaah, Dr F K E Nunoo and Sisters Lily Adjei and Irish Nunoo, according to the minutes of the meeting. Another part of the 'Airport dream' had become a reality.

Following its inauguration as a preaching post, the leadership of the church mooted the idea of building a gallery at the Association International School for the church's worship services and other activities. Unfortunately, this idea came up against major legal obstacles principally, on the ownership of the structure. The land belonged to an entrepreneur and owner of the school. Under the Church's Standing Orders, any property, moveable or immovable that is acquired or built by any society immediately becomes the property of the Methodist Church Ghana.

So, the idea of a gallery was dropped. By this time, the facilities at Association International School were no longer adequate for the growing church. Additionally, the Accra Metropolitan Assembly legislated heavy charges on all churches that worshipped in schools that were owned by the assembly, as Association International had earlier been seized by a previous government and was, therefore, being run by the Assembly. A sister mentioned the availability of facilities at the nearby Englebert School. The leadership approached and received approval from the proprietors of the school and so we moved to Englebert soon afterwards.

### Some names worth mentioning

Many members made generous contributions in financial and other terms in the challenging years before the new Church moved into its own premises. However, some individuals put their personal comfort online and even risked their very lives, to get the new church going. It is for these reasons that it seems proper that some individuals must be mentioned by name, even though I know some of them will not like the idea. Without those sacrifices, the church could not have made the amazing progress it made in such a short time span. I also believe that it is for such purposes of appreciation that St Paul often specifically mentioned names in his pastoral letters, the epistles, as we know them today.

At the start of the "Evening Service", Brother Titi Dei who had retired for several years, was one of the oldest members of the Society, but as Chapel Steward, he was there every Sunday morning at six o'clock without fail. In his characteristic white shorts and a white T-shirt or 'jumper', he would sweep the filth that the school children would have left in the classrooms before any 'helpers' arrived. He usually worked till all the desks and chairs were properly arranged and wiped clean, before dashing back home to fetch his wife, Auntie Mary, and return to the church premises before service began at 8 o'clock. After Service, he ensured that the chairs were all folded and moved back to Brother Abbey Sam's house before he went home, often making several trips in his car.

Brother Dei continued this routine after the membership increased and canopies were set up on Sunday mornings, to accommodate the increased numbers, right through the move to Englebert School when the Church had to relocate to that new site. He continued to play that role until he sadly passed away that fateful March 6th afternoon in 1998. May his illustrious soul continue to rest in peace in the Lord.

Brother Dan Sam took over from me as Secretary to the "Elders' Meeting", when my duties (as Society Steward, Building Committee Secretary, Local Preacher and Bible Class Leader, among others), became too many. The seasoned civil servant that he was, Brother Dan Sam set up the administrative structures of the Church and later served as its first Leaders' Meeting Secretary until he sadly passed away about 2006.

Brother Fiagbe as a branch manager of Stanchart, set up the bank accounts and account reporting procedures after I had attended a special "Methodist Accounting" Induction course by Brother Ekuban who was then serving as the "Accounts Manager" at Calvary. Brother Andy Quartey was later elected Assistant Society Steward and with his vast experience in banking, helped to move the Church forward in its financial reporting, with Brother PK Arhin guiding us in the "Methodist Auditing Procedures." Brother Quartey continued in that position as Society Steward long after I had moved back to England to join my family until he passed away in 2008.

On the day of the Church's very first 'Harvest' at the new site had Brother Fiagbe not been an experienced banker who had dealt with members of the public for many years, with tons of experience in moving large sums of money from one point to another, armed robbers would have attacked him with possible serious consequences.

Apparently, those robbers had remotely observed the proceedings at the church during the whole service and determined that Brother Fiagbe was the person who was going to carry the money home. They began to stalk him as he left the church premises on his way to his house at Labone. As he told the church leaders later, he noticed after a while, that the robbers' car which was occupied by several men and followed a few cars behind his, repeated every move he made. He parked by the roadside to see what they would do. They also stopped and parked their car. That was when he realised the danger he was in.

By this time, he had gone past the Airport Police Station but was too far away from Cantonments Police Station to take refuge there. He decided to make a dash for it. Being a long-time resident of Labone, he knew the numerous turns and crossroads. He snaked his way through his neighbourhood, lost his pursuers by taking a less travelled side road, went home, hid the money and drove out of the area by another route and by so doing, outwitted those robbers, by the grace of God.

By the following year's harvest festival, Brother Fiagbe had moved to Winneba on transfer and Dr Erica Dickson and her husband Ebo, were the ones that were making the bank payments. After the Harvest offerings were counted, some church members formed a large convoy of cars and vans, with decoys, to ensure their safety and the safety of the money they were taking to their flat at Switchback Road, to be deposited at the bank the next day.

It was after Ebo and Erica had been paying the monies for nearly one year that I discovered by accident, that most Mondays when they went to the bank to pay in the offertory, there were shortages either due to wrong entries or torn notes. They were making up the shortages with their savings, without telling anyone (as a steward of my church here in England, I can identify with that, although not at their scale of losses.)

Additionally, Sister Erica had been the "Church Doctor" right from its "Evening Service" days. Many members, including some in my own family, followed Dr Erica Dickson to the 37 Military Hospital with everything from a slight headache to malaria, even on her busy days. Sister Erica still carries that responsibility.

Ironically, when the time came to write the history of the Church for its twentieth-anniversary celebration, Ebo and Erica were not even mentioned in the anniversary brochure.


## A new Church Hall


Sometime in 1998, one of my estate agent friends informed me about a large tract of land that was going in the Spintex Road area, close to the Kotoka International Airport. This was one of the numerous 'agents' that had tried to find us a house during our long house search in Accra. He was a very pleasant person who had kept in touch with me, although he had not been able to find us a house as he had wished.

He came up with the idea that I could acquire one or two of these plots, as an investment, even if I could not develop it immediately. After what I had been through looking for a house in Accra and building at Gyaman, I had no appetite whatsoever for building another house anywhere in Ghana. However, the church had discussed the idea of looking for land to put up its own permanent buildings. This could be the opportunity we had been looking for.

After my friend took me to see the layout of the land, I reported it to the Leaders' Meeting which showed interest in the land. At about the same time, Brother Emmanuel Botchwey, a member of the Church and his RegieManuelGray Real Estate Company were looking for new land for the next phase of their estate development. I introduced him to my friend who took Bro Botchwey to show him the land. He liked the location and size of the land on offer and went into immediate negotiations. The layout of the land included the site for a Church.

The company acquired the land and gave the portion that had been designated for a church building to our church, free of charge. Additionally, Brother Botchwey informed the church that his company could provide artisans for direct labour with little or no cost to the church if we could provide the materials. Since his company bought building materials in large quantities, they could also purchase materials for the church as and when they were needed, which could save the church in transportation and storage costs, as their company had large haulage trucks and secure storage facilities.

## Design and construction of the Church Hall

Sometime later in 1998, soon after the donation of the plot of land by RegieManuelGray, a Building Committee was formed by the Leaders' Meeting to put together a proposal for building a Church Hall for use as a place of worship, so a more permanent chapel could be planned at a later date. The Late Rev J K Bassaw who was serving as Assistant Administrative Secretary at the Methodist Headquarters at the time also exercised ministerial responsibility for our new church. He was the chairman of the committee, with Brother Abbey Sam as his vice, while I served as secretary.

At its first meeting, the committee decided to commission two architects, Dr A K Blankson and Mr Ken Ampratwum, to produce conceptual designs for consideration by the committee for the construction of a church hall on part of the newly donated land, as its place of worship.

Mr Ampratwum was married to Sister Naana Ampratwum, one of the group leaders of the Airport Bible Class and a very active member of several of the new church's committees, including the building committee. Although Mr Ampratwum was an Anglican who worshipped at Ridge Church, Accra, he was very supportive of his wife and attended all the important functions, especially harvest festivals and other fundraising occasions at Calvary Methodist Church. Dr Blankson was a member of the Methodist Church and had been involved in or personally designed several church buildings and halls of Methodist Churches around the Accra Diocese and beyond.

At the end of the meeting, I was tasked as secretary, to write to the two architects to inform them about the Committee's decision. I wrote the letter, got it signed by Rev. Bassaw and the two gentlemen were served with their copies.

A foundation stone laying service was held on Sunday, June 1, 2002, at which The Most Rev Yedu Bannerman, then Chairman of the Tema District of the Methodist Church Ghana, officiated. It was at that service that Mr Ampratwum unveiled the design of a massive church building, complete with offices and manse at an estimated cost of over two billion cedis at the time. To put it in the right perspective, this was at a time when the mother Church Calvary, with a membership of close to 2000, grossed around two hundred million cedis at annual harvest.

Dr Blankson presented his conceptual design estimated at seven hundred million cedis. Naturally, the church leaned towards Dr Blankson's design and opted for it. This decision did not go down well with Mr Ampratwum, who believed that the Church had commissioned him to design a Church building.

The matter ended at the desk of Most Rev Dr. Asante-Antwi, then President of the Methodist Conference. Most Rev Dr Asante-Antwi queried Rev Bassaw about what seemed to have been a breach of contract. Rev Bassaw was convinced that the Church had asked for "conceptual designs for consideration" and not a contract, otherwise, it could not have been signed with two different architects. This happened at a time the Church did not have any permanent structures and no filing system; ministers were temporary. Fortunately, I had kept a very detailed filing system in my house, a kind of mobile office for the church. I fished out the letter that had been sent to the two architects, made several copies and sent them to the Leaders' Meeting. That was how the matter of the conceptual design of the Church Hall was resolved.

With that resolution, the construction of the Church Hall, using Dr. Blankson's design, began in earnest and on Sunday, October 24, 2002, the Church held its first service at the new site in a half-completed church hall.

The Late Rev John Onwona arrived as a minister-in-training to serve the new church during a very important phase of the construction of the Church Hall. As mentioned earlier, it had been decided that the work would be done by direct labour. Brother E K Y Ewool was tasked to buy the lighter materials (the bulky items were purchased and brought to the site by RegieManuelGray), for the construction. On a number of occasions, I drove to Trinity College to wake Rev Onwona at six in the morning, to sign cheques for the purchases. I went early so I could beat the traffic and return home in time to go to work at Tema, to face my own 'trials and tribulations' as Acting Chief Executive Officer of GNPC.

Fortunately, Rev Onwona's roommate at Trinity College was another very tolerant person who always overlooked my early 'rude' interruptions, after they had studied through the night and would be struggling to catch some sleep before attending early morning lectures.

## Ministers of the early church

The late Rev John Onwona was not just the one who led the early phase of the construction of the Church Hall, he was the one who established and nurtured the spiritual foundation of the church. The late Rev J K Bassaw established the "Methodist Standing Orders," the theological structures of the new church, to be continued by Rev Dr Kow Ghunney, another astute administrator, but Rev Onwona's Sunday evening Bible Teaching was the glue that bonded old and young together in the church. A number of young members who had been attending teachings at the "Charismatic" churches returned and stayed because of those Sunday evening teachings. A number of members experienced various miracles in their lives from those teaching and prayer meetings, which often attracted non-members from other churches and Calvary too.

## Positions in the Church

. . .

In addition to my position as Society Steward and Bible Class Leader at Immanuel Methodist Church, I was also Secretary to the Church Hall Building Committee. From these two positions, I had direct, sometimes difficult issues with the purchases of materials for the construction of the Church Hall.

As mentioned earlier, the building of the Hall was done by direct labour. The Church bought all the materials for the contractor to carry on with the building works. As a Society Steward, I had to raise purchasing orders and write cheques for purchases. At the end of the quarter when I balanced the Church's books, I was required to attach receipts and purchasing orders to the accounts. This ordinarily should be a very simple procedure, but at the beginning of the project, those in charge of purchases would often report that they found a certain item cheaper on the open market and therefore did not have receipts for one item or the other.

My reaction was always that I needed receipts for the cheques that I wrote and would therefore not accept any items that were not covered by receipts. Naturally, the Methodist Standing Orders (SOs) supported my position and I was not really bothered by what was said either in my presence or behind my back!

In the middle part of 2000, I was delegated by the Quarterly Meeting of the North Accra Circuit to supervise the election of officers of the Circuit Lay Movement Council. The Lay Movement, a very important wing of the Methodist Church Ghana, is the lay equivalent of the Conference of the Ordained Ministry. The Ghanaian Church's numerical expansion since its inception in 1835 and most of its major projects, whether local, circuit, diocesan and connexional, have always been spearheaded by the Lay Movement.

While the ordained ministers are very particular and supportive of their 'society', in many circuits around the country, the Lay Movement is usually left in the hands of a few "diehards." That is what was happening at the North Accra Circuit in 2000. A few people had been running the movement for many years, well over the three-year term, as stipulated by the Church's Standing Orders. Some members of the

North Accra Executive Committee of the movement had actually abandoned their positions as a result of the lack of interest among the generality of the Church.

On the day of the elections, there were so few people that although I was only there to lead the devotions and then supervise the elections, I ended up being elected Chairman of the Circuit's Lay Movement Council.

We worked really hard to drum up support for the Movement in the circuit and through co-operation with other circuit executives of the Accra Diocese managed to raise the image of the Lay Movement in the Diocese. With the Diocesan Council Chairman, Mr Ato Essuman, we pushed the motion for the Movement's anthem, "I will build my Church", to be sung at Sunday morning services throughout the Connexional. It was that revival that made it possible for Bro Ato Essuman to be elected Lay President of the Church at the 2002 Conference in Kumasi.

In 2001, I was also elected Vice Chairman of the Men's Fellowship of our Immanuel Society. I had decided earlier that I would never join the Men's Fellowship because, with its weekly meetings on Monday night, it would have meant being out for a meeting virtually every day of the week. That I believed was not good for family life, especially with respect to the boys' school homework and supervised home studies of which I was very particular.

In the end, when I decided to join the family in England in late 2002, I resigned from all these positions. Eventually, in consultation with the Church in Ghana, I became an accredited Local Preacher of the English Church and I am currently serving my second term as a Steward of my local Church. It has been a humbling, but amazing walk with the Lord, who continues to uphold me by His grace.

# CHAPTER 16

# ... AND TEN MONTHS OF REVELATION

left Accra for London on Thursday 9$^{th}$ December 2000, two days
after the first round of the third Presidential and Parliamentary
Elections of the Fourth Republic not knowing when or if I would
return to the country any time soon. Through a bit of arm twisting by a
Giant friend, I had written four memos for Candidate Kufuor earlier in
the year. I had signed the first two memos. Those memos were certain
to have been part of the documents on his personal computers when
his office was broken into in the course of the election campaign. I
would be a marked man.

Then the presidential election went to a run-off between Mr Kufuor
and Professor Atta Mills, which Mr Kufuor won. I was still
contemplating my options up to the day of the inauguration of now
President Kufuor. Not long after Mr Kufuor's inauguration as the
second President of the Fourth Republic of Ghana, I received a
telephone call from one of my nephews who was living in our Airport
house in which he said among other things that my old GSTS "Uncle"
Nii Ayi Ayite had come looking for me and wanted to speak to me
urgently.

I decided to return to Ghana at the end of January. The day after I
arrived in Accra, I went to see Uncle Nii, as we all called him, and he

promised to make an appointment for me to meet a friend of his. He did not give me any details of the meeting.

## Major changes at the Corporation

In October 2000, GNPC went through possibly the biggest shake-up in its sixteen-year history. The Chief Executive, Mr Tsatsu Tsikata who had been part of the Corporation's directorate, first as a member of its first Board, as Chairman and Acting Chief Executive and then as Chief Executive Officer for several years, was moved to the Ministry of Energy as a Special Adviser and Nana Asafu-Adjei who had been the Exploration Manager since the crisis that saw the deportation of Mr Stinson, was made Acting Chief Executive Officer. That was during the run-up to the general and presidential elections just two months away.

In that shake-up, the then Vice President and now Presidential candidate, Professor Ata Mills, was put in charge of the national economy, with additional responsibility for GNPC. The ripples of this reorganisation would lead to even more drastic changes in the fortunes of the Corporation in the next six months.

## Off to Research and Development (Plot 83)

On Monday 29th January, I reported for work as my annual leave had ended the previous Friday, the day after I arrived back in Accra. At the office, I found a letter to the effect that I had been appointed head of Research and Development and was therefore to report to the GNPC data storage and research facility on Spintex Road, popularly known as Plot 83. This was the facility for which I had travelled to Calgary, Abidjan and also inspected Petrobras' research laboratories in Rio de Janeiro.

The Department had been headed by Prof A K Addae since its inception after he was moved from the position of Acting Managing

Director of the Corporation in the mini-reshuffle of 1989. I am not certain as to what happened to him, but it would seem that he had retired at the end of 2000, as the new government had appointed him together with the former Director of the Geological Survey Department, Mr G O Kesse, to look into the affairs of GNPC and propose a programme to restructure the Corporation. I actually appeared before that committee later in the year.

Apart from the big warehouse which served as storage for 9-inch seismic field tapes, the facility also housed the Corporation's geochemical, thin section and paleontological laboratories. It also maintained a large collection of exploration reference books and magazines. Additionally, the offices of the GNPC Ada Songhor Salt and Power Projects were located on the large compound of the facility, and so were the masts and equipment of the corporation's communication subsidiaries, Westel and the Connexsat Satellite station.

The Corporation had taken over the equipment that had been installed in the Ada-Songhor area of the Volta Region by the late S.A. Appenteng's Salt Company following a disagreement with the chiefs and people of the area. Subsequently, the Corporation entered into an agreement with a Cuban state company to mine and refine salt in the Songhor Lagoon and brought in staff of the Cuban company to help set up and run the salt extraction and refining operations. The project was just about taking off at the time the new government came into office.

As mentioned earlier, GNPC had already commissioned a power barge in anticipation of the gas to be produced in the Tano fields. The Aboadze dual fuel power generating plant had been commissioned and was beginning to produce power that was fed into the national grid through the Corporation's extension to the national power transmission grid in the Western Region

The satellite station was set up to provide effective communication with the Corporation's 'marine assets' like drilling rigs, supply and chase boats in Ghana and around the world. With excess capacity, the station also provided communications cover for Ghana Commercial Bank's branches across the country and the internal operations of the Ghana Civil Aviation Authority, among others.

Westel was set up with an American telephone company, as the second landline provider for the country. The original agreement was for the company to roll out five thousand landlines for customers across the country every year, beginning with Accra and the Greater Accra Region. As it became evident later, the company found "call completions" much more lucrative and therefore abandoned the idea of rolling out landlines.

With the inauguration of the new government and the policy to limit GNPC to its core business of finding oil for the country, the managers of these subsidiaries had already been sent on extended leave and because these subsidiaries were located at the site of the Research and Development Department, all except the Salt and Power Generation subsidiaries became my responsibility after I assumed office at the facility.

Having worked on most of the Corporation's seismic data acquisition projects, I knew that the field tapes of several seismic acquisition programmes were still locked up in warehouses in Europe and North America. I set out immediately to organise the field tapes and drilling core samples at various locations so we could catalogue them for storage locally and also offsite, for safety and security reasons.

## Uneasy lies the head that wears the crown

About one month after I assumed duty at the Research Laboratories, Uncle Nii called to say he wanted to see me at his official residence in East Cantonments. Our two families had been regular visitors to each other's homes, first of all, because our children attended the same school, Christ the King International at Flagstaff House and were friends. Secondly, our boys and Uncle Nii's children were trained in Tai Kwan Do by his personal trainer, in his house. I also visited him regularly at his Kabelmetal office in the Tema Light Industrial area. Often, when he had an evening funeral or other function in Accra, he would call me to come along and I usually drove on such occasions. So, I did not think much about this invitation to his house that night.

When I arrived at his house, Uncle Nii introduced me to the newly appointed Minister of Energy, Mr Albert Kan Dapaah and said he was the person he wanted me to meet. I had met Mr Kan Dapaah at a "financial reporting" workshop that was organised by one of the United Nations agencies on behalf of the Ministry of Energy when he was either Chief Accountant or Controller of the Electricity Corporation of Ghana. I believe it was that experience that got him the job of Minister of Energy.

His first comment after the introduction was: "Oh, the government is planning to disband your GNPC." My immediate reaction was, "No, you cannot do that, we are this close to finding oil for Ghana." "Then we shall move it to the Ministry." I said, "No, what the Corporation does cannot be done within the civil service. Additionally, we have signed binding agreements with international organisations as a Corporation and distinct entity from the government. And as an entity, the Corporation can sue and be sued." "In that case, we shall reduce the Corporation to just the Exploration Department." "How about the Drilling and Engineering Department?" I asked. His response was, "Oh, as for engineers, we can always bring some from Tech!" That was the first sign of trouble.

It reminded me of my late grandaunt. When I returned to Ghana in late October 1984, I went to Gyaman for the first time in December, to see my mother, this grandaunt, siblings and other relations. This, the last of my grandaunts, Nana Addow, as we called her, was 103 years old, but was still very sharp. Even her eyesight was so good she could make me out as I entered the lane to the family compound some 25 metres away. As I shook hands with her, she said, "Kobena, I hear you are now a doctor, get me some medication to straighten up my knees and back."

Here we were in a country that had no department for even the most basic training of petroleum professionals in any of our universities. We had managed to train staff elsewhere over several years in reservoir, drilling and even production engineering and yet with the stroke of a pen, we could send them home and replace them with "engineers from Tech?"

The staff strength of GNPC in January 2001 was 977. Of that number, the whole technical staff, Exploration and Production – Geophysics, Geology, Geochemistry, Reservoir, Drilling and Production Engineering was thirty-three. After haggling for some time, we finally agreed on a total of 75 staff members, made up of all the thirty-three technical staff, plus forty-two from all other divisions. In other words, we were going to get rid of 902 people!

### Formal announcement

A few days after my meeting with the Minister, I received a formal letter signed by him appointing me as Acting Chief Executive Officer of the Corporation. I was asked to assume duty at the head office with immediate effect. Nana Asafu-Adjaye, the Acting Chief Executive Officer at the time, had been asked in a separate letter, to hand over to me and proceed on leave.

When I assumed duty at the Research and Development site, I decided to retain the secretary to the head, Miss Agatha Amos, who had been Professor Addae's Secretary for several years. Agatha was a very bright young lady who had sailed through Ghana's rather long and cumbersome secretarial training system very quickly and had been appointed a teacher at one of the top institutions in the country before she joined the Corporation. She was a good Christian lady who worshipped and also sang in the choir at Christ the King Church where our boys attended school. I informed Agatha that I would like to take her with me to the head office, to which she agreed.

One of the first and possibly silliest policies any new government of Ghana, including the military ones, has ever made was the announcement by the incoming government of January 2001 for all heads of department, corporations and institutions to "proceed on leave with immediate effect."

As a result of that policy, many departments and institutions lost incalculable amounts of data, documents and other resources, including computers and software, and GNPC was not spared that misfortune.

On my first day back at the head office, as I moved from one office to the next, I nearly threw up with disgust. The sight of sheer destruction that stared at me from office to office, with the exception of Geology and Geophysics, was most distressing. There were official files and documents strewn on the floors and tables. There were partly shredded documents and partly singed papers all over the place.

Whole computers had vanished from departments, while some electrical gadgets had their power sources cut off. I still retain remnants of documents that some junior officers rescued from the incinerator. It was one of the saddest days of my life. The Public Affairs Department was the worst culprit. That was the state of the Corporation I inherited and the problems I faced for the next ten months have stayed with me till today.

Even though I qualified for an official car, as even staff far down the ladder in the scheme of things were assigned Corporation cars as part of the benefits that came with their positions, I had never been assigned a self-driven Corporation vehicle. At best I always had a driver who picked me to and from work. Sometimes, I shared the vehicle and driver with one or more members of staff. While other officers of the Corporation enjoyed the use of Corporation vehicles on a twenty-four-hour basis, I only used the assigned vehicle during the week. Not even when I assumed responsibility for Research and Development was I assigned a Corporation vehicle. The excuse this time was there were no roadworthy vehicles

However, within minutes of arriving at the head office as Acting Chief Executive Officer, there was a scramble to find me a vehicle. I arrived at the office in my private Opel Rekord and at the end of the day, I drove one of the Corporation's Audi 6 cars home, leaving my driver to drive my personal car to the house. When this 'new' official car developed an electrical fault within two weeks, I was told I could use the "special" Toyota Crown saloon car which had apparently been reserved for very special guests of the Corporation.

•   •   •

## The blessings of my Superintendent Minister

The week after I took over at the head office, I presented Immanuel Methodist Church's quarterly account for the January-March Quarter, together with the four Class Books of the Church to the Superintendent Minister, Rev Essuah-Sekyere. The Superintendent Minister congratulated me on my new appointment, prayed for me and encouraged me to continue with the work that I had been doing in the Lord's vineyard despite what he believed would be a very busy and possibly, stressful schedule. He was convinced that the Lord would provide the strength and wisdom to carry me through.

In addition to membership of the North Accra Circuit, for which I also served as Lay Chairman, I had also served on the Board of the Calvary Vocational Institute for several years under his chairmanship. Rev Essuah-Sekyere had always valued my contributions at the meetings of the Board. He and the headmistress, Mrs Christiana Odoi always insisted on my presence at the meetings even if it was for a short time. I thanked him and promised to do my best and asked him to always remember me in his prayers.

## Empty Coffers

The first thing I did after I got to the head office was to call the accountant for a briefing about the Corporation's finances. It was a harrowing story. The coffers were completely empty. Not just that, it also owed close to one billion cedis to local institutions, organisations and individuals. One creditor had gone to court in the Western Region and garnisheed the Corporation's account with the Ghana Commercial Bank at Half Assini. Any money that was paid into that account was immediately swallowed up.

The former landlord of the former Chief Executive, Mr Tsikata was also owed eight months' rent which had accumulated interest into several hundred million cedis. Rent at the Airport Residential Area where this house was situated, was quoted in dollars and converted to cedis.

The Corporation owed utility bills to Ghana Water Company, Electricity Corporation of Ghana and Ghana Telecom. An American company, Intelsat, which provided satellite cover for the Corporation's satellite station at the Research Centre and the marine assets that were scattered all over the place, was owed several months' subscription and the owner was threatening to cut the satellite cover, a disastrous situation for every entity that depended on GNPC for its operations. Meanwhile, Ghana Commercial Bank, Ghana Civil Aviation Authority and other institutions that depended on the Satellite station for their communications and internal operations had paid their subscriptions for the year to GNPC and their payments had been swallowed up in the Corporation's financial debacle.

The Social Security and National Insurance Trust (SSNIT) hospital that provided medical care for staff and their families at their facilities at their Tema and Accra Hospitals had not been paid for months and had, therefore, cut the credit facility they provided for the Corporation. Under the prevailing "cash and carry" system that was operating in Ghana at the time, staff and their families who attended any of the hospitals had to put down deposits to be reimbursed by the Corporation, which had not been paid for months.

The local and foreign contract staff on the rigs offshore Saltpond, Brazil, Angola, and Gabon had not been paid for months. In fact, fuel supplies for the generators on the Saltpond rig had become a problem. The rig was often in darkness and was beginning to pose a major navigation risk to shipping and fishing vessels. The two Americans on board the rig that was moored off the coast of Rio de Janeiro were threatening to abandon the vessel. At the end of March, one of them called me to say that he had sold one of the refrigerators on board so he could travel to America to visit his sick wife.

The Corporation was embroiled in a court case in the English courts with Société Générale, a French Bank that had financed the Corporation's hedging programme that had run into debt. By a court injunction, the bank had seized the rig in Oman as it tried to sail to an abortive drilling contract in India.

The repayment of a credit facility that was apparently made available by Consolidated Discount House (CDH), to facilitate the operations of the drilling rig Discovery (D) 511 was long overdue. As soon as I moved to the head office, the Managing Director of CDH, Mr Fred Apaloo, began to call me on a daily basis. Within a week of taking office, he was actually coming to the house every morning at about 7:30. He was in trouble with his board because the facility that was supposed to be short-term was dragging on for months. The amount involved was so huge that a default, he believed, could bring the whole Ghanaian financial system crashing.

The Corporation had invested in EcoBank at its inception and that investment had yielded excellent returns. According to Mr Apaloo, the understanding was that even if the rigs were not self-financing, the sale of the Corporation's shares in EcoBank and or interest on the investment in the bank would be used to repay the loan. By February 2001, the Corporation had already begun to take advance payments from EcoBank in order to settle its indebtedness elsewhere. At the end of March, we actually had to go to Mr Akah the Managing Director of EcoBank, for some advance payment on the yet-to-be-declared dividends, to be able to pay salaries.

Mr Jean Akah was born a twin in Côte d'Ivoire, to Ghanaian-Ivorian parents. I met his twin brother who took Ivorian citizenship as an adult when I first visited Petroci's (the National Oil Company of Côte d'Ivoire) Research and Development facility outside Abidjan. He was a manager of one of the company's outfits. I became friends with his senior twin, Jean when we met later in Accra and I told him that I had met his twin brother.

The Corporation received 15% of the price of every litre of any petroleum product that was sold in Ghana, commonly known as the exploration levy, part of what was known as petroleum price build-up, towards its exploration activities. The Ghana Highway Authority also received a percentage that went into a road fund which was used for the maintenance of roads in the country. The oil marketing companies paid these and other deductions to the Bank of Ghana, which then paid to the relevant organisations on a quarterly basis. Here again, GNPC had made withdrawals on its account at the Bank of Ghana in anticipation of the levy for the quarter.

## Dousing fires

About 85% of my ten months as Acting Chief Executive Officer of the Corporation was spent dousing one kind of fire or other. It began as a negotiation of the repayment of outstanding debts. Then there were the court cases and finally the reorganisation and redundancies.

## The Kibi ambush

The owner of Intelsat, the provider of satellite cover for the Corporation's satellite station had apparently been calling the ministry before I took over at the head office. On Thursday 12th July 2001, he called and spoke to Mrs Veronica Wiredu, the Chief Director of the Ministry, warning that there was a bill of $8,000 that had been due for payment for several weeks and that if it was not paid by the following Monday, his company would cut coverage to the GNPC station and begin proceedings in the international courts, to recover that and other bills owed to his company.

Mrs Wiredu called and told me about the latest crisis and asked what we could do. She knew our situation because she was aware of my constant trips to the ministry and our total indebtedness. By this time the minister had travelled and even if it had that kind of money, only the sector minister could authorise payment. She promised to call a few people and get back to me.

On Friday morning, she called and told me that I had to put off whatever I was doing the next day, Saturday because we would travel to Kibi in the Eastern Region on that day. She explained that the only person who could help us was the President himself, but we could not see him at such short notice and he was scheduled to travel outside the country on Sunday night.

She had found out that the President would attend the funeral of the Okyenhen's mother and an aunt of Nana Akufo-Addo (his Attorney-General and current President of Ghana). She had spoken to Nana Akufo-Addo. The President was scheduled to arrive at the funeral at 8 a.m. and would be there for just about one hour because he had other engagements for the day. If we could get to Kibi before the President arrived, Nana could get him to see us for about ten minutes.

Mrs Wiredu told me, "I am a good driver, I have a four-wheel drive vehicle, you can trust me." We arranged to meet at the Shell Station opposite the University of Ghana at 7 o'clock so we could travel in her car to Kibi. I arrived at the station at 6:45 and went to ask permission from the station manager to park my car in the vast parking area for a few hours, to which he readily agreed. Mrs Wiredu arrived at 6:59 am and we took off.

We arrived at Kibi just before 8 o'clock. Nana Akufo-Addo met us just inside his vast and very pleasant compound ushered us into a room and served us water. Thirty minutes later, we heard some commotion outside. It signalled the arrival of the President. A short time later, Nana Akufo-Addo took us to another room where the President was seated. After the initial greetings and introductions, Nana left us with the President.

The President who had obviously been briefed about our mission, listened as Mrs Wiredu narrated the problem that had created the 'ambush.' At the end of it, the President turned to me and remarked in Twi, "*Eno dee se woye* bankrupt." I smiled sheepishly and nodded my head.

After a few moments, the President turned to Mrs Wiredu and said, "I will speak to Yaw (Osafo-Maafo, the Finance Minister) later today. Call him on Monday.

Early on Monday, Mrs Wiredu called Mr Osafo-Maafo who confirmed that the President had spoken to him on Saturday and that the money was ready to be transferred to the gentleman if she could provide his bank details. She did and about lunchtime, the gentleman sent a telex to say that the money had been received and therefore, the immediate threat of closure had been lifted by his principals. I called Mrs Wiredu and thanked her for all the good work she had done. We both heaved a sigh of relief. There was relief, even if for a short time.


**The court cases**


As a sixteen-year-old in Form Two at GSTS, I loved to sit quietly in the public gallery at the old High Court at Koforidua to listen to civil cases. Uncle Nyarko's office at the Ministry of Agriculture was close by and the Regional Library was also around the corner. Occasionally, I had to go to my Uncle for something which then took me to the courts, but most times I would be on my way to the library. Justice J B Short was the High Court Judge at the time.

Then in the summer of 1976, I appeared before a county judge in State College, USA, to plead a parking fine. While I was on a geophysical field trip in southern Pennsylvania and Maryland, I lent my car to a Ghanaian friend to show his visiting relative around. In the course of the weekend, he parked at the wrong location and was given a parking ticket and never said a word about it. About a month later, I received a writ from the court saying that I had violated the county's traffic rules on a specific day and refused to pay the parking fine and should, therefore, appear before the court to show why a more drastic action should not be taken against my person.

I was terrified because I only used my car at the weekends and only for grocery shopping, and sometimes, bargain hunting at the mall some ten kilometres away from campus, all locations that had free parking in those days. Student parking at the vast campus car park was also free. Then I looked more closely at the ticket and realised that it was the time Kwamena was driving the car.

When I asked him, he admitted seeing the ticket on the windscreen and just ignoring it. I pleaded guilty to the charge and paid the fine of $60, which had increased with interest from $10. Those were my only experiences in a court of justice until I assumed the helm of affairs at the Corporation. From the very first week, I seemed to be involved in one court case or another every week.

First, there was the class action case that a group of casual workers had taken at the High Court against the Corporation. According to Ghana's and International Labour Organisation (ILO) laws, an employer who engages a casual labourer on the same assignment for more than six months is under obligation to make such an employee a permanent member of staff. Some of these casuals had been working in the same jobs for up to eleven years and were still classified as "casual employees" of the Corporation.

I appeared in court on two occasions with the Corporation's Lawyer, Mr Joe Ghartey, to seek postponement of the case. Then there was the case against my person that was filed on behalf of the government by the former General Secretary of the New Patriotic Party, Mr B J da Rocha, who at that time held a rather nebulous position of some kind of "Elder Statesman" within the party, and on the sidelines of the government.

As I mentioned earlier, GNPC had taken a facility from Consolidated Discount House in connection with the running of its rigs and had been unable to settle the account as promised. By the time I took over, the loan had grown from Three Billion cedis to Thirteen Billion. I met with the company's team of lawyers led by Professor Mike Ocquaye, the current Speaker of Parliament, who would later assume lead cabinet positions in the government and Mr Yeboah Amoa, and agreed to hold the facility at Thirteen Billion cedis if we would agree to at least pay a quarter of it within two months. This was June 2001.

According to Mr da Rocha, the government considered this loan which was on the Corporation's books and had actually been captured in the budget that had been presented to the government for consideration, as having been taken under questionable circumstances and therefore illegal. I had no business entering into any agreement about that loan. He had taken action against me, the Corporation's Legal Counsel, Mr G K Abankwah and the Director of Finance and Administration, Mr TT Fabyan. That case was never called until I left the Corporation but I heard later that the

Corporation settled it out of court to the tune of Nineteen Billion cedis!

## The Discoverer 511 affair

By far, the most intractable of the court cases was the one concerning the drilling rig, Discoverer 511. The Corporation purchased five marine drilling rigs, one land rig and a drilling platform at a cost of $46.78m and refurbished them for another $33.38m.

The D511, the most viable of the lot, was the only one that was ever used to drill two wells in Ghanaian waters, the best of which was botched, as described earlier. It was later used on a contract in Mexico which grossed $20m, although the high cost of maintenance and remunerations of its mostly expatriate staff made the net profit of little significance.

As part of the Corporation's assets and liabilities, the handing over notes stated that the D511 had been used as collateral in a hedging programme that was financed by a French Bank, Société Générale, a deal that had gone sour and had therefore, become the subject of litigation in the courts in London. The notes and the related correspondence indicated that GNPC owed a total of $47m (including accrued interest) to Société Générale and that at the same time as the case was going through the courts in the United Kingdom, GNPC was negotiating with Société Générale to settle its indebtedness out of court. However, there had been a stalemate with Société Générale asking for $12m and GNPC offering $10m.

As a result of the Corporation's indebtedness to Société Générale, the vessel had been detained in international waters in Oman, as it travelled to India, to undertake a contract which was aborted as the vessel was on the high seas to the Indian location, through a court injunction that had been secured by Société Générale.

As at the time I assumed office, the Corporation had spent some £65,000 on legal fees and the Lawyers, Bindman & Bindman, were owed an outstanding bill of £8,000 for which the law firm had served several urgent notices for payment. The Legal Counsel estimated that it would cost a minimum of another £50,000, to conclude the case either way.

Mr Abankwah stated further in the Legal Counsel's section of the handing over notes that the government had officially informed him and the Corporation that the defence of the suit had been taken over from Bindman & Bindman and handed over to the Attorney-General's Department. Therefore, all files on the case had been transferred to the Department and all correspondence was to be sent to the Attorney-General's Department. Subsequently, each time the lawyers sent a fax or letter which was usually addressed to Mr Abankwah, he would make a copy for our files, a copy for the Ministry of Energy and the original was sent to the Attorney-General's Department.

Bindman even sent a letter, warning that unless payments were made immediately in respect of certain processes that the company had filed on behalf of the Corporation, those processes would be dismissed. All these letters and faxes were duly sent to the Attorney-General's Department.

By this time in early July 2001, the Corporation's cash flow position was so dire that I and Miss Agatha Amos were taking turns buying printing paper to be able to respond to external correspondence, including memoranda to the Ministry. Consequently, there was no way we as a Corporation, could continue with the court case in the United Kingdom, and neither was even the Attorney-General's Department. However, we believed that the Attorney-General could use his clout within the government to ask the Ghana High Commission in London to send a representative to the court, to seek postponement, while the government sorted itself out or concluded the parallel negotiation with Société Générale.

Bindman & Bindman sent letters to say that as their former lawyers, they had a moral obligation to warn that the Corporation's continued absence in court and without representation or excuse, could cause Société Générale to obtain a default judgement against it. And that is exactly what happened and once they obtained the judgement, they were no longer interested in the out-of-court settlement. They wanted their pound of flesh. The bank went back to their $47m! That was when the President mandated Mr. K T Hammond, the Deputy Minister of Energy, to go and negotiate a settlement with Société Générale.

## The sale of the D511

Mr Hammond stayed in touch with me throughout the negotiations and I went to see him in his house in Enfield just north of London during a visit to my family in England. He was still negotiating with Société Générale. Then I went to Houston a few weeks later and returned his call from my hotel room, which cost an arm and a leg. When I went to check out at the end of my stay in Houston, I realised I did not have enough money to pay for this telephone call. I was scheduled to catch my flight back to London in a few hours.

When I returned to Ghana in 1984, I cancelled all my credit and bank cards, for fear of theft and fraud. Anytime I travelled to London and needed money, I went directly to the bank and cashed it with my passport. I had also closed my bank account in Bartlesville, Oklahoma, because of the excessive charges on the current account that I had maintained for several years after leaving Phillips Petroleum.

God being so good, an old friend, Chris Wilmot who owed me some money for work I had done for him several years earlier, had an office about five minutes' walk from the hotel, and for once had not travelled outside Houston. I went to relate to him my predicament and he readily gave me the money, plus a little extra. Although he did not give me as much as he owed me, it was such a huge relief and I have been ever so grateful.

As the rightful owner of the D511, Mr Hammond needed a Power of Attorney from the Management of GNPC with the official blessing of the Attorney-General in accordance with the Laws of the Land, to represent GNPC and the Government of Ghana in the negotiations with Société Générale which culminated in an amicable settlement of the Corporation's indebtedness to that bank.

Earlier, the Corporation's own technical committee had sought and obtained an evaluation of $20m for the D511. Mr Hammond sold it for $24m and managed to beat the bank's demand from $47m to $19.5m. He paid $19.5m out of the sale price of $24m to the bank, leaving a balance of $4.5m. Expatriate and Ghanaian staff on the rig were owed remuneration and there were port handling charges, making a total of $900,000. On 27th July 2001, I wrote to the ministry detailing the list of the rig's creditors, with their bank details, so they could be paid. The law firm that Mr Hammond used in the negotiations charged $100,000, making a total of $1m.

Commenting on the $20m purchase price of the D511, one of the foremost oil industry drilling rig brokers, Messrs. Bassoe Offshore Consultants, noted that "nobody has paid more than USD 20 million cash for a drillship similar to the Discoverer 511 for 15 years (and 1997/98 experienced the highest market for 15 years in the oil industry). And true to their word, the rig market fell so drastically within two months of the sale of the D511, it would have fetched about $15m if it had been sold just eight weeks later.

There was initial confusion about what exactly happened to the balance of $3.5 million payable to GNPC on behalf of the Government of Ghana. Apparently, that money was paid into an account that was opened by the Ghana High Commission in London for the purpose, although the money was eventually traced to America, as having been utilised by the Ghana High Commission in London.

When Mr Hammond returned to Accra after the sale of the rig, I asked him what had happened to the balance from the sale of the rig. His reaction, half-jokingly was, "You did not send me anywhere. I was sent by the President and I have accounted to him." Of course, technically, the rig belonged to GNPC and we had every right to know, especially at a time when that kind of money could have paid off most of our debts and brought our finances into the black again.

When I got to the office, I wrote officially to the Minister of Energy with a copy to the Deputy Minister, asking for a full accounting of the sale of the D511. I received a response after several weeks, with a breakdown of the sale and disbursements, but not how much of it was to come to the Corporation. I am glad I did, as I had to appear before a Commission of Enquiry on the sale of that rig some twelve years later.

The rig belonged to GNPC and could therefore never have been sold without the consent of the Corporation. We had to issue a Power of Attorney to Mr Hammond, appointing him as the "Grantor's true and lawful attorney for it and in its name, place and stead to do any and all of the following:

(1) to sign any addendum or addenda to a Memorandum of Agreement dated 20th June 2001 ("the MOA") made between the Grantor and Frontier Drilling ASA of Norway (the "Buyer");

(2) to execute in favour of and to deliver to the Buyer a bill or bills of sale in respect of the sale by the Grantor to the Buyer of the Grantor's Panamanian flag self-propelled drill ship called "Discoverer 511" ("the vessel") for the sum of twenty-four million US dollars (US$24,000,000) as provided in the MOA;

(3) effect physical delivery of the Vessel to the Buyer and to date, sign, execute, deliver, register or otherwise render perfect all such protocol or protocols of delivery and acceptance, letter or letters of undertaking, applications, oaths, documents, deeds or other instruments as may be necessary or desirable in connection with the delivery of the Vessel by the Grantor to the Buyer;

(4) to receive the purchase price of the Vessel and to receive any other sums which may be due from the Buyer to the Grantor in connection with the sale pursuant to the MOA;

(5) to maintain up to the Closing the Vessel on the Panamanian Register;

(6) to execute all documents and to take all such acts and things as may be necessary or appropriate in connection with the sale of the Vessel."

The Power of Attorney which was executed on 3rd July 2001 was witnessed by Miss Ursula Owusu Adjei, Special Assistant to the Attorney-General and Minister for Justice and Mrs. P.J. Dontoh, Chief State Attorney at the Attorney-General's Department. Attached to the Power of Attorney was a Resolution of the Ghana National Petroleum Corporation (GNPC) passed in Accra, Ghana, on the 29th day of June 2001. Among other points, it was resolved that (1): "The sale by the Corporation of the Vessel to the Buyers for the sum of twenty-four million US dollars (US$24,000,000) be and is hereby approved, confirmed and ratified; (2) The terms and conditions of the MOA and the execution thereof by Kobina Tahir Hammond for and on behalf of the Corporation be and are hereby approved, confirmed and ratified in all respects."

Generally, one person who came out with credit on this whole sordid D511 affair was the former Deputy Minister, Mr K T Hammond, and should have been highly commended for the positive outcome of the affair. Instead, he has been hounded by the left wing of the Ghanaian electronic and print media, using so-called "energy experts" who have no clue about the difference between a seismic section and a street map!

One of the five rigs, the Production Pioneer, was purchased for $3.3m and refurbished at a whopping $6M and was costing $50,000 per month in running costs. At that stage of the Corporation's exploration activities, the most viable of the rigs, the D511 had a maximum draught of 300 metres. The GNPC technical committee recommended that the vessel be upgraded again to bring it to about 500m draught. The rig capacity required to drill in deep water, which was the point the Corporation had reached in its exploration effort, drilling in deep water areas, was of the order of 2000 metres or deeper. Yet some Ghanaian "experts", including technical staff of the Corporation, faulted the government of the day and Mr Hammond, in particular, as having severely damaged the nation's exploration effort by selling off the rigs that were costing the Corporation and the nation some $250,000 per month, while doing absolutely no useful work!

## Do not say it, write it

Prominent among the items in the "welcome package" that was given to new employees at the old Petroleum Department was a memo pad with the title, "Don't say it, write it." For the avoidance of doubt, staff were strongly advised at all times, to write things down, whether it was a request to assist with work on hand, buy stuff from the market or deal with an outside agency, instructions were written down rather than just voicing them out. Not long after I joined the Department, a family friend also advised me, "Don't ever accept verbal instructions from anyone, especially the politicians. I have sat on two commissions of enquiry in the past five years. They always plead I am only a lawyer, teacher, and businessman, I took the decision on the advice of the technocrats." I took this caution to heart to the point of sometimes irritating people about wanting to "see everything in writing" until the restructuring process came up.

There had been neither staff evaluation nor salary increases for the majority of the staff for about five years. Some members of staff had been promoted for five years but had not been able to assume their new positions for that long. In some cases, while others had received elevations and salary increases "through the back door", others had also assumed their new responsibilities with all the headaches and extra hours that came with them, without the corresponding remunerations and benefits that should have come with their new positions and responsibilities. With the impending redundancies, these issues shot to the forefront.

With both the Unionised staff and Senior Staff Association, there were legal implications about the severance to contend with, in terms of the redundancies. The junior staff of the Corporation belonged to various unions under the Ghana Trades Union Congress, while the senior staff came under an association (GNPC Senior Staff Association) that was recognised by the Corporation under the Laws of Ghana and relevant statutes of its incorporation.

Under the Corporation's service conditions, there were clear terms under which staff could be made redundant, whether voluntary or compulsory. Under those terms, a staff member who had been promoted but not been officially recognised as such for any length of time was sure to lose out in a redundancy situation. The Unions and the Senior Staff Association met separately and petitioned management that if the Corporation was going to be so severely decimated, then all pending promotions and outstanding salary increases ought to be implemented before any calculations of severance benefits could be effected. That way, those who would be let go could not be unduly disadvantaged in terms of their terminal benefits.

The initial proposal from the joint Unions-Senior Staff Association Negotiation Team was a salary increase of 180% with all benefits backdated to the year the promotions were made or the number of years for which staff had not received salary increases. This proposal was made with the understanding that the Corporation was going to revert to its core business of finding oil for Ghana. In that case, subsidiaries like Ada Songhor Salt, Mole Game Reserve, Cocoa plantations and the numerous rigs and chase boats that were not contributing anything to the exploration effort but still receiving so much unnecessary attention and costing so much in maintenance and refurbishment should be sold off to pay the redundancies. The excess could then be channelled into serious exploration.

I must admit that if this had been done immediately, there would have been enough money to even carry out the 3D seismic survey, processing and other studies that would have enabled Ghana to own a much higher percentage of the discoveries that were literally handed over to foreign interests on a silver platter!

Naturally, the quantum of increases that were put forward by the Union-Senior Staff team was completely unacceptable to management. They came back with a drastically reduced 85%. This new position was put before the Ministry. It was while the negotiations were going on internally that the government appointed the Ghana Institute for Management and Professional Public Administration (GIMPA) to implement the restructuring exercise.

About the same time, the government also engaged PriceWaterhouseCoopers to undertake a forensic audit of the Corporation's finances, an exercise which turned out to be a complete waste of time and resources.

Sometime in late April or early May when I had to travel to London, I needed to see the Minister. Parliament was meeting in the Banquet Hall of the State House (Job 600) at the time. The GNPC Board had not met for more than two years and with the restructuring, was sure to be dissolved. The Minister through the Ministry exercised direct oversight of the Corporation. So, I needed to inform him about all my travels, especially outside the country.

After the discussion of my trip, he said, "By the way, you have to write to the staff about the redundancy, we need to get the process of restructuring off the ground now." For once, I ignored my own advice and the departmental principle of, "Don't say it, write it." I wrote and signed the circular. It was a fatal mistake! When the letters went out and the staff began demonstrations in Tema and Accra, the Minister denied ever instructing me to send out that memorandum.

I had numerous friends among the Corporation's workforce, from cleaners through labourers and drivers to managers, but the reaction of the staff at my first appearance at the head office overwhelmed me. When things turned nasty later as a result of the redundancy letters, several attempts by individuals and groups within the Corporation, particularly the unions, to burn the offices were revealed to me by my "friends', often going along with the plots on the inside and revealing them to me privately. Had it not been for the actions of those friends, Ghana's oil discovery would have been pushed back by decades, since all the relevant data were housed at vulnerable locations within the Corporation and were easy targets for sabotage. Sadly, I do not believe much has changed even today.

With respect to the redundancies, four members of the technical team, the Chief Geologist, Mr Agbesinyale, and three other members of the Drilling and Engineering Department, George Khoury, Philip Oduro-Kwarteng and Emmanuel Abledu opted for redundancies, giving us room for four more support staff members. We ended up with a staff strength of 79 out of 977.

## The end-of-service debacle

In the late 1980s, the Corporation instituted an end-of-service scheme whereby staff contributed a certain percentage of their salary which was matched by the Corporation and invested in various investment vehicles, state bonds, shares and later, the Ghana Stock Exchange. A panel made up of representatives of the Unions and senior Staff Association and chaired by the Financial Controller, Mr Tabereyang was put in charge of the scheme.

This scheme was instituted because those who had retired over the previous five years since the incorporation of the former Petroleum Department had not done very well with respect to the Social Security and National Insurance Trust (SSNIT) pension scheme. For junior and middle-level staff, the bulk sum paid under the SSNIT scheme had not been much and the time it took between retirement and payment of the bulk sum made it a lot worse, up to one year in some cases, which made life really difficult.

Being an internally managed scheme, pay-out could be made very quickly and staff could actually go into small-scale businesses to support themselves as they waited for their SSNIT bulk payment and monthly pension to kick in. The periodic statements that were issued to individual members of the scheme showed that the scheme was working very well.

When the idea of restructuring was mooted, the Union and Senior Staff Association met independently and decided that staff be paid their entitlements under the scheme as a means of easing the effect of the disengagement.

Rumours had been circulating in the office that senior members of the oversight panel had taken their portions of the scheme and invested them elsewhere. Others actually claimed that monies had been misappropriated. To try to nip the rumours in the bud, management decided that individuals' contributions for the previous quarter be paid to them, while arrangements were made for a complete pay-out. That was when the facts began to emerge.

Firstly, it took quite a while for that meagre amount to be put together for payment. Then in the course of payment, it emerged that every member of the panel, including very senior members of management, had taken out every cedi of their contribution as well as the Corporation's portion.

Finally, it became clear that there was no money at all to pay even a small portion to staff. Part of the money had been invested in a dubious "pyramid" scheme that had collapsed and, in the attempt, to recoup the money, our University of Ghana graduate of a Controller and chairman of the scheme, had allegedly carried the rest of the money in a suitcase to a "jujuman" in Togo "to double it" and in so doing, had lost every cedi of the Staff End of Service Scheme!

The case was reported to the police and the gentleman was arrested by the National Bureau of Investigations (BNI). Mr Tabereyang was a soft-spoken seemingly intelligent gentle giant of a man who one suspects was brought to the Corporation as part of the policy to involve more people of northern extraction in the upper echelons of society.

I went to visit him at the BNI cells near the Water Resources Research Institute of the Council for Scientific and Industrial Research, a short distance from the 37 Military Hospital. This gentleman had the temerity to look me in the face and assure me that the money was there intact that he had been wrongly detained and that as soon as he was freed from detention, he would make the money available.

I naively reported back to the staff that the man had assured me that the money was intact and that he would make it available as soon as possible. It turned out to be a big lie and at a staff durbar later that month, one of the junior members of staff that I had believed to be a friend called me a liar in the face, for believing Tanareyang's fibs.

Immediately, my mind went back to the Alhassan-Shardow Saltpond Oil field misappropriation case that petered out after a few months when the "Northern Card" was evoked to stifle any attempt at prosecution. Eventually, the Corporation absorbed the end-of-service benefits debt into its debt portfolio and paid off staff and I believe Tabereyang got away with it.

## The new GNPC Board

In October, an eight-member Board including myself and one woman, Ms Holdbrook-Smith with Dr Kwame Donkoh Fordwor as Chairman, was announced. The Board also included Mr Adu-Gyamfi, an Agricultural Engineering graduate of the University of Science and

Technology who ran a pharmacy shop at the Airport Residential Area at the time and a retired diplomat, Mr Haruna. As it turned out later, Mr Adu-Gyamfi, a close friend of President Kufuor apparently represented the interest of the President, while Mr Haruna represented the interest of the Vice President, Mr Aliu Mahama.

Following the inauguration of the Board at the Ministry of Energy, the Board Chairman had a long meeting with Mr Joe Klemesu who had worked briefly for the Corporation and had been seconded to the Ministry and later confirmed as Director of Petroleum.

When he emerged from that meeting, the Chairman reported that he was co-opting Joe to the Board as an additional "technical expert", since I was the only technical person on the Board.

### First signs of trouble

Before the Board was announced, I was hoping that I would be consulted about its constitution. One of my UST friends who had done very well on the international oil and gas scene had offered to serve on the Board pro bono. I was never consulted.

Before the announcement of the Board, Mr J E K Taylor with whom I worshipped at Calvary Methodist Church and whose son, John, was a member of my Airport Bible Class and had become a family friend, called me on the side at Calvary after church service one Sunday morning and informed me that his friend Dr Donkoh Fodwor had been pencilled in as Chairman of the yet to be announced GNPC Board. Could I write for him a summary of the Corporation and its activities? I wrote a twelve-page summary of as much of what I knew of the Corporation as possible, including as much of the Corporation's scattered assets as I knew.

I left out the technical details, knowing that Dr Donkoh Fordwor was an economist-finance man. He obviously did not appreciate my idea of a short summary of the Corporation's activities. So I went back to the drawing board and expanded the summary to twenty-three pages.

I had ever met Dr Donkoh Fordwor at his house in London. I mentioned it to him the first time I met him at his house at Cantonments when the Board was announced and before the inauguration.

He had been Special Assistant to General Kutu Acheampong when he assumed the position of Finance Minister of his Supreme Military Council (SMC) government. Following the junior officers' uprising of June 4, 1979, Dr Donkoh Fordwor went into exile in London. When my in-laws were coming to our wedding at the end of August 1981, a mutual friend of theirs gave them a parcel to be given to Dr Donkoh Fordwor. The parcel had been addressed to his house in Golders Green, which was only a short bus ride from our flat in West Hampstead. We took it to him after church service the following Sunday morning.

I still remember very vividly the location of the house on a side street off the main Cricklewood-Golders Green road, but he did not seem to remember that visit and I did not push it.

## Our boy in Tarkwa

After the inauguration of the Board, the Chairman invited the members to a sumptuous lunch at his house. We had drinks in one of the guest areas before lunch. It was during the 'drinks' session that one of the Board members drew me aside and said to me in a low tone, "One of our boys in Tarkwa did so well for our campaign we would like you to find him something at the Corporation when things settle down." I couldn't believe my ears. Was I hearing right? Here we were getting rid of more than ninety per cent of our staff, some of them after several years of intensive training, because of compulsory redundancy and this man was telling me to fix their man in Tarkwa!

Naturally, I told him I would look into it, but never gave it a second thought over the following ten months and somehow, I think from the look on my face at the mention of the matter, he never raised the issue again. Of course, later after I had left the Corporation, I learnt that government functionaries brought in drivers from upcountry who lost their way travelling between the office in Tema and the Ministry in Accra.

## Writing four speeches in a single day

Two weeks after the inauguration of the Board the ministry organised a two-day seminar at the Akosombo Hotel at which the Senior Minister, Mr J H Mensah, the Minister of Energy and the Chairman of the GNPC Board were billed to speak. The Senior Minister was scheduled to give the keynote address at the conference and I was tasked to write his speech, while Mr Cato Browne, the former GNPC Director of Marketing who had been attached to the Ministry together with Mr Joe Klemesu and another Giant and housemate of mine, Martin Asare, were asked to write the Minister's speech. I gave no thought to my Chairman's speech. I was asked to deposit the Senior Minister's speech at the Ministry of Energy when it was done.

When I returned to the Ministry with the speech, I discovered that the people who had been assigned the job of writing the Minister's speech had managed just two paragraphs of the speech. The minister asked me to stop by and help them write it. After just a few minutes, I realised that there was no way we could ever finish that speech if I did it with them. I told them not to worry and that I would go back to my office in Tema and write it.

I returned to the ministry after about two hours with the draft speech. The Minster liked it so I asked his secretary to retype a final version for her boss but promised to have my secretary do another copy which I would carry along to the conference the next day, just in case.

From the ministry, I had to pass through the Board Chairman's house to give him a copy of the programme for the conference. When I mentioned that I had delivered the Minister's speech to him, he asked me where his speech was as Board Chairman. I scratched my head and assured him that he would get his speech before morning. I went back to Tema and wrote a speech for the Board Chairman. By the time I delivered it to his house, it was past seven and I had not done the slides for my own presentation. I had to go back to the office. While thanking me for his speech, the Chairman advised me to take it easy.

I returned to the office and did my overhead projector slides which were printed early the next morning before we set off for the conference at Akosombo.

## Sense of gratitude

About a week after the conference at Akosombo, contractors for the construction of the South Tano development power barge, Ansaldo and Mitsui arrived in Accra for a discussion on the financial arrangements in connection with their contract. The Senior Minister who by this time had been assigned the oversight of GNPC's local and foreign debts called a meeting at the Ministry of Energy, to discuss the issue.

At the end of the meeting, as we filed out of the ministry, Mr J H Mensah remarked, "By the way, who took the minutes of the meeting? I hope the minutes will be ready in a few days." There were blank faces, nobody had taken any minutes of this three-hour meeting.

I have always had the habit of writing notes for every meeting I attend, even if I am chairing it. That was something I picked from my first boss at Phillips Petroleum, Mr Curtis Bratt. He had a very efficient secretary who took minutes of our weekly departmental meetings, but Curtis as he preferred to be called, made his own notes and would often compare with the shorthand notes that the secretary took.

I broke the silence by saying that I had made some personal notes at the meeting and would try and put something together. Back at the office, I composed my notes into minutes and got my secretary to type them. I went through the draft and sent it to the ministry to be given to the Senior Minister.

Later that day, he sent a handwritten note through an assistant to say how very grateful he was for the minutes and how pleasantly surprised he was that I had captured everything that had been said at the meeting.

## Why is that man so angry with you?

Sometime in late October 2001, the Ministry of Energy organised a workshop to which every institution in Ghana that had anything to do with natural resources, including the Geology Department at the University of Ghana, was invited. The Ministry also got the British Government to sponsor three British 'experts', a Geologist, a Geophysicist and a Petroleum Lawyer, to participate in the workshop.

There had been this rather wrong perception by people outside GNPC that the reason why Ghana had not made a major commercial oil discovery was that the fiscal terms in the model Production Sharing Agreement (PSA) were too harsh on the contractor. If those were toned down, according to the Corporation's detractors, the country would be more attractive to the multinationals to do more exploration.

This notion was obviously wrong because even at that time, we were in serious negotiations with three different consortia and two more were far ahead in their exploration programmes in fulfilment of their contractual obligations.

As I parked my car at the forecourt of the hotel to attend the workshop, Kofi Coomson, the editor of 'The Chronicle' came running to me and asked puffing, "Why is a certain "big wig" of the ruling party so angry with you?" He mentioned the name of a man who lived not too far away from our house at the Airport Residential Area and asked if I knew him. He added that he was a very close confidante of the President.

I said I knew him and I had actually been to his house a few weeks earlier. He warned that he was very influential and that I should be careful how I dealt with him.

Then I remembered that a few days earlier, two Norwegian Geophysicists had come to the office with proposals for the maintenance and management of the Corporation's seismic data. It was the kind of enquiry that was regularly handled at the senior exploration staff level and they had merely come to pay a courtesy call before going into discussions with the geophysicists of the Exploration Department. Two senior officers of the Corporation had accompanied these Norwegians to my office. We talked about our ongoing exploration programmes for about fifteen minutes and they left to begin their meeting.

At the end of their meeting with the exploration staff, the Norwegian delegation passed by to bid me farewell. A short time later, as we were preparing to go home at the end of the day, the leader of the Norwegian group came and reported to me that they had held fruitful discussions with my officers, thanked me and left.

The next day, the GNPC officers who had held the meeting with the Norwegians brought me a report of the meeting saying that the Norwegians had made a proposal to scan, digitise and vectorise all our seismic data and put them on a website for promotion to the international oil and gas community and give the Corporation something like 20 per cent of the proceeds. In response, the GNPC officers had said no to the proposal, in no uncertain terms and the minutes of their discussions made that very clear.

Apparently, the Norwegians had gone to report to this man who had obviously been their contact man in government that "I was trying to thwart a huge investment they were bringing to Ghana", thus his anger at me. I was not even at the meeting!

Around this time, with government direct subvention virtually dried up, the sale of data and the exploration levy were the main sources of exploration financing for the Corporation. We were selling that data, which was our own in the first place and pocketing 100 per cent of the sales. We knew the geology, we had acquired and processed the data and were, therefore, better placed to answer any questions any potential buyer might have on the data. Who better to promote or sell Ghana's data than the Corporation's exploration staff?

**Chris Wilmot and Western Geophysical Company**

• • •

In an almost identical development, my old friend Chris Wilmot went to the Deputy Minister, Mr K T Hammond and told him that he had a very juicy proposal for GNPC. To his eternal credit, the Deputy Minister after listening to the proposal told him that since he was not a technical person, he would like him to make the presentation in my presence and ask for my opinion.

He invited me to his then-temporary accommodation at the Ahmadiyya Mission at Osu. Chris Wilmot represented Western Geophysical Company. Western had bought Geophysical Services Incorporated (GSI, the company that did the 3000-kilometre 2-D speculative survey offshore Ghana in 1983) in the late 1980s and assumed ownership of the Ghana speculative data by so doing. Under the original agreement, GSI was to return the data to the Corporation after it had recovered its investment.

After hearing his repeat presentation, the Deputy Minister asked for my reaction. I told him that Western had held on to the Corporation's 3000 kilometres of seismic data for over eighteen years and had apparently not been able to recover its investment, why should we give them 60,000 kilometres of 2-D and 3-D seismic data when they had not been able to sell 3,000 kilometres for eighteen years?

Mr Hammond asked if it was true that his principals were holding on to the Corporation's data, to which Chris answered in the affirmative. With that, the Deputy Minister said, "That is not on, is there another issue, otherwise, the meeting is over." And that was it.

Apart from the financial implications, neither the Norwegians nor Western geophysical possessed the facilities for digitising and vectorising seismic data at the time. They were both going to use third parties to carry out the main programme. We could also go to the companies with those capabilities and do the same thing and promote and sell the data by ourselves.

**More travel woes**

. . .

In early September 2001, I travelled to Houston with the Minister of Energy and his Director of Petroleum, Mr Joe Klemesu, at the invitation of the Ghanaian community in the city, mostly people involved in the oil industry, a city that could easily be described as "the Oil Capital of the world."

The Minister was out of the country and was to meet us in Houston. Joe and I flew to London on an overnight British Airways flight and were to take the first of two flights to Houston. We went through the transit, customs and immigration procedures and parted ways. We had more than two hours before our flight so I decided to get some rest at a downstairs rest area where I believed I could see flight information on the screens. I forgot completely that security procedures could take up to thirty minutes. I was constantly looking at the screen to see if our flight would appear on the screen. I was at the wrong location! Apparently, my name was announced on the intercom system several times before the gate was closed. For security reasons, not only my luggage but Joe's as well were taken off the flight.

Eventually, when I got to the relevant screens, I discovered that my flight had taken off. Fortunately, there was a second flight to Houston that day. I was booked on that without hassle, but our luggage would not arrive in Houston for another two days. Mr George Owusu, who would later be rather unfairly embroiled in the Kosmos-EO Group hullabaloo, heard of our plight and took us to a shop on the outskirts of Houston to buy a few toiletries, change of shirts and underwear, to get us going until we got our luggage. Mr Owusu who impressed on us to pick a few more items in case our luggage did not arrive in two days, as promised by the airline, generously paid for our purchases at the till against all our protestations.

Fortunately, our luggage arrived intact after two days, as promised by the airline. We completed our presentations and meetings late Friday, 8th September. The Minister left the next day, Saturday the 9th. Joe Klemesu left early Sunday to spend some time on the east coast someplace, before returning to Ghana. I left on Sunday night and arrived in London on Monday the 10th, to attend scheduled meetings in London and spend a few days with my family before returning to Ghana.

The first of the meetings I attended was with Lloyds Insurers, the company that insured the GNPC rigs and other marine vessels. The insurance cover on two rigs, one moored offshore Angola and the other off Gabon, had elapsed and the vessels had also gone out of classification. To be able to buy insurance for the vessels, they needed to be taken to the drydocks, but they could not be moved until they had insurance cover and the insurers were reluctant to provide insurance cover without classification.

The Corporation's insurance man, Mr Neequaye, had flown to London to speak to the insurers and I was required to be there to assure the insurers that the Corporation would pay them for any outstanding debts and that it was important they extended the cover for the two vessels. That was Tuesday, 11th September and while we were still engrossed in our negotiations, the television screens began to display the bombing of the Twin Towers in New York. It was 9/11, the catastrophic event that would change air travel forever. I had just made it back to the United Kingdom. Joe Klemesu was stuck in the United States for nearly two weeks, while most major American airports were closed.

It was a close call for me because having missed my flight for no good reason with my luggage taken off the flight would have meant lengthy questioning or even detention in America if it had happened after "9/11!"

# CHAPTER 17
# MY RESIGNATION FROM GNPC

The Ghana National Petroleum Corporation has operated a satellite receiver station on the premises of its laboratory and storage facility at "Plot 83" on Spintex Road, as a subsidiary, for many years. That was the facility I was appointed to head, following my return from England after the new government came into office in January 2001. At the time I took over the running of the facility, the satellite station provided data coverage for fourteen branches of Ghana Commercial Bank, eight branches of Merchant Bank nationwide, the Ghana Civil Aviation Authority, for the internal flights of Ghana Airways, as well as the corporation's data transmission and communications with supply boats and rigs dotted around the globe.

By the time I was appointed Acting Chief Executive of the Corporation, the Ministry of Energy had earmarked that subsidiary as one of the many subsidiaries of the Corporation to be disposed of. I wrote a memorandum to the Ministry explaining that the station was essential to the operations of a slimmed-down GNPC and that it would be prudent for the Corporation to maintain a certain minimum equity at least, in its operations. This proposal was eventually accepted by the new Board of Directors of the Corporation, after its inauguration.

Before I took over as Acting Chief Executive, an American IT company, IP Telecom, owned by one Dr Lawrence had signed a Memorandum of Understanding (MOU) with the Corporation in a bid to join in the running of the subsidiary on structured commercial lines. Following the assumption of the new government and the new policy to restructure the Corporation, three other companies, including Comparex of South Africa, that had been invited by the Chairman of the Board, Dr Donkoh Fordwoh, were invited to look into a joint partnership arrangement with GNPC.

Subsequently, the Board set up a sub-committee to review the proposals that had been submitted by the companies and recommend one, two or all three, to run the subsidiary with GNPC. Privately, the Ministry of Energy's preference was for the subsidiary to be run by a Ghanaian partnership because of the security implications of satellite communications; others had their own ideas.

Around the beginning of February 2002, Dr Lawrence, the owner of IP Telecom called to say that his company had shipped some equipment to the Kotoka International Airport for some tests towards the commercialisation of the facility and could GNPC clear the equipment from the airport. I told him that in view of the prevailing situation whereby proposals from various companies, including one from his own company, were being evaluated towards the new direction of the subsidiary, the Corporation could not clear the said equipment.

He pleaded that the equipment was quite expensive and ran the risk of being vandalised if they were left at the airport for any length of time. He cited the existing MOU between his company and GNPC. He also mentioned the fact that a similar thing had been done in early 2001. After a long discussion, I agreed and offered to assist.

Three days later, Dr Lawrence's representative in Ghana, one Mr Abrefa-Kudom presented a letter with an airway bill covering the shipment. I passed the airway bill to the Corporation's shipping officer to deal with it. Three days later, the officer came to inform me that the equipment had not been consigned to GNPC as should have been done. I told her to forget about it in that case. Before then, Mr Abrefa-Kudom had called to say that he was travelling to the United Kingdom for a few days and that one Alhaji Yusif would be the contact man in his absence.

When Alhaji Yusif learnt that the Corporation was not going to clear the equipment, he called to ask why. I told him that the equipment had apparently not been consigned to GNPC. He promised to go back to Dr Lawrence to get him to re-consign them to the Corporation. I informed the shipping officer to that effect. A few days after this discussion, a substantive Managing Director was appointed for the Corporation, and I was made Deputy in Charge of Exploration and Production. So, I moved to assume my new role.

Unknown to the Corporation, Alhaji Yusif had contracted Henry Palm, who used to work at the Corporation's shipping department, to clear the equipment for IP Telecom. Three days before I handed over to the new Managing Director, Henry Palm came to my office with one Timothy Oklu who had worked for the Corporation as Acting Head of the Satellite subsidiary, to ask for the corporation's exemption certificate, to be able to effect the clearance of the equipment. I called the shipping officer and asked her about the request.

She advised that the certificate was issued specifically to the Corporation and was therefore non-transferable. She advised further that if IP Telecom wished the Corporation to clear the equipment, they should pay Henry Palm off and engage the Corporation to do the clearance on their behalf. I communicated this decision to Alhaji Yusif who agreed to do just that. With that, my involvement with the equipment ended, since my new role did not include control of the satellite subsidiary.

At the beginning of March, the new MD came to my office one afternoon and asked if I knew anything about labourers who were excavating at the satellite hub site in apparent preparation for the installation of some new equipment. I told him that I did not know any group like that and explained that a company that maintained an MOU with the Corporation had asked for assistance to clear test equipment for the hub, but when we discovered that the equipment had not been consigned to the Corporation, I instructed the shipping officer to cease any involvement in the process.

The company's representative promised to get their principals to re-consign the shipment but I had not heard any more about the matter since I moved to my new role. When I enquired as to who had sent the labourers, the MD responded that the labourers had told him that a contractor had sent them there but they did not know who the contractor's employer was. In any case, the new MD had driven the labourers away.

Subsequently, I called Alhaji Yusif to ask if he knew anything about excavation for installation. He said he didn't and that he was in the middle of a meeting in Kumasi and would call as soon as the meeting was over. He did not call until later the following day, which was Saturday. He still maintained that he did not know anything about the excavations but promised to investigate and call me.

On Monday, I called Dr Lawrence to ask if he knew anything about the excavation. Dr Lawrence did not know anything about it either but promised to call his people in Accra and come back to me. He never called back.

The next day, Tuesday, while I was preparing to leave the office at about 5:30 pm, the MD called and asked me to write a report on the matter of the IP Telecom equipment for the Board meeting that had been scheduled for Thursday 7th March. This report and another he had asked for, were ready by 9 o'clock that morning.

At 10:30, I was sent for by the Board. After some brief introductions, I was asked to go back to my office and would be contacted if I was needed. I was called back to the meeting an hour later and asked to explain the circumstances surrounding the shipment and clearance of the equipment that was supposed to have been shipped to the satellite station for tests. I narrated the story as detailed above, why I had instructed the shipping officer to cease any dealings with the equipment and how I had not heard anything since I had ceased to be Acting Chief Executive.

There were questions from members as to why I had aided my friends in using the Corporation's exemption certificate to clear their dutiable equipment. I explained that none of the people involved was my friend and that I had spoken to Dr Lawrence on the telephone on several occasions but I had never met him in person. I explained that he had drawn my attention to the fact that there was an existing MOU between the Corporation and his company. It was on that basis that I had initially referred the airway bill to the shipping officer to see to its clearance. However, I stopped her immediately, I discovered that the equipment had not been consigned to the Corporation.

Under the GNPC Law, equipment that was imported into the country by the Corporation's business partners and associates could be cleared by the Corporation's officers if they were consigned to GNPC.

Members of the Board, and the Chairman, in particular, did not take kindly to the fact that I had tried to override a Board decision to "stay off any action on the satellite hub until a decision had been taken on the future of the subsidiary." The Board Chairman informed me that under the circumstances, the Board had decided that I could either resign or the Board would take its own decision about my future. He stated that if I resigned, I would be paid whatever I was entitled to. He went on to say that, "if I resigned, he would not be in my way if any of the oil companies operating in the country wished to employ me in any capacity at a later date." He said in terms of technical ability, I was one of the best he had ever come across but in terms of administration one of the worst. I didn't care much about that.

When I asked if I could go and think about the matter, the Chairman pointed to the chairs in the corner of the boardroom and said I could sit on one of those and think about it. I had worked for the Corporation for seventeen years, mapped every basin in the country and been involved in every seismic acquisition and processing the Corporation had ever undertaken, saving the Corporation and the country huge sums of money in consultancy fees. If I could only sit in a corner and think about a matter like that, it was not worth my time. I offered to resign. The Chairman thanked me on behalf of the Board and I left to write my resignation letter. I submitted the letter on the afternoon of Friday the 8th of March.

On Monday the 11th, one Mr Keelson, a journalist from "The Independent" newspaper called to ask if I had been forced to resign from my position with GNPC; and if I had helped my friends to evade taxes. I answered in the negative. I had caught some kind of stomach bug over the weekend and had been running all weekend. I told the gentleman I was ill and if he could call back another time or leave a number by which he could be reached. He hung up.

The next day, the newspaper reported that I had been forced to resign from my position at GNPC because I had used my position to help my friends evade taxes to the tune of 43 million cedis and cleared their goods from the port. We would learn later that the equipment had not even been cleared. They were still waiting at the airport!

I called my lawyer and narrated my side of the story. He asked me to write a rejoinder to the newspaper article. I wrote and he asked me to meet him in his office so we could go through it together, and then send it off to the newspaper and the Media Commission.

I was out all day that day. When I got home in the evening, I received a message that the Deputy Minister of Energy, Mr K T Hammond had called and wanted to see me. In the meantime, the Deputy Minister who was in the same law school class as my lawyer had asked my lawyer to hold on to my rejoinder until he had spoken to me. The rejoinder was never published. When I got to his office the next morning the Managing Director was already there. Mr Hammond asked and I narrated my side of the story. The MD said he did not remember if the Board Chairman asked me to sit in the corner and decide whether I was going to resign or not.

Subsequently, the Deputy Minister asked for the minutes of the Board meeting. First, the MD promised to provide the minutes. Later, he informed the Deputy Minister that the Board wanted him to write officially for the minutes. He wrote and he was informed that the minutes could not be released until they had been approved at the next Board meeting on the 11th of April 2002. While he was waiting for the minutes of the Board meeting of March, the Deputy Minister who was responsible for Energy and Power (GNPC, Ghana Oil (GhOIL) and GhAIP, the refinery), asked me to write a letter to withdraw my resignation from the corporation, which I did. Over the next several weeks I saw the Deputy Minister on several occasions, each time promising to settle the matter, without the publication of my rejoinder.

Eventually, the Deputy Minister left a message for me to the effect that he had got Dr Donkoh Fordwoh fired from GNPC and as far as he was concerned, that was it. I travelled to London at the end of the year and resolved that the well-being of my family was more important than anything I could get from GNPC. Besides, I was convinced that between me and my God, I had given back to society as much or even more than I had received from it. I had done my bit.

Sometimes when the Lord speaks to us and we do not listen, He uses a donkey. GNPC was my donkey, and that was a revelation.

**End piece**

Leaving GNPC at the time I did has turned out to be the best decision I have ever made in my personal life in the last forty years. I had been travelling on a rickety vehicle with booby traps for sixteen years, and it took ten months at the helm of affairs to discover that. I sacrificed my comfort, savings and in many instances the comfort of my family for the Corporation. In so doing, I established my footprint on the path to the commercial discovery of oil for Ghana. I had paid my dues to society. It was time to move on.

I pray that the efforts of the people with whom I battled the elements in the marshes of Elubo, Edu, Tekinta, Ebbwazo, Kabenlasuzo and other places will benefit generations of Ghanaians unborn. Amazingly, the Lord has blessed me so much in the seventeen years since I left the Corporation that I could not have asked for any better.

# APPENDIX A

regions of the sub-basin. In which case, the structural locations of these stratigraphic prospects would not be favourable. However, since these turbidite-like features are, in most cases completely encased in shales, they must be of major exploration interest.

## 6.0 CONCLUSION AND RECOMMENDATIONS FOR FURTHER WORK

i.  A detailed interpretation exercise has been undertaken in the study area. The quality of the available data, especially the 1988 vintage, has been found to be reasonably good, although they will benefit from specialised processing for stratigraphic interpretation.

ii. Structurally, the study area is very complex, having gone through several phases of faulting and vertical and lateral movements. The study area is consequently bounded by faults on its northern, southern and eastern boundaries, all of which seem to be related to the Atlantic megashear zones.

iii. The study area seems to be divided into two structural provinces along a line west of the Cape Three Points-1 well location. To the west, the structural features trend east-west while the ones in the east trend northwest-southeast.

iv. Available data seem to indicate that Upper Cretaceous source rocks have the best potential for hydrocarbon generation in the sub-basin. However, there is the potential for other deep seated sources particularly in the Lower Albian, to generate hydrocarbons.

v.  Several of the structural highs have been tested with limited success. A series of tilted fault blocks seem to be the remaining structural features with the potential for the accumulation of commercial volumes of hydrocarbons.

vi. Generally, Upper Cretaceous sands appear to be the best developed reservoirs in the area. Thus the tilted fault blocks and stratigraphic features that were discussed in sections 5.2 and 5.3 respectively, need to be studied in more detail. The Upper Albian structural nose described in Section 5 has a very good potential for finding oil in the Cape Three Points area. Because the feature is big, any oil find in it is likely to be commercial. With respect to the structural features that were mapped, the two closures designated D and E at the Middle Albian level, are the only ones worth further attention.

Printed in Great Britain
by Amazon

47664649R00145